ANTON HARBER was a founding co-editor of *The Weekly Mail,* later known as the *Mail & Guardian.* He was the chair of the Conference of Editors in 1991, the National Association of Broadcasters in 1998, and the Freedom of Expression Institute in 2010. He serves on the board of directors of the Global Investigative Journalism Network and the Center for Collaborative Investigative Journalism. He is an adjunct professor of journalism at the University of the Witwatersrand, a columnist for *Business Day*, and the co-editor or author of five books.

SO, FOR THE RECORD

Behind the Headlines in
an Era of State Capture

ANTON HARBER

JONATHAN BALL PUBLISHERS
JOHANNESBURG · CAPE TOWN · LONDON

Originally published in South Africa in 2020 by
JONATHAN BALL PUBLISHERS
PO Box 33977
Jeppestown 2043

ISBN 978-1-77619-068-3
ebook 978-1-77619-069-0

Website: www.jonathanball.co.za
Twitter: www.twitter.com/JonathanBallPub
Facebook: www.facebook.com/JonathanBallPublishers

Cover design by MR Design
Cover image: Gallo
Design by Martine Barker
Set in Fieldwork/Adobe Garamond Pro

To the whistleblowers.

AUTHOR'S NOTE

This book attempts to demonstrate how elusive – and how essential – is the journalistic aspiration to accuracy and fairness. Some of those I've criticised for errors and misrepresentations will, I expect, be eager to point out my own. I apologise for these in advance.

CONTENTS

PART III
'DUPES OF DECEIVERS'

CONCLUSION

PART 1

FAST JOURNALISM

A story of many beginnings

A great deal hangs on when one begins a story. Different beginnings lead to different endings. And that was the case with the Cato Manor 'death squad' story.

It is sometimes said, particularly by those close to the story, that it originated with a well-known KwaZulu-Natal human-rights activist, Mary de Haas. She sent an email in September 2010 to the *Sunday Times* with a tip-off about allegations of irregular killings by the Durban Organised Crime Unit's Cato Manor team. De Haas attached a letter she'd sent to the unit telling them of taxi operators who were in hiding because their rivals, 'allegedly operating in collusion' with police, were threatening their lives.

De Haas's tip-off was cited as part of the journalists' argument that there was a legitimate public-interest story to be investigated. The trouble was that this origins story wasn't quite true.

The reporters of the *Sunday Times* investigations unit have given oddly different versions of where it began. Stephan Hofstatter wrote in 2015 that the story emerged when they received a flood of calls after the arrest of his colleague Mzilikazi Wa Afrika in 2010, some of them from disgruntled police officers, several of whom told them about 'a police unit gone rogue ... controlled by one Major General Johan Booysen'. Wa Afrika said on one occasion that it came from senior officers in the Crime Intelligence division of the South African Police Service (SAPS), an agency that tracks criminal elements within the country.

An unattributed *Sunday Times* article on 1 July 2012, though, said that Hofstatter and Wa Afrika had got the tip-off while interviewing a senior police officer in Pretoria on 14 August 2010.

What the reporters told their editor when questioned about it in 2017 was that the story began with a telephone call from former Commissioner of Police Jackie Selebi to Wa Afrika in August 2010.

Selebi had been sentenced for corruption and was awaiting his appeal. It had been a spectacular downfall for someone who'd been a senior figure of the African National Congress (ANC) in exile and in government, and he was an angry man. He phoned Wa Afrika to sympathise with him after Wa Afrika was arrested in August 2010, and to share their mutual dislike of Selebi's successor, Bheki Cele, who was believed to have been responsible for Wa Afrika's arrest. Then Selebi dropped it into the conversation: 'Have you heard about Bheki Cele's death squad in Durban?'

Selebi died in January 2015, so we can only speculate about why he might have made a point of telling Wa Afrika about the Cato Manor unit – or why the reporters still feel a need to protect him if he was their source. Was he seeking revenge on those responsible for his downfall, particularly his successor, Cele? Was it part of the ANC's internal battles, as Cele was from the Zuma faction of the ANC, while Selebi was firmly in Mbeki's camp? Selebi was highly critical of the new ANC leadership, often arguing, as Hofstatter put it, that 'Zuma and his henchmen such as Cele were turning South Africa into a gangster state'. Was it an attempt to win favour from Wa Afrika? Was it part of an information-swopping deal with the journalist, as is so often the case: I'll tell you something because I want to ask you something?

One thing we can say for certain is that it's unlikely that it was out of a concern for human rights. If that were the case, Selebi could have tipped off the Independent Complaints Directorate (ICD, since renamed the Independent Police Investigative Directorate, IPID), a civilian agency responsible for investigating all deaths as a result of police action or while in police custody and other public complaints of police abuse, or the Human Rights Commission.

If Selebi told a journalist, he had a political reason to do so.

In 2020, Hofstatter would only say to me that he'd 'received a tip-off from a high-level police source about what the source called "Bheki Cele's death squad".' The source, he said, 'though implicated in corruption himself, was a Thabo Mbeki loyalist' who often criticised President Zuma and Cele. Mbeki was South Africa's second president, ousted in a bitter battle with Jacob Zuma that split the ANC into two camps. This version fit the story that it was Selebi who told the reporters about the 'death squad'.

Wa Afrika didn't pay attention to the tip-off until some weeks later, when the note arrived from De Haas. Then he and Hofstatter, who at that time were the core of the *Sunday Times* investigations unit, travelled to KwaZulu-Natal to look into the allegations.

De Haas introduced them to two taxi operators who were in hiding, and these operators repeated their accusations that Cato Manor policemen were taking sides in taxi conflicts. One of them had a recording of a policeman threatening to kill him. The problem was that taxi violence was endemic, as were allegations of police involvement, and the views of two of those deeply embedded in this messy business couldn't be taken at face value.

These operators introduced the reporters to three or four others with similar complaints. And Hofstatter said they spoke to other human-rights campaigners, including some involved in helping families bring civil cases against Cato Manor detectives who'd killed their kin. There were also local journalists who had investigated the Cato Manor unit's killings, and who introduced them to other sources, including within the police.

They were building their story. But it was a murky semi-underground world they were learning about, and in this world allegations – like life itself – were cheap, and witnesses few.

He said, they said

It was more than a year later, in December 2011, that General Johan Booysen, head of the KwaZulu-Natal arm of the Directorate for Priority Crime Investigation, also known as the Hawks, had his lawyer contact *Sunday Times* editor Ray Hartley. Your reporters have been snooping around here, the lawyer said. I hear they're working on a story about Booysen's men in Cato Manor. When are you going to talk to him about it?

Mzilikazi Wa Afrika and Stephan Hofstatter had been working on the story in those months, systematically gathering witnesses, evidence and other material. Journalist Rob Rose had joined the *Sunday Times's* investigations unit when the story was quite advanced, and worked with them in crafting it.

They'd been told horror stories of what appeared to be cold-blooded killings by the Cato Manor unit, which seemed to have been given a free hand to be ruthless in pursuit of violent criminals. They'd been given photographs of what appeared to be members of the unit celebrating after killings, sometimes in the presence of the bodies or mourning family members. They'd spoken to forensic experts about what these photos showed.

When Booysen asked to have his say, the team was in the last stages of the investigation and was getting ready to send the police a string of questions. Professional best practice and the Press Council Code of Ethics and Conduct required that they give reasonable time for responses, but the *Sunday Times* had lost a few scoops before, when their subjects had used the time to pre-empt them by issuing a statement, to give a different story to another journalist to muddy the waters, or even to rush to court to try and prevent publication. It had therefore become regular practice on the newspaper to make the obligatory call as late as possible, to keep the initiative and avoid such pre-emptive action.

Sometimes they waited until the Friday afternoon before publication, sometimes the Saturday morning, sometimes even later, though the first edition of the paper went to press early on Saturday evening. The effect was to catch the person off guard, not give them time to gather evidence or consider their views, and reduce their capacity to influence the narrative. What that person said was usually too late for the reporters to do more than drop a quote or two into the story. Seldom at this late stage – with the deadline looming – could they reconsider the story on the basis of anything new learnt from the interviewee. It was little more than a formal ticking of the right-of-reply box.

This time, though, editor Ray Hartley decided to hold the story for that week, and Hofstatter flew down to Durban to speak to Booysen. Wa Afrika joined the interview by telephone from Johannesburg.

It was a crucial conversation. Having worked on the story for months, having got the material from Booysen's detractors, it was the chance for the reporters to hear the other side.

*

The two parties – the policeman on the one hand, and the reporters on the other – gave me accounts of this conversation that differed in key aspects. Investigating these two versions told its own story about the difficulties of finding the truth in journalism.

Booysen told me that in the interview he'd challenged aspects of the reporters' story, and had pointed to evidence or ways of getting evidence that would bear him out. The reporters, for example, had said Booysen had arrived in a helicopter within minutes of a shooting in the Maryvale area, to congratulate his men on the killings. This was important because it put Booysen at the scene of the alleged crime, while he argued he wasn't involved in the day-to-day activities of the unit.

Booysen said he'd been at head office when he heard about the shooting, which was some distance away. He'd wanted to drive to the scene but was warned that he would hit peak-hour traffic, so instead he drove to the police air unit and was flown from there in a helicopter. He got to the scene of the shooting at least ninety minutes later, so it wasn't true that he was on the scene within minutes of the shooting, he said. Booysen told me that he'd told the journalists that they could go themselves to the air unit, check the helicopter logs and speak to the pilot to verify this.

Booysen said that Hofstatter had shown him pictures of what were apparently the shootings, but that these were just standard crime-scene photos from the police's own records, and he told the reporters this. One of them was of an event that didn't even involve the Cato Manor unit, and he pointed this out to them.

Hofstatter denied showing Booysen any pictures.

With two versions of the same conversation on the table, it looked like I'd have to rely on the traditional journalism practice of presenting both and leaving the reader to decide which was more credible. This was an unsatisfactory shortcut, but sometimes the only way to deal with factual disputes.

Then Booysen told me that both sides had recorded the conversation. I asked him if I could listen to his recording. He agreed, but said he'd have to dig it out from a container-load of material that he kept in a hidden place. He'd need to set aside a day on the weekend to locate it.

Weeks passed, and I heard nothing. I wrote to Booysen and he promised that he'd do it as soon as he could.

I wrote again. Months passed and I began to doubt whether his recording existed, or if it showed what he'd said it showed.

Eventually, I wrote to him to say that I couldn't wait much longer and would have to presume the recording didn't exist. He said he'd go to find it that Sunday.

That weekend, he messaged me to say that he and his wife had spent the whole day looking through masses of material and hadn't found it. But back home, his wife remembered that he had one box of CDs in the garage, and he'd found it there.

Please send it to me, I said.

No, he said, you must come and listen to it with me so that I can make sure you hear it all and understand what's going on in the audio.

Some weeks later, I met up with him to listen and we spent a good part of the day going through it.

*

The recording provided insight into how the *Sunday Times* reporters conducted the interview – and some pointers on how not to do it.

The interview started with formalities. They got Wa Afrika on the line from Johannesburg, summoned a police spokesperson to be present, and agreed that both parties would record the conversation. Booysen asked for assurances that they would deal with all the allegations they had and not do 'half a story'.

Hofstatter kicked off with a redacted version of what information they had and where they'd got it. In the course of their work, he said, they'd 'come across some court papers' that had raised 'this intriguing spectre of the actions of your Cato Manor unit'. He cited a report of an attempt to extort money from Booysen on the basis of photos of his men behaving irregularly. 'Was there anything in those pictures that would cast your unit in a bad light?' Hofstatter asked.

It wasn't unusual for a reporter to approach an issue from a side angle and avoid coming at the interviewee head-on, but Hofstatter didn't lay out the evidence and allegations they had and intended to print, thus leaving Booysen in the dark about the context and extent of their story.

As the interview progressed, Hofstatter's comments and questions were general: 'Some people are saying that the Cato Manor unit is a hit squad'; 'Is it just coincidence that over and over again suspects are killed in what is claimed to be self-defence, and experts question the evidence for this?' It isn't easy to refute broad general accusations rather than the specifics of cases where you can check the details.

Wa Afrika's questions were long and rambling, and often unanswerable because they involved matters over which Booysen had no control (like the slowness of post-mortem reports or the safety of witness-protection programmes), and sometimes they were bizarre: 'Can the general confirm or deny that the pictures of these incidents were stolen from the house of the Commissioner of Police?'; 'How many times in your career since 1976 have you seen a suspect shot by police in the head?'; and, when asking why Booysen had shaken hands with his men after arriving at the scene of a shootout, 'If Stephan walked into your office carrying a dead body, would you shake his hand?'

At one point Booysen said of a question being put to him: 'I can't believe what I am hearing.'

The recording confirmed that Booysen had dismissed the photographs: 'Every single one of them are actually police photographs ... None of those photographs can cast [the unit] in a bad light because they are normal crime-scene photos taken by police photographers.' And he pointed out that some of the pictures were misleading and might have been slipped in with malicious intent: 'Some do not even relate to cases investigated by the Cato Manor unit ... so whoever supplied the photographs didn't have all their facts straight ... They slotted in a few others, by default or by design I do not know.'

The recording also confirmed that Booysen had told the reporters that they could check the helicopter logs to see when he'd arrived at the Maryvale shooting. 'Whoever is giving you this information is absolutely and completely wrong. And it is easy to establish, because these chopper flights are all logged, and we can make that log available to you.'

Asked about arriving at the Maryvale shooting and congratulating his men, Booysen was dismissive: 'When you came in here, Stephan, I shook your hand. Was I congratulating you?'

Booysen was adamant that the Cato Manor squad was just one

of about ten units that fell under him. He was based at head office and not involved in the units' day-to-day operations. This became an important issue because as the story unfolded, the reporters pinned it all on Booysen rather than the immediate unit commanders. 'The picture that has been painted for you is that I am in direct command. Nothing could be further from the truth ... I am not operationally involved. I sit in management meetings,' he said.

Wa Afrika asked him about photos of the men drinking at a braai shortly after a shooting. It was an image that would have resonated with South Africans who recalled the notorious descriptions of the apartheid killing unit at their farm Vlakplaas, holding a braai after burning the bodies of their victims.

'Isn't this a little bit callous, a big party two hours after a killing?' Hofstatter asked.

Booysen said he hadn't been at the event, and took issue with the reporters calling the incident 'a killing': police only shot in self-defence when they were shot at, he said. 'I might ask the same question of a journalist. Journalists, during a day's work, get exposed to gruesome scenes, they get shot at, some of them lose their lives, and I am sure after hours back at the hotel, they also may have a beer or two.'

'Fair enough,' Hofstatter replied.

Then Hofstatter approached – still gently – the central question: the Cato Manor unit's kill rate. 'I have been looking at the statistics,' he said. 'Doesn't it suggest that things have got out of hand?'

But those statistics applied to all the police in KwaZulu-Natal, not just this unit. 'Go get the proper facts,' Booysen told him. 'I am not going to comment on those. I can only comment on my own unit.' Then he called the unit head to get their arrest statistics, as he wanted to show that their arrest success rate was high (although he didn't ask for their kill figures, the ones that he was telling Hofstatter to get).

There was a bizarre interruption while they were talking: one of the reporters' phones rang, and the ringtone was of President Jacob Zuma singing his favourite song: 'Umshini wami' ('Bring me my machine gun'). There was an awkward moment as they hurried to shut it down. On the recording, Booysen laughed.

Hofstatter told Booysen that experts who'd seen the pictures had thrown doubt on the police version that they were shooting in self-defence. 'If, over and over again, independent experts cast doubt on the version of events of the Cato Manor unit, isn't it a little suspicious? The same men – five names crop up again and again in these shootings – the same doubts are raised every time. Doesn't it cause some disquiet?'

Booysen cautioned them about relying on only photographs. 'Are you going on what an ex-policeman says, not having been to the scene, not having attended the post mortem, not having access to any of the statements?'

Hofstatter replied, 'I am calling them experts in their fields, and they say that, given the preliminary evidence that they have seen, there are serious questions and doubts raised that they think warrant a much more thorough investigation.'

'Don't jump to conclusions prematurely,' Booysen said. He could not accept untested evidence from experts who were paid to give their testimony, 'who are paid to come with a different opinion', he said. These opinions were often shot down in court.

Booysen told them that in every case of a death at the hands of the police, the ICD was immediately called, as was required, and they investigated.

But, Hofstatter said, there were concerns that the ICD wasn't investigating properly.

That was out of his hands, Booysen said. He could only make sure everything was reported to them, and who was better placed than the ICD to assess whether there had been wrongdoing?

The reporters quoted eyewitnesses who'd spoken of cold-blooded police killings, but refused to come forward because they feared for their lives. 'We have several accounts of people in at least two cases where they say the Cato Manor unit members executed the suspects, there was no evidence of any firing back, and the scenes were doctored afterwards … They have no reason to lie to us. I don't know, if they are under oath they might say something different, but isn't that a concern that the unit might have gone rogue?'

Booysen urged the journalists to be careful with such untested evidence. It was easy to make allegations and then hide behind claims that you were scared to come forward, he said. People with allegations must be talked to and put at ease, and must sign affidavits with their evidence and be brought into the witness-protection programme. Then their claims could be investigated and tested by the courts, he said.

Wa Afrika and Hofstatter questioned the safety of the witness-protection programme, and Booysen pointed out that not one person in the programme had been killed, and that there were examples every day of people giving evidence against policemen. He himself had arrested members of his unit for all sorts of wrongdoing, and the members of the public who'd given evidence against them hadn't been harmed.

Hofstatter said that journalists couldn't force people to come forward or sign affidavits, but that the many cases they'd found that had raised questions about the Cato Manor unit meant they had a public-interest obligation to report a worrying pattern of deaths. 'You can see our conundrum,' he said. 'If people have seen police executing someone, how are they going to take it to [the] police to report [it]?'

'That is my conundrum too,' Booysen responded. 'There are laws, there is the ICD, there is the witness-protection programme. If they come forward and make statements, then whoever is responsible will be arrested. If they don't, what do we do?'

'I accept what you are saying,' Hofstatter said, then challenged Booysen on whether he would accept an independent inquiry into the shootings.

'Absolutely,' Booysen said immediately. 'I would have no objection to something like that, maybe to prove once and for all what happened, because the picture that has been created has been completely skewed.' In some of the shootings, for example, Booysen said, his unit had been accompanied by the National Intervention Unit, which assisted local police with high-risk policing duties, specifically at incidents of violence where normal policing was deemed inadequate – and they had done some of the shooting.

Meanwhile, the reporters should be very careful regarding what they wrote about how suspects had died, Booysen cautioned. 'You can only go with a post-mortem report, not a photo, not a witness. The sole document that will say how a person was shot is the post-mortem report.'

But most of the post mortems were incomplete, Hofstatter said.

Booysen: 'You cannot expect me to respond to that.' Post mortems were performed by the Health Department. It was out of his hands.

Booysen then made a crucial point: the unit was operating in violent areas and against the most ruthless criminals who were often more heavily armed than them. 'This unit doesn't deal with white-collar crime,' he said. 'Ninety-nine percent of their cases are the most serious violent crime. The people they are dealing with are murderers, rapists, police killers, serial killers.'

He cited one of the cases where the reporters had raised questions about how the suspects had died. 'The victims in this murder had their throats slit. The man, the wife and the son bled to death. They were slaughtered like animals. This is the type of criminals we are dealing with.'

Hofstatter: 'That does not justify breaking the law of the land.'

Booysen: 'Absolutely not. That is why we have courts and the judiciary to deal with it. But if people make loose statements, make assumptions and conjecture without coming forward with the facts and having them tested, there is nothing you or I can do about that. Let's have these cases investigated and sent to the prosecutors for their decision.'

Booysen urged Hofstatter to find out how many of the more than 500 police killings in the province had been done by the Cato Manor unit, and how their record compared with those of other units.

'We will definitely do that,' Hofstatter said.

The three agreed that Hofstatter would email detailed questions that could be best answered by the unit members present at each shooting. Booysen said he would give the men permission to talk to the journalists, but warned that they were unlikely to want to talk while investigations were still open.

Booysen asked Hofstatter if he thought it was fair to spend many days investigating the claims, and then take just ninety minutes a few days before publication to hear the other side.

'I think it is fair,' Hofstatter said. 'Some other journalists would give you much less time.'

*

This interview highlighted how difficult it was to get to the bottom of such stories when the justice system wasn't operating effectively. These allegations should have been tested by the ICD, and then by prosecutors and the court system. Witnesses should have made sworn statements and been cross-examined, and been protected if necessary. Post mortems should have been completed quickly.

Journalists have limited tools at their command: they can't demand evidence, they can't force witnesses to make statements, and they have often to rely on untested witnesses and secondary interpretations of evidence such as photographs, which may be strongly suggestive but which are seldom conclusive.

Booysen had deferred to the men on the ground on the specifics of each shooting but a major obstacle was that investigations were still under way. Hofstatter told me he'd informed police communications officials of every person who would be named or pictured in their story, and requested an interview with all of them. But, as Booysen had warned, these men were unlikely to talk while investigations were incomplete. 'We were informed that [interviewing them all] would not be possible and we could interview Booysen on their behalf,' Hofstatter told me in 2020.

What the recorded interview did make clear was that that Booysen had challenged Hofstatter and Wa Afrika's version of events, and warned them to be careful what conclusions they drew from the so-called evidence, especially since some of it appeared to be tainted. He patiently and meticulously dealt with the issues they raised, and was adamant that his men shot and killed only in self-defence. In the recording, hints of Booysen's frustration with some of the questioning came through, but he painstakingly worked through the issues the reporters raised with him.

This fit with the Booysen I came to know: he was willing to go into deep detail about what had happened, and was open to scrutiny and questioning; and while he wasn't willing to trash his men, he was willing to listen to criticism of them and occasionally to agree with it. This is important, because a journalist takes note of someone who's confident enough to go over their story repeatedly, who doesn't respond defensively under questioning, and who's calm and consistent.

When Booysen later complained to the Press Council, he said that the journalists had 'afforded themselves scant opportunity to investigate or verify my version ... they were content to hear me, but did not bother to investigative my version ... During the interview it became evident that they were merely going through the paces ... they had clearly set their mind on printing the story and the interview was of academic value.'

Wa Afrika wouldn't (and still won't) speak to me. Hofstatter, meanwhile, offered plenty of different reasons for not fully opening up to me or others: he had to protect sources, he had to protect his colleagues, he was bound by confidentiality agreements, he didn't trust me, and so on. It didn't help his cause that he remained cagey about many of the details, even years later, and that he and his colleagues sometimes gave conflicting details of what had happened.

Hofstatter took a different view to mine of the interview. He and Wa Afrika had been 'scrupulously fair to [Booysen] at all times', he said, but Booysen had 'deflected' and 'obfuscated'. I had some concerns about this – perhaps Booysen's recording was incomplete – so I asked Hofstatter for his recording so that I could compare them.

'The interview took place over eight years ago and I no longer possess the recording,' he said – to my surprise, as any reporter would want to keep such a record of what became a much-disputed story. He had detailed notes, he said, but would only show them to a formal, independent inquiry.

*

What do the journalists do with a story that's so hard to pin down? Do they let it go, when other targets of the Cato Manor unit might die as a result? They have an obligation to put allegations of police brutality in the public eye, at the very least to let the policemen know they're being watched. If they use anonymous sources, the journalists have to decide if they have enough corroborating evidence to back them up, and they have to ensure that they convey it as just one version of a multi-faceted story. They have to put it into context, and the context Booysen gave it was of police confronting violent, heavily armed criminals in tough conditions.

The journalists had, at best, evidence of a pattern of killings that raised questions about the unit. They should have made it clear that their witnesses wouldn't swear to their evidence, or identify themselves, and that many of the cases were under investigation. They had an obligation to do more work – to track down the exact Cato Manor police-killings figures, for example, and compare them with those of other units; to check the helicopter log; and to pursue the details of each allegation with the individual unit members involved. And they were obliged to convey Booysen's argument that they had to take into account the violent and harsh context of these shoot-outs.

The Sunday Times *treatment*

'Shoot to kill' was the *Sunday Times* headline on 11 December 2011, just two days after Stephan Hofstatter and Mzilikazi Wa Afrika's interview with Johan Booysen. Above it was the strapline, 'Inside a South African police death squad'. The story kicked off: 'Today the *Sunday Times* lifts the lid on killings committed by an elite police unit.'

The Durban Organised Crime Unit based at Cato Manor had allegedly committed scores of assassinations, the story said, some in retaliation for suspected cop killings and others related to ongoing taxi wars.

Seven members of the unit were under investigation. The article cited killings going back to 2008, including that of a taxi boss who'd taken out an interdict to prevent police from harassing him, and a woman who said police had entered her house and killed her husband, and four cop-killers who'd died while sleeping on a mattress in their house.

The headline would have been familiar to many, as 'shoot to kill' was the controversial phrase attributed to Commissioner of Police Bheki Cele, who'd militarised police structures and encouraged a tough approach to criminality when he came to office in 2009. He'd later denied this phrase, which had drawn sharp criticism from human-rights organisations, claiming he'd said, 'Police must not die with their guns in their hands,' but the words were linked with him in public memory. The newspaper was suggesting that the conduct of the Cato Manor unit was the result of this get-tough attitude.

The story had gone through what insiders called 'the *Sunday Times* treatment', undergoing multiple edits to get it into the paper's house style. The draft would go to the news editor, then a subeditor, then the chief sub would take a look because it was a big story, as would the legal editor and at least one assistant/deputy editor, and finally the editor. This is normal newspaper practice, but at the *Sunday Times* it was designed to knock the story into a style that was a source of some internal pride. It had to be short – preferably no more than 800 words – and succinct: every extraneous word would be removed, every long sentence shortened, every multisyllable word substituted with a shorter one. It had to have real human beings at its centre so that it wasn't abstract and would matter to the reader.

Most of all, it had to be as unequivocal as possible – do we have to keep saying that things were 'alleged' or 'believed' to have happened, editors would ask; do we need quote marks around words like 'assassinations' or 'death squad'? Don't leave the reader wondering if the story is true: assert it, firmly – if we believe it to be true, the newspaper must swing its weight behind it, was the *Sunday Times* attitude.

Each editor would take out some qualifiers and nuance that might temper the story. The cumulative result was that the story was clear and firm, hard-hitting. It was a style developed over years, and with efficacy proven in the newspaper's sales figures. But in the process allegations often became assertions, assertions sometimes became fact, claims became evidence, and evidence became proof.

All this was then reduced to an eye-catching headline of just a few words – usually the starkest description of the story, with no qualifiers and little subtlety. And with the print deadline looming, all this had to happen within minutes. The team might have worked on the story for many months, but many of the crucial decisions – and those that would haunt the paper for years – would be made in the last few high-pressure minutes.

The paper had also established a policy on the byline, which identified those who'd reported the story: everyone who'd contributed anything to the piece would share the credit equally in a prominent joint byline, sometimes with half a dozen names in it. The first name was the lead writer, the person who'd pulled the contributions together and knocked it into a coherent story; sometimes this person was also the lead reporter, and sometimes their role was only to write and edit.

This shared credit was the result of longstanding competitiveness over the byline on the front-page splash – the main story spread across the front page – and the question of how much a writer had had to contribute to be included in it. The problem was solved by putting everyone in – which had the combined effect of sharing credit and spreading responsibility, so that it was sometimes not clear who was responsible for what. Raise a problem in a story, and almost everyone could point to someone else, either another author or an editor who'd worked on the text.

More than one reporter has said they would sometimes wake up on a Sunday to be surprised by what they saw under their own name. Hofstatter put it this way in an email to me:

> All bylined writers were given the chance to vet the stories prior to publication. In practice, there was often

very little time to do so. There were instances when my byline appeared on a sidebar I hadn't written, containing passages I didn't recognise, with errors I hadn't picked up because I hadn't looked at the proofs too closely.

None of this, he quickly added, applied to the Cato Manor stories.

This '*Sunday Times* treatment' ensured that this story had unambiguous wording: 'death squad', 'assassinations', 'scores'. It was a strong human-rights story, a stark illustration of the dangers of Cele's tough talk. It went so far as to compare the unit to Vlakplaas, the brutal extra-legal police hit squad of the apartheid era.

This was a long way from Hofstatter saying there were patterns of police killings that had raised concerns, or that experts had raised questions about the unit's conduct.

The story quoted Booysen briefly from the reporters' long interview with him, saying he 'strongly disagreed' with the *Sunday Times*'s interpretation. 'Their [the Cato Manor Unit's] lives were at stake; they defended themselves in a shoot-out.' They dealt with the most violent criminals and had a high success rate, Booysen said.

It was only a broad, general, routine denial, one that did no more than allow him the formal, minimal right of reply, giving the impression that he'd brushed them off rather than spent time going through the evidence with them. And there was no indication in the story that Booysen had shown a willingness to take a closer look at the evidence with them or that he welcomed the idea of a formal inquiry.

The reporters didn't look into the Cato Manor unit's claimed success rate or check out whether the unit had a higher killing rate than its peers. Their report said the unit was responsible for 45 of the 527 police killings in the province over three years, which was not disproportionately high.

They didn't check out the helicopter evidence. They used the picture of Booysen alighting from the helicopter and said he had 'apparently congratulated officers'.

It was only in retrospect that it became clear that readers would have to trust the *Sunday Times* if they were to buy into the story. The evidence the newspaper offered was vague and anonymous: police who'd looked at photographs of the bodies said these 'appeared' to have been executions. The journalists had, the report said, 'testimony and copious evidence from dozens of people about the killings, including hundreds of death scene photographs and expert ballistics reports. Three senior police officials, a pathologist and a ballistics expert had examined the images and 'concluded that they appeared to have been executions'. Little specific evidence was offered to the reader, and none of the witnesses gave their names to add to the credibility of the story.

And it was only later that the question arose why Johan Booysen was named at the very top of the story as the officer who had 'ultimate command'. The reporters could have chosen the two layers of leadership between him and the actual unit, or the layers above him. Instead, those in charge of the day-to-day operations of the unit, and the multiple layers of command between them and the top, were barely mentioned. Why were they so intent on targeting Booysen, and not conveying his disclaimer that he wasn't involved operationally?

Out of the blue, in the article the reporters said Booysen's appointment the previous year had 'caused a stir among provincial top brass' because of his unit's 'disproportionately high kill rate of crime suspects'. There hadn't previously been any report of such a controversy.

Prominent on the page was a powerful photograph of members of the unit apparently celebrating after a shoot-out: some of them were bare-chested, waving guns and cups in the air. It looked bad: a show of bravado and machismo after a killing, apparently mixing guns and alcohol in contravention of professional rules.

There was another picture, of bodies lying in the back of a bakkie after a shooting. It was the photograph that Booysen had specifically told them was unrelated to the Cato Manor unit: members of the police-dog unit and flying squad had carried out this shooting, not the Cato Manor unit.

Four years later, on 27 December 2015, the *Sunday Times* apologised for this error, and for another minor misquote. When they did so, they used these errors to trumpet their accuracy: 'After conducting a review of 28 articles and more than 20 pictures, covering 20 incidents resulting in 90 deaths, we would like to correct [these] two errors ...'

*

Various follow-ups appeared on the *Sunday Times* front page over the next few months, each one an escalation of the story. 'Rogue unit "executed" 51' was the splash on 19 February 2012. The alleged hit squad was now being investigated for many more killings, which were now all escalated to 'executions', including one in its offices and one in its toilets, the paper reported. Booysen was the only person named, as the one who had 'ultimate command'.

A week later, the paper had interviewed some of the families of those killed. 'We'll come back and kill you' was the front-page story, telling of policemen crowing after showing off the bodies of two men they'd just shot. Again Booysen was named, even though he wasn't even alleged to have been present when it had happened.

In August 2012 the *Sunday Times* raised the stakes further. 'New details emerged this week of how the rogue Cato Manor cops were "guns for hire", contracted to hunt down and kill members of a taxi association involved in a turf war,' it claimed. Again the unit was compared to Vlakplaas, and again Booysen was the commander named. It was now stated as fact that the unit had 'gone rogue' – a term that was to be used often by the *Sunday Times* in a number of its controversial stories.

Most significant, though, was that at no time in these many stories did the journalists give more than two short paragraphs to Booysen's counter-narrative. He had pointed to the extreme violence of the taxi bosses, arguing that his men had shot in self-defence. He had highlighted the high murder rate in the area, how heavily armed the criminals were, and the strong pressure from above and from the public to act firmly on criminal violence. He had kept pointing out that while he took responsibility for those under his command, there were a number of layers of authority between him and them. Why did they always go for him?

This was the '*Sunday Times* treatment': there could be only one version. A counter-narrative would only confuse the reader and weaken the story. So the newspaper stuck with its rule: choose what you believe to be true, and go with it.

*

The *Sunday Times* has for over a hundred years been a leader in national news. For much of this time it was the only really national newspaper and the one that could be found in a wider cross-section of middle-class households on a Sunday than any other. Apart from a few years in the early 2000s, when the populist tabloid the *Daily Sun* overtook it, it has long been the country's biggest newspaper, and numerous attempts to compete with it in the weekend market have fallen short. So when the *Sunday Times* took a position, when it targeted wrongdoers or hailed heroes, it mattered. A lot.

The 'paper for the people' was launched in the early 1900s with a dedicated staff of just two, the editor and an assistant. It got off to a difficult start, facing active church resistance: many pastors called on their congregants to eschew this invasion into their holy day. But the paper's sensationalist mix of hard news and social gossip was an instant success, and on its launch day on 4 February 1906 an extra 5 000 copies had to be printed immediately, on top of the original 10 000, to meet demand.

At the launch, the colourful, outspoken founder-editor, George Kingswell, tried to placate the churches by saying the paper would break with the tradition of putting adverts on the front page, and put news there instead, so as not to contaminate the sabbath with commerce. He soon realised that the news he intended reporting – crime, divorce, rape, social scandal – would be even more provocative on the front page, so he used birth and death notices and a large cartoon up front. Kingswell, contemptuous of all politicians and brazenly racist, set the tone for the paper that would sell well for years to come – a rich mix of outspoken politics, celebrity gossip and salacious news. 'Dip your pen in bile,' he told newcomer Langley Levy, who was to become editor. 'Don't be afraid of libel. They threaten all kinds of things here, hoping to gag the press. But they can't gag the *Sunday Times* ... Say what you think!'

The editor who perfected the paper's rich mix of populism and power to maximise its sales and profits was Joel Mervis in the 1960s and 1970s. Mervis, though, was cautiously liberal and decidedly anti-apartheid, and gave his newspaper's backing to the hapless parliamentary opposition, the United Party. The relentless support of the country's biggest newspaper never raised this party from the dead, nor did Mervis ever move beyond the strict bounds of white parliamentary politics.

The United Party pushed for a milder, more caring racial separation, and that was as far as Mervis would take it. His mix of ruling-party scandal and intrigue with a back page famous for gossip and mildly risqué photos meant financial success but a politics prescribed by the white parties of the time and reflecting all the contradictions and limitations of white liberalism in South Africans living under the constrictions of apartheid: speaking out against petty discrimination, pushing for reform and exposing government corruption, but unable to embrace the rising black political movements in the streets, on the factory floors and in exile, and forced to enact in its own operations the rules of segregation and censorship. Its coverage, its voice, its news choices reflected the inequalities and inequities in the society it reported on.

Within these constraints, the *Sunday Times* was nonetheless big and strong enough to do as it pleased, and made enough money to scare off anyone who wanted to take it on. There was something in the newspaper for everyone in the family within its target market, from comics to a weighty business section. And if it was on the front or back page, it was a talking point for the week – and the rest of the media followed.

The paper grew consistently until it hit 500 000 copies in the 1970s – more than twice its nearest rival – and only stopped there because management put a cap on the print order, realising that they couldn't push their advertising rates any higher. The paper was a massive cash cow. Even today, it's the only significant – if diminished – profit-maker in the extended Arena Holdings media group.

The dapper Tertius Myburgh was the editor in the 1980s, known by his staff as 'Smiling Death' for his capacity to make you like him as he knifed you in the back. He pivoted the paper to the right, backing the reformists in the apartheid ruling party rather than the opposition. This included a crucial call to vote 'yes' in the 1982 referendum on the government's tricameral system – a half-baked reform move that sparked the township uprising that was to lead to the end of apartheid.

Myburgh was accused of being a government plant in the opposition media, notably by journalist John Matisonn. The evidence was largely circumstantial, though it was clear that Myburgh delivered the paper's support to the ruling party, demonising the liberation movement and backing the National Party's promise of cautious and partial top-down reform.

Myburgh was followed by Ken Owen in the early 1990s. More of a classic liberal, Owen was furiously independent, and with a pen and management style that dripped with Kingswell's bile. The paper's circulation rose to a record 560 000 during the period of the first democratic election in 1994, ensuring its voice remained dominant in the public sphere. I knew its clout well, as my friends and I ran what was then *The Weekly Mail* – and it was galling to know that the news we broke would have much greater impact if the *Sunday Times* picked it up, even though they often didn't bother to credit us.

'If it's not in the *Sunday Times*, it isn't news,' was their line of swagger, 'and it's not news until we say it is.' And they changed their masthead slogan from 'A Paper for the People', which had run since the beginning, to '*The* Paper for the People', as if to embed their ascendancy into their title.

They were top of the heap. They were making pots of money. They didn't have to pay much attention to their rivals and competitors. So when the world began to change around them, the *Sunday Times* newsroom – like so many big, traditional newsrooms – was slow to take on the full import of it.

David Bullard was hired as a columnist in 1994, just as the paper was entering a period when it would have to grapple with its identity, its history, its internal makeup, and its place and voice in the new democracy. That it should at this time hire a right-wing British expat whose column, 'Out to Lunch', pictured him with a cigar and a glass of champagne, is the best illustration of how deep ran the contradictions in *the paper for the people*, and the challenges of editing it.

Bullard's wit catered for an element of white South Africa that would see itself as liberal and open-minded, but was deeply cynical of majority rule and the democratic transition, which might have characterised the *Sunday Times* readership of old, but not the new. It was an oddity in a newspaper running to catch up with the massive demographic, political and cultural changes happening around it.

The *Sunday Times* was an historically 'white' newspaper in a society in which the media were sharply and deliberately divided by race and language. In the first 90 years of its life, its owners, its editors and most of its writers and readers were white. Change began in the 1980s, as black staff were hired and black readership grew, but the paper remained firmly within the paradigm of white parliamentary politics, fearful of losing its wealthy white advertising base.

With liberation in the 1990s, there was immediate pressure – internal and external – to transform. As black editors were appointed, the focus shifted to issues of content, particularly when the media were critical of the ANC government. This led to an intense debate about whether the newspaper's criticism was genuine, independent and credible, or rooted in its historical hostility towards the liberation movement. Black journalists – including those who'd asserted a fierce independence – were often accused of being nominally in charge but pandering to white interests and values.

The *Sunday Times* grappled to find its voice in this atmosphere, to define its independence and its attitude to the new order. Bullard's survival as a columnist on the paper was a symbol of its dual and shifting identity. It couldn't last.

The contradictions came to a head with a Bullard column in 2008 headlined 'Uncolonised Africa wouldn't know what it was missing', which had more stereotypes per sentence than anthropologists would consider possible. ANC leader Pallo Jordan said Bullard's writing was 'like coming into someone's living room and defecating on the carpet' and he was 'the sort of person South Africa does not need within its borders'.

Editor Mondli Makhanya, who oversaw the paper's centenary, had tolerated – even defended – Bullard when he'd been sued a year earlier by President Jacob Zuma for a column headed 'Stupidity a mitigating circumstance for Zuma'. But by publishing this latest column the paper was 'complicit in disseminating [Bullard's] Stone Age philosophies', Makhanya said – and fired him.

It was a tale that told of the slowness and difficulties of changing the paper.

Booysen speaks

The Cato Manor death-squad story won a string of prestigious local and international awards: Stephan Hofstatter, Mzilikazi Wa Afrika and Rob Rose scooped the Story of the Year, Journalist of the Year and Investigative Journalism categories at the 2012 Sikuvile Journalism Awards, the runner-up prize in the 2012 Taco Kuiper Award for Investigative Journalism (the country's biggest journalism competition), and joint first prize in the 2013 Global Shining Light Award of the Global Investigative Journalism Network.

I was a judge for two of these competitions, the Taco Kuiper and the Global Shining Light, and I can only say that there was little to suggest at the time that the story was anything but a solid piece of public-interest reporting. Like most people in and outside of journalism, our panel of judges trusted the *Sunday Times* and its investigations unit.

As a result of the bad press it had got, the Cato Manor unit was disbanded and Johan Booysen was suspended. He fought his suspension in court and won reinstatement.

He and a number of his men were arrested in an orchestrated public event in August 2012, with television cameras and *Sunday Times* photographers present, and charged with murder and racketeering. *City Press* reported that the ICD had wanted to charge others, not Booysen, saying 'there was no case against him'. And the ICD had wanted to negotiate a 'quieter, less aggressive surrender process' rather than the show arrests staged for the benefit of the national broadcaster, the South African Broadcasting Corporation (SABC), and the

Sunday Times. But different orders had 'come from above', though they never said exactly where from.

The *Sunday Times* took the arrests as vindication of its reporting. 'Now that the dust has settled ... it would be useful to deal with the facts of the matter,' an editorial stated, reaching deep into the newspaper's stock of righteous indignation.

To those who queried why the *Sunday Times* and the SABC had been tipped off to record the arrests as a public show, the newspaper said the death squad's victims had never been given the courtesy of arrest, and had allegedly been shot after surrendering – double standards, the paper charged.

The editorial showed contempt for those who believed the policemen could be innocent, dismissing them as children: 'Well, there are many people who believe that the tooth fairy exists – but that does not make it true.' It said there had been a long investigation that had shown that the police had tampered with crime scenes to mislead investigations, had threatened witnesses, and had planted weapons on victims to make it seem as if they, the police, had acted in self-defence.

What the editorial didn't say was that the police spokesperson had said at the time of the arrest that Johan Booysen and his men had targeted the victims in order to gain merit certificates and incentive rewards. But when, after a night in custody, they appeared for a bail hearing, it was shown that none of them had received any such certificates, promotions or rewards.

Police said that in searches of the unit members' homes they'd found explosives, illegal weapons and counterfeit money – but it turned out the 'explosives' were police-issue teargas canisters, the 'illegal weapons' were a single weapon licensed to a recently deceased family member, and the 'counterfeit money' was part of a numismatic collection. These might have been just the errors of the incompetent, but it looked more like a deliberate attempt to frame Booysen and his men as rogue policemen.

It was also a mystery why they should proceed with a mass trial and include Booysen. Normal process would have used individual cases to establish a pattern of wrongdoing and then gone after any commander who'd been implicated by the evidence. But that would have left Booysen out of it, for a while at least.

The charge of racketeering was knocked down quite quickly. It took seven years – and most of Booysen's pension funds – to clear the rest of the charges, which were finally dropped in 2019.

The dust had not settled.

*

Every interview a reporter carries out on a story gives more information, every perspective adds another layer of insight – if, that is, the reporter goes about the story in the knowledge that every story is made up of multiple versions and viewpoints, and if the journalist respects each of the perspectives obtained from different people.

This is not to say that the journalist treats all viewpoints as equal, as some are more credible than others. The journalist's task is to sift through the versions for credibility, and make those choices clear to the audience. As we teach in journalism school, if someone says it's raining, and another person says it's not, your job isn't to report both claims, but to stick your head out the window and see if it's raining.

To get a full picture, the reporter has to embrace complexity and contradiction, and get as many versions as possible, when the temptation – and the demand from editors – is to offer the reader simplicity and clarity, and do it at speed.

I felt this strongly as I researched this book. Some interviews turned everything on its head, while others allowed the correction of an apparently minor fact or even just the qualification an assertion. In any given instance, just when I thought I understood what had happened, I would do one more interview and find that it added another level to my understanding.

Of course, when you're writing a book, you can add interview upon interview, and version upon version, sometimes to a point at which

31

you have to stop yourself or else you'd go on forever. A weekly newspaper has far less time to spend researching a story – although much more time than a daily to fill out a story with multiple perspectives. Dailies – memorably called 'the first rough draft of history' by *Washington Post* publisher Philip Graham – rely largely on a formula of reporting conflicting versions side by side, and doing no more under pressure of time than guiding the reader towards an understanding of the various perspectives. This leads to the 'he said, she said' shortcut of journalism – helpful on a breaking story but not the best way to establish the truth, as the reporter hasn't done the task of weighing up the relative veracity of each version.

On a weekly publication, there should be more time to gather and weigh up multiple versions, to discard those that lack authority and to guide the reader towards those that stand up the best. Much depends, though, on a newsroom's practices and values: does the editor want simplicity and clarity, or can the audience deal with contradiction and complexity? Do they want heroes and villains, or do they want to convey the nuances of human interaction?

Newsroom processes shape these questions: do editors and sub-editors see their role as hardening up a story or verifying it? Do they have the skill to improve it without distorting it, or do they carve it up to fit the need for an eye-catching headline? The editor's job is to shape these processes and values, which in turn shape the product.

Sunday Times editors opted for fast journalism, sneering at those who went slowly. They gave the investigative team more leeway, sometimes allowing the luxury of months on a story, only for the team to be forced to rush it when an empty front page was looming.

*

My sister, Stephanie Miller, had worked alongside Booysen when she was a peace monitor in the 1990s and he was a policeman assigned to work with those trying to contain the KwaZulu-Natal violence in the build-up to the country's first democratic election. He was a solid, old-style professional, she told me. He didn't have a lot of social graces, but he did his job without fear or favour. He was the sort of policeman who could be relied on to stay away from the politics of apartheid – interested in building a career as a professional, ready to work under any government. She appreciated working alongside him, and had respect for him, the two of them having seen some difficult things together.

My first interaction with Booysen was when he contacted me in 2018 to ask me, as a judge in the Taco Kuiper Awards, to rescind the *Sunday Times's* runner-up award for the Cato Manor story. He then accidentally copied me in on a note intended for someone else: 'He is very terse,' he wrote about me. 'Sounds like one of these lib-tarts who has difficulty to be answerable to a ex police general and an Afrikaans speaking one nogal.' [sic]

When I pointed out that he'd sent this to me by mistake, Booysen didn't seem embarrassed. 'Actually, it was meant for someone else. But for your information I mean it and make no apology for it ... You seem to think you are immune to be questioned and hence is not answerable to any one ... It is the same arrogance by the journalists that has culminated in this sordid saga.' [sic]

It wasn't a good start.

Face-to-face, though, he was unpretentious and helpful. He started the story from an entirely different place when I visited him in December 2018 in his new office on the huge Midrand campus of one of the country's largest private-security companies. He'd forgotten that there was a fire drill that morning, so when I arrived scores of people were milling around the office-block courtyard, relaxed and chatting.

Booysen sneaked me into the empty building so we could do our interview uninterrupted. His office had the stark anonymity of a government workplace, with nothing but a map on the wall and a picture of his family on his desk, though the furniture was new and modern, as you would expect in a corporate headquarters.

I found Booysen to be a mild-mannered man who talked with the quiet confidence of someone who knew he'd done little wrong and just had to keep saying and showing it, so that the truth would eventually come out. He was proud of having risen through the police ranks, and had had every reason to believe he would carry on doing so. This was a man whose world had been torn apart around him. All his certainties of being a career policeman had been shattered, and he'd had to rebuild a new life.

He had meticulously collected and stored all the evidence of what had happened to him, and hidden it in a huge container in a secret place. He was still locked in legal battles to clear his name, and wouldn't give up. By this time, after the fall of President Zuma, the state had set up the Zondo Commission of Inquiry to look into all aspects of the allegations of 'state capture' – of private interests seizing control of state institutions, particularly the large parastatals and their powerful boards, and twisting them to their own purposes – and Booysen gave me the first draft of the statement he'd prepared for the inquiry. It consisted of scores of pages of detailed and methodically gathered evidence.

Booysen told me he'd had an unblemished record in the police, rising through the ranks over forty years. This had changed when he became involved in an investigation of fraud and corruption by well-connected local businessman Thoshan Panday.

He'd inherited the Panday case when he took over as regional head of the Hawks in 2010. Panday was under scrutiny for suspect deals with the SAPS to provide accommodation worth R45 million during the 2010 World Cup. The evidence was that Panday and a Colonel Navin Madhoe, who'd worked in the SAPS regional procurement office that handled purchases and tenders, had conspired to inflate quotations and share the proceeds.

When Booysen learnt that an outstanding payment of R15 million was about to be paid to Panday, he informed SAPS financial services that they shouldn't release the money until his investigation was complete.

Early in 2010, Panday approached a member of Booysen's Cato Manor unit and indicated he knew exactly where the evidence against him was kept, and asked this person to steal it – or to burn down the building. 'Name your price,' he said. Booysen said he set up a sting, but it fell through. It appeared Panday had been tipped off.

Booysen then came under severe pressure to drop the case. He got a call in May 2010 from the provincial commissioner, Lieutenant-General Mmamonnye Ngobeni, telling him to end the investigation – 'there was enough going on in the province' and 'the police could not be embarrassed any further', she said.

Booysen wasn't happy, but called in the investigating officer to tell him to stop.

A few days later Ngobeni phoned him again and, Booysen says, shouted at him: 'What is wrong with you people? ... I told you to stop the investigation, but you people are still continuing.'

Shortly after this, Booysen was called to a meeting in her office and Madhoe – one of the accused – was present. 'She accused us of being more concerned about finances than the lives of the public,' Booysen stated. Booysen didn't want to discuss the matter in front of Madhoe and asked to see Ngobeni alone. Booysen told her that he believed they had an obligation to pursue the matter, but she assigned the case to another officer.

Booysen was again called to Ngobeni's office. This time, astoundingly, Panday, the civilian who was under investigation, was present. Once again, Ngobeni told Booysen to stop his probe.

However, Booysen being Booysen, he continued to follow the evidence. Twice more he was called in to Ngobeni's office, and both times Panday was there to hear him warned off. 'These meetings caused me some level of discomfort,' Booysen said with studied understatement. 'Panday levelled several allegations against the investigators and threatened to sue us.'

Ngobeni even instructed Booysen to turn the investigation on one of his own men, and she later phoned Booysen at home to complain that he hadn't stopped the investigation.

In 2012 it emerged in newspaper reports that Panday had paid for an extravagant birthday party in 2010 for Ngobeni at an Umhlanga Rocks hotel. An investigation was opened into Ngobeni's alleged corruption.

When Booysen was granted search warrants for Panday's premises, he found something remarkable: Panday had a copy of a confidential report on the investigation that Booysen had provided to Ngobeni. Someone high up was working with the accused, Panday, to frustrate the investigation.

Booysen said he discussed it with the national head of the Hawks, Lieutenant-General Anwa Dramat, and national commissioner of the SAPS, General Bheki Cele. They instructed him to continue his investigation.

Then another piece fell into place. Booysen received an unexpected visit from Edward Zuma, son of President Zuma, some time around June 2010 in his Durban office, Booysen said. Edward Zuma asked Booysen to release the money owed to Panday; he told Booysen he was a 'silent partner' in the deal and wasn't getting his dividends. He'd come to try and use his name to unblock the flow of funds.

The following year, Colonel Madhoe, who'd been accused with Panday, approached Booysen to show him crime-scene pictures that appeared to show the Cato Manor unit's bloody trail of killings. 'My interpretation was that he was subtly trying to intimidate me,' Booysen said.

Madhoe said that Panday would pay 'two bar' (R2 million) for Booysen's 'cooperation'. Booysen decided to set up another sting. He went to the National Prosecuting Authority (NPA) and got authorisation to go along with the bribe offer and record it, so that there could be no confusion afterwards and it would be valid court evidence. A meeting was set up and Madhoe transferred a bag containing R1,3 million in cash from his own car boot to Booysen's.

Madhoe was arrested that same month, as was Panday.

As part of the investigation, Booysen had received legal permission to tap Panday's phone. Shortly after the sting, the tap revealed Panday complaining to a Deebo Mzobe – another relative of President Zuma –

that he'd been set up. According to Booysen, they were recorded saying that Booysen 'had to be taken care of because he was standing in the way of everything' and that his 'wings must be clipped'.

Soon after this, a further attempt to stymie the investigation came from the NPA, when advocate Laurence Mrwebi from the Pretoria office wrote to inquire why Panday and Madhoe were being charged. The local prosecutor, advocate Bheki Manyathi, wrote a lengthy opinion, setting out the substantial evidence against the two.

This laid bare how state capture worked. State tenders, often at inflated prices, went to those with political connections, and President Zuma's family and friends were often involved. When honest officials tried to stop this, they themselves were targeted, and institutions that had been 'captured', like the NPA, interceded on behalf of the corrupt. Those who stood by the evidence and their professional principles were pushed out. Manyathi, the local prosecutor who'd resisted dropping the case against Panday and Madhoe, was overlooked for promotion and left the public service.

*

Booysen had inherited another politically sensitive case when he took office that he believed set him up against powerful people.

Two provincial politicians, Peggy Nkonyeni and Mike Mabuya-khulu, and businessman Gaston Savoi were charged with corruption in the supply of water plants for hospitals. The regional Acting Director of Public Prosecutions in KwaZulu-Natal, advocate Simphiwe Mlotshwa, was coming under pressure to drop the charges.

Advocates Laurence Mrwebi, again, and Anthony Mosing, from the NPA, summoned the investigators to Pretoria to argue that the case wasn't strong enough to proceed. Booysen asked his people about the evidence, and was assured it was strong. The case went forward.

Mlotshwa was an obstacle to those interfering with the process of justice, because he was doing his job: proceeding with charges against the accused even if they had political influence, and declining to go after Booysen because the evidence in that case was insufficient.

It was during this time that the *Sunday Times* was given the handful of photos and other evidence about Booysen's 'hit squad' and the first attempt to prosecute Booysen was initiated. Acting NPA national head Nomgcobo Jiba pressured advocate Mlotshwa to prosecute Booysen, but he said there wasn't enough evidence.

Mlotshwa was replaced in July 2012 by advocate Moipone Noko, who within days withdrew the charges against Nkonyeni and Mabuyakhulu, as well as against Panday and Madhoe. Charges against Booysen soon followed.

'This is one example of how the capturing of the NPA started to manifest itself. Prosecutors who stood for justice and who prosecuted without fear or favour were systematically worked out and replaced by pliable prosecutors who acted towards political objectives and not in the interests of justice,' Booysen wrote in his Zondo Commission affidavit.

Similarly, after Dramat was ousted as head of the Hawks in 2015 and Berning Ntlemeza was plucked out of nowhere to replace him, 'the new regime in turn made changes to the structures downwards that were calculated to seize complete control of the Hawks by Ntlemeza by placing pliable people in strategic positions. This resulted in a mass exodus of competent skilled personnel.'

There was also, according to Booysen, direct interference from Minister of Police Nathi Mthethwa, a man who had shown his willingness to intercede on behalf of President Zuma and his friends. He met with the prosecutors to push them to act on the Cato Manor unit because he'd heard there were human-rights abuses, even though he'd previously defended the Cato Manor unit publicly and had filed an affidavit in its support in a civil case.

It was becoming increasingly clear that there was a posse after Booysen. In the Cato Manor story these people had found a vulnerability – and in the *Sunday Times* they had found willing listeners.

*

When the *Sunday Times* editor Bongani Siqoko later said they believed they'd been manipulated in the handling of this story, they said they didn't know who was manipulating them and dismissed the idea that it could be Thoshan Panday. Hofstatter told me that Panday had offered them the photos of the Cato Manor Unit's killings, and asked in return that they introduce him to Anwa Dramat, head of the Hawks. The *Sunday Times* team told him they already had the photos, and that anyway they didn't do such deals.

Journalists from other newspapers later said that Panday had also offered them the Cato Manor photos, but that they'd been sceptical of his motives and trustworthiness.

Booysen discovered that Panday had paid someone to steal the photos from the police computer system. That person had spoken about it because he said that he'd been promised R50 000 but been paid only R5 000. So it seems that the photos had originated with Panday, although there had been intermediaries who'd passed them on.

These were all the dealings that Stephan Hofstatter admitted to the *Sunday Times* team having had with Thoshan Panday. But when police were investigating Panday, they were granted a warrant to tap his phone. According to Booysen, they recorded conversations between Mzilikazi Wa Afrika and Panday, including one in which Wa Afrika asked Panday to steal a docket that implicated Booysen in a shooting. Another recording has Wa Afrika arranging to fly to Durban to get from Panday a video that allegedly implicated the Cato Manor unit. But when Wa Afrika arrived in Durban, he called Panday, and Panday told him that the video had been sold to TV programme *Carte Blanche* and was no longer available. *Carte Blanche* managers, though, knew nothing of this recording, which in all likelihood never existed.

Booysen said that at one of his court appearances in Durban he confronted Wa Afrika about working with Panday. Wa Afrika said it was Panday who'd called him with information, not the other way around. Booysen, who'd heard the telephone recordings, knew this to be untrue: 'I told him it was him who made contact with Panday and that I found it unbecoming that a journalist collaborates with a suspect in a criminal investigation to undermine that investigation. He again denied it.'

Booysen said to me, 'If Wa Afrika denies my version, I will tell him to his face he is a liar.'

It is clear that at least some of the *Sunday Times* team were working with Panday, who they knew was trying to undermine Booysen. Admittedly, journalists sometimes use unsavoury sources with dubious motives but in this case it did mean that they would have been alert to Panday's agenda, and should have been sceptical about using his information and cautious about serving his ends.

Even if they didn't see it at first, they would in the course of their investigation have read Booysen's court papers, which gave a detailed enunciation of how he believed he was being framed for political reasons. They would've had to ignore what rival newspapers such as the *Sunday Tribune* were reporting: that Booysen was being targeted because he was investigating corruption. And they would've had to ignore their own reporting, as they themselves had exposed Panday: they had reported in 2011 on the police-accommodation scandal that Booysen was investigating, and how Cele himself had irregularly signed off on the deal with Panday; and in 2012 on how Panday had paid for holidays, a car and tuition fees for the families of police officials.

The *Sunday Times* team argued that Booysen had only investigated Panday when he'd had no choice but to do so, and was using Panday as a diversion from the Cato Manor story. But there is no evidence to back this up.

The *Sunday Times*'s treatment followed the well-established pattern. As the evidence grew over time that there was more to this story than met the eye, they doubled down on their version and ignored the alternative one. The normal practice would've been to tell the reader about the other version, even if they didn't give it much credit, or to show why it wasn't credible if that was what they believed – not to ignore it. But it was more dramatic and effective to stick with one straightforward, apparently uncontested, narrative. That was the *Sunday Times* way.

They even turned around the incident in which Colonel Navin Madhoe had paid Booysen a bribe and Booysen had trapped him. 'There was much more to the tale,' the *Sunday Times* investigative team wrote, giving credence to Madhoe's claims that Booysen had initiated the attempt to buy the Cato Manor photos from him. This was not a credible explanation, because the photos were mostly standard crime-scene photos and therefore of little value, Booysen had obtained legal permission to conduct the sting, and Madhoe had been caught red-handed.

'Rogue unit "executed" 51' the *Sunday Times* screamed on 19 February 2012. In fact, this was the number of deaths being investigated, and there was no suggestion that they were all cold-blooded killings. Some of them had been investigated already, and ruled to be legitimate acts of self-defence.

On 4 March the newspaper ran an opinion piece titled 'Truth is first casualty' in which the three writers – Stephan Hofstatter, Mzilikazi Wa Afrika and Rob Rose – took on those who'd spoken out in defence of Johan Booysen. This was the only hint they gave that their narrative was contested, but they painted the conveyors of the counter-narrative as themselves corrupt or as far-right-wingers who were in favour of police killing criminals.

Noseweek *weighs in*

One publication that did carry Johan Booysen's narrative was Martin Welz's monthly investigative magazine, *Noseweek*. This small, cheeky, canary-in-the-coalmine magazine mixes investigation, rumour and speculation with tongue-in-cheek fun at the expense of anyone who holds or hangs around with power and wealth. *Noseweek* is often the first to signal when something or someone is worth watching, because Welz is prepared to say what other journalists are thinking.

Welz, a trained lawyer who'd built up a substantial reputation as a muckraking investigator on papers such as *Rapport* and the *Sunday Express*, started *Noseweek* as his personal project in 1993 and has run it almost singlehandedly ever since. Under the slogan 'News you're not supposed to know', he's been relentless in his dogged pursuit of corporate malfeasance, but also sometimes veers eccentrically off into areas of personal obsession.

Noseweek took on the *Sunday Times* in a series of long, detailed pieces over many months. 'The award-winning *Sunday Times* exposé of an alleged police "death squad" based at Cato Manor ... is rapidly falling apart,' *Noseweek* wrote in July 2013. It suggested that the *Sunday Times* team had got its pictures and other material from Thoshan Panday and Navin Madhoe, who'd offered a CD of the material to other newspapers, which had snubbed it because of where it came from – the men Booysen was investigating, so not exactly credible sources.

The *Sunday Times* threesome said it was 'poppycock' to say this was where they'd got their evidence. Wa Afrika would only tell *Noseweek* that they'd got it from a senior person in Crime Intelligence.

Wa Afrika also denied ever having met Panday, although *Noseweek* said they had 'a first-hand account' of the meeting. Hofstatter, however, admitted to having been at the meeting, but denied they'd used any information from Panday.

Noseweek described some of the shoot-outs between the Cato Manor unit and the criminals they were chasing to highlight how heavily armed and dangerous the criminals were – a context ignored by the *Sunday Times,* yet critical to assessing whether the Cato Manor Unit was 'rogue'.

The *Sunday Times* treated *Noseweek* with all the contempt it could muster. When Martin Welz wrote a piece for the *Sunday Tribune* and the *Weekend Argus* that challenged their story, they responded with an article that called his version 'pure invention'. It was a strange overstatement, as Welz may have disputed their facts and interpretations but it wasn't invention.

The *Sunday Times* continued, 'We have tried to follow the dictum "never argue with a fool"' but with 'Welz's latest diatribe based entirely on a false premise, we decided it was time to set the record straight'. The *Sunday Times* said the *Noseweek* story was 'without merit and false ... riddled with distortions, defamatory insinuations and lies'. And they nitpicked *Noseweek's* reporting: it wasn't Wa Afrika who'd got the CD of pictures, and it hadn't been from Crime Intelligence head Lieutenant-General Richard Mdluli, they said.

In perhaps the strangest part, the *Sunday Times* asked how going for the Cato Manor unit could derail the fraud and corruption investigations into Panday and Madhoe because the unit didn't deal with these crimes. But it was Booysen who was overseeing these investigations – and it was Booysen's name that kept appearing high up in the *Sunday Times* stories.

The *Sunday Times* didn't deal with the substance of Booysen's version, only restated its own investigation and evidence. *Noseweek*, the writers said – with more than a touch of the righteousness that had infected the paper – had rushed to protect the powerful, whereas the *Sunday Times* had spoken for the voiceless victims.

A further *Sunday Times* article in February 2015 gunned for *Noseweek* reporter Paul Kirk who, they said, had a dubious record, citing a 2003 court judgment that had found him to be 'a liar and a coward' who'd planted false evidence to implicate someone in fictitious crimes. Kirk had fed them information on the story, they said, and then had made a 'dramatic about-turn ... [writing] a series of articles in *Noseweek* claiming that we'd got our facts wrong'. 'Normally we ignore such small fry,' wrote Hofstatter, Wa Afrika and Rose, 'but we believe our readers deserve to know the full story.' This was an amazing claim, since they themselves had certainly not covered all sides of the story.

This spat between one of the country's biggest publications and one of its smallest was important because it pitted one version against another. After months of exchanges, only the most dedicated reader could make sense of the conflicting versions and not get lost in the intricate minutiae of the exchange.

But what is important is that *Noseweek* outlined the competing narrative, weighing up the counter-evidence. The *Sunday Times* chose only to denounce the little monthly and its reporters, avoiding much of the hard evidence. They doubled down on their version, and then they trebled down.

The Sunday Times *digs in its heels*

The internet, and good search engines, have made fact-checking, that most basic journalistic function, a lot easier and quicker. A reporter can quickly look up names, titles, places, histories and other details – although care has to be taken, as the internet is also full of errors.

Using the net, you can see what locations look like through readily available satellite imagery. You can check what the weather was like in a certain place on a given day. You can check the movement of planes and ships in real time. And if you have the skills, you can learn an enormous amount from people's social media about their background, their circle of contacts, their movements and their habits.

Fact-checking is built into newsroom processes. News editors guide reporters doing their story. Have you spoken to this person, or that person? Have you considered this? How do you know this fact? Have you gathered the documentation? The story idea is presented at a news conference, where the whole team of senior editors is expected to raise any concerns they may have about difficult stories and share ideas of how to track down the facts. And it's usually presented at another conference when it's ready for publication, for another round of scrutiny.

The written story goes through other senior hands, who cast a second and third eye over it, check that facts and allegations are well sourced, that the piece is balanced and includes the views of all parties, that key people have been given a right of reply, that names are spelt right, and that ethical considerations have been taken into account. Sometimes it's referred to a legal expert, who might advise changes.

If it's a major or risky story, the editor or deputy editor would be expected to take a look, and ask some hard questions and make necessary changes before giving it final approval. And once the story is placed on the page there will be a last look, usually by more than one person.

Each of these people is expected to have a heightened awareness of the red flags of poor journalism, such as vagueness, lack of proof, loose generalisations, missing links and unnamed sources.

Some years back, the *Sunday Times* introduced its own additional step: when a journalist finished a story, he or she had to collar a colleague and together they had to go through a list of standard questions on their sources and evidence. A form had to be ticked off and signed by both of them, and filed away in case there were ever queries.

Little of this happened on the stories that caused all the trouble at the *Sunday Times*. Because the *Sunday Times* investigations unit would often put their stories through late, the checking process was often truncated. Shortcuts were taken. You'd think that their stories would go through special, additional scrutiny, but the status the unit held in the newsroom, the way they had negotiated less oversight, and their cockiness meant that their work slipped through with less oversight than it should've had.

Editor Phylicia Oppelt, who was at the helm of the Sunday weekly from early 2013 to the end of 2015, told me that on her watch the stories went through all the normal processes. Others, however, including seniors who would normally be part of the scrutiny, told me they often didn't know about the investigations unit's stories until they saw them on the page. And if they did, the status of the unit and the arrogance of some of its members meant that you had to think twice about questioning them.

In 2013 the *Sunday Times* investigations unit came up with what appeared to be new evidence from a whistleblower. Ari Danikas was a former police reservist who'd worked closely with the Cato Manor unit for a decade before leaving for Greece, his country of origin. In an article headed 'Cato cop comes clean on "hit squad"' on 24 February

2013, they quoted him saying the unit was 'trigger-happy'. They had 'no respect for human life. They torture, use excessive, brutal force and alter evidence on a crime scene. This I witnessed myself first-hand.'

Danikas detailed 'numerous atrocities', including how Cato Manor members 'executed' a crime suspect days after Booysen told him to 'put a bullet in his head'. He backed up what he said with videos, one of a naked man being tortured in 2004, and one of police standing around as a man bled to death. This latter was alleged to implicate Booysen, though he wasn't clearly identified in it.

Booysen was quoted in the story rubbishing Danikas's versions as 'fraught with so many improbabilities'. He was unreliable and had left the country under a cloud, Booysen said. 'If he had witnessed any of the things he said he did, he'd definitely be one of the state's witnesses [in the murder charges against Booysen and the unit] – and I know for a fact he is not.' Booysen described Danikas as 'deranged'. 'I challenge him to make an affidavit and come to South Africa and testify,' Booysen said.

Buried in the *Sunday Times* story was a mention of an allegation that Danikas had been suspended from the police reservists and left the country. It seems the newspaper didn't check this, slipping it in only as an untested allegation and therefore making it difficult to assess the man's trustworthiness.

The same witness featured in a documentary Stephan Hofstatter and Mzilikazi Wa Afrika made for television channel Al Jazeera in 2015. *Echoes of Apartheid* contended that extrajudicial killings and torture were continuing in the new South Africa. They presented a few cases but 'most shocking', they said, were thirty questionable killings over four years by the Cato Manor unit. '[When] the people who were at the scene are almost the same people,' Wa Afrika says on camera, 'you start asking yourself a question: is this a coincidence or what?' Booysen's face featured strongly in the film, which blamed the killings on him and his 'very close' group.

In this documentary, Danikas says that when he confronted Booysen about the torture, Booysen's response was, 'We get the job done.' There was no mention, though, of the charges that Danikas was less than reliable or why he wasn't being used as a prosecution witness.

Hofstatter to this day cites Danikas's evidence against Booysen.

This is 'confirmation bias', in which journalists eager to get backing for a story on which their reputations depend see only the evidence that supports their version and ignore that which throws doubt on it.

*

Johan Booysen worked slowly and steadily to challenge the *Sunday Times* story. He gave his version and his evidence to other, more sympathetic journalists. He challenged his suspension and his charges in court, waiting to be exonerated. He noted that the *Sunday Times* reported in detail when he was arrested and charged, but minimally when charges were withdrawn – it was clear that they would only report what supported their story, and conveniently avoid what didn't. Editorially, it was deeply dishonest.

Booysen complained to the Press Council in 2015, having waited for internal disciplinary and legal actions to play out. And he initiated civil action in the courts. He wrote to the convenors of the country's journalism awards to demand they review their recognition of the story.

The *Sunday Times* didn't budge.

The rise of the investigations unit

Few journalists had the connections and contacts of Mzilikazi Wa Afrika. He seemed to know everything going on in government and the ANC. He was famous for his contact book and his capacity to get anyone on the phone, and have them talk to him.

As an example, Phylicia Oppelt told how when no-one in her newsroom could get anything on the murder of legendary soccer player Senzo Meyiwa in 2014, and the newspaper was faced with a big hole in its coverage of the story of the week, she turned to Wa Afrika. Always the showman, he made a performance of coming in to her office and using her phone, on speaker, to get Meyiwa's manager on the line to talk to him. 'That's Mzi,' she said. 'When no-one else could deliver, he could. That's why he had the position he had on the *Sunday Times*.'

Wa Afrika's 2015 memoir, *Nothing Left to Steal*, is a memorable read that captures – often in an unintended way – a great deal of this large character. As one reviewer put it, the book would be easy to dismiss as an overwritten, poorly edited exercise in self-glorification, but it's more than that. It's about the battle for identity and recognition of a young outsider from rural Mpumalanga who fought his way up the journalistic ladder with determination and fortitude, making his mark in the epic battle to expose corruption and dishonesty – and immensely proud of his achievement as a black African in a world still predomi-nantly white. His florid language and tendency to hyperbole – such as when a wrongful arrest becomes a kidnapping, or when he repeatedly quotes his friends and colleagues showering praise on him – say a lot about the man, but not as much as the story of a young man who was prepared to take on anything and anyone to build, against the odds, a life and career of note.

How he named – or renamed – himself says a lot about his identity. 'An African proverb says a good name is better than riches,' he writes, and he took this literally. He was born Leonard Ndzhukula, the son of Simon and Deyiye Ndzhukula of Bushbuckridge, in what is now Mpumalanga, and rejoices in recounting his clan history. As a teenager, he got his hands on a DVD of Alex Haley's *Roots,* and watched it repeatedly. 'I was touched, moved, motivated and inspired. I thanked God a million times that I was an African. I was, and still am, proud to be black and African,' he writes in his memoir. That might explain why he dropped the name Leonard but not why he dropped his family name. 'Mzilikazi means "little path", and this would be the road of my journey in life.' It was also, of course, a reference to the 19th-century nation-building giant, King Mzilikazi.

Online, Wa Afrika sometimes used the identity 'mzeetheicon' and that was how he saw himself: no less than *the* icon for young journalists. A journalistic hustler, he was a muckraker with a fondness for the muck, and that was both his great strength and his great weakness.

Wa Afrika joined the ANC underground in the 1980s, making him an ANC insider, a position that gave him access to the ruling party over the coming years but also rendered him vulnerable to pressure around where his loyalty lay.

With the arrival of democracy, he turned from activism to journalism, starting as a freelancer for a local paper, *Witbank News,* in 1995. A couple of years later he joined a local news agency, African Eye News, started by journalist Justin Arenstein in the booming capital of Mpumalanga, Nelspruit.

Wa Afrika learnt the reporting ropes at African Eye, covering courts and crime. His first breakthrough story was about a string of murders in Mpumalanga and neighbouring Limpopo province. He pieced together a number of murder cases to show that there were two serial killers at work – a classic case of taking available information and digging deeper.

His next big story came from a conversation he'd overheard on a bus from Nelspruit to Johannesburg about how easy it was for Mozambicans to buy a new identity from the Home Affairs office in Johannesburg. He took himself off to buy a new identity – and confronted the local Home Affairs boss, who admitted his involvement. It was his first big *Sunday Times* break: 'We bust fake ID racket. For just R300 you can buy a new life – and an illegal vote', the paper shouted on 7 March 1999.

Home Affairs director-general Albert Mokoena took what was to become a standard line. 'Morena,' he said to Wa Afrika, 'why are you doing this to your black brothers just to please your white bosses?' That defence-through-racial-identity was to become important in the tensions that played out at the *Sunday Times*, with many over the years putting its exposés down to race-baiting.

It was a mistake to rub Wa Afrika up the wrong way. He responded to Mokoena by taking a closer look at the man and started asking around about him. He found that Mokoena ran a Premier League basketball team from his government office, and used his influence to give local identities to foreign players. Nine months of stories followed, until Mokoena resigned in late 1999.

According to Wa Afrika, he proposed an investigations unit to *Sunday Times* editor Mike Robertson in 1999. Across town, the *Mail & Guardian's* investigations team (what was to become *amaBhungane*) had led the way for some time, with its exposés giving the paper a prominence and influence out of proportion to its modest size and readership.

Robertson quickly embraced the idea, found 'a handsome budget' for the *Sunday Times* investigations unit, and set it up in its own little office in the corner of the newsroom. Its task was to provide a flow of front-page splashes.

Experienced editor Jocelyn Maker headed the start-up unit, and hand-picked the best of the newsroom to work with her: Wa Afrika was the core of the team for the longest time; André Jurgens and Jessica

Bezuidenhout, and later Stephan Hofstatter, Rob Rose and Piet Rampedi were brought in; and others, like Pearlie Joubert and Malcolm Rees, worked with the unit from time to time on particular stories.

Wa Afrika broke many stories, knew everyone and everything, and had the best contact book in the business – but he did things that made his colleagues throw up their hands. He was a journalistic diamond but a rough one. He was vulnerable to gullibility, wanting to believe everything he was told, a couple of his teammates told me, and the unit had to work hard to verify his material and get it into shape for the newspaper.

The unit did brilliant work that won a string of awards. Its pre-eminence in the newsroom was built on a series of stories that set a cracking pace. Coleman Nyathi was the Mpumalanga director-general known as a corruption-buster when Wa Afrika showed that he'd spent government money to buy his doctorate from a fake online university and had lied about his citizenship.

In 2003 Wa Afrika nabbed Zimbabwean Information Minister Jonathan Moyo in a massive shopping spree in Johannesburg. 'Hey, big spender' was the splash headline, followed by 'Mugabe's spin doctor stocks up on food in SA as millions starve at home'. Alongside it was a story of the police being called after Moyo assaulted his wife at a Joburg hotel.

Next in line was a kingpin of South African soccer, Irvin Khoza, a man with a dark history that Wa Afrika had been pursuing for years.

The biggest catch of all arose out of the Strategic Defence Package, or 'arms deal', a multibillion-rand military acquisition by the South African government, and the ANC's first major foray into the world of multimillion-rand tenders. It ended up costing the state over R70 billion, and spawned allegations of large-scale corruption, with millions of rands of public money lost to bribery and other irregularities.

The investigations unit's look into the allegations flying around about corruption in the arms deal during the 1990s homed in on a relatively minor but easy-to-prove element: that then ANC chief parliamentary whip Tony Yengeni had failed to declare a dubious discount on his expensive 4x4 Mercedes. The unit pieced together a range of documentary evidence that showed that a company linked to the arms deal had ordered the vehicle as a 'staff car', that the company that had supposedly financed the purchase had not actually done so, and that Yengeni had only started paying instalments on the car when there was talk that it had been an improper 'gift'.

The *Sunday Times* headline on 25 March 2001 was unusually cautious: 'Tony Yengeni, the 4x4 and the R43-billion arms probe'. The word 'bribe' wasn't used. They hadn't cracked open the arms deal, but they had – as is so often the case with investigations like this – found a side story that nailed a few of those involved.

Yengeni went to prison, and Wa Afrika – described in the text of the story as an 'award-winning investigative journalist' – and the *Sunday Times* investigations unit were riding high.

Then Wa Afrika was fired.

*

Wa Afrika's first banishment from the *Sunday Times* and from the fraternity of journalism arose from the political scandal that became known as Travelgate. Members of Parliament (MPs) had been found to be working with a travel agency to defraud the institution through their travel claims. In the midst of it, it emerged that Wa Afrika had tried to broker a property deal in Mozambique with the travel agency. There was nothing intrinsically wrong with the deal, but Wa Afrika hadn't declared this side business and the conflict of interest it entailed, and was summarily dismissed.

In his time of professional exile, Wa Afrika turned to his other great love, his weekend special, the music industry. He wasn't without success in this area, having released a few albums and run his own recording company. He also did time with a smaller newspaper, the *Sunday World*.

Allegations that he was often doing business side-deals were to haunt him. When, in 2013, he was part of the investigative team that took down the Minister of Communications, Dina Pule, she brought this up: 'You will recall that a few years ago, Wa Afrika was fired by the former *Sunday Times* editor Mondli Makhanya for conflict of interest because of his tendency to develop unsavoury ties with sources. While he was out of work, Wa Afrika became involved in many business ventures and pursued various business opportunities. It is these extensive business networks that Wa Afrika pursued that have now come back to disgrace the *Sunday Times*.'

Pule lost her post and Wa Afrika came back to his first love, journalism that tackled the powerful. But the allegations and rumours didn't quite go away. It emerged that Martin Welz had briefly employed him on *Noseweek* but had let him go when he started to have doubts about Wa Afrika's ethics. When Wa Afrika reappeared at the *Sunday Times*, Welz warned then editor Ray Hartley, only to be brushed off. And when there were allegations of the reporter having taken money from a secret police slush fund, Hartley brought in crack cross-examiner advocate Wim Trengove to investigate, and they came up with no evidence.

So when the *Sunday Times* took Wa Afrika back, they were taking a chance, and they knew it. But the fact was that the paper needed him. Hartley said that when he took over in 2010, the newsroom was depressed and demoralised. 'I had never seen anything like it. I said we had to get back to what we did best, and the investigations unit was exactly what I thought we wanted. They had an unblemished record for breaking complicated factual stories. To my mind, they were doing it the right way.'

Wa Afrika was nonetheless put on terms: the newspaper's management was watching closely for any further hint of untoward side activities.

And Wa Afrika wasn't the only disgraced journalist who was rehabilitated. Political reporter Ranjeni Munusamy had been dismissed in 2004 after the *Sunday Times* had declined to run a highly controversial story she'd submitted, and she'd passed it on to their rivals at *City Press*. After two years working for the presidential campaign of the then-aspirant Jacob Zuma, already known for his corruption and dubious sexual conduct, she reinvented herself as not just a critic of Zuma, but the most ardent and vociferous of them all. In 2017 she was back at the *Sunday Times*, this time elevated to Group Associate Editor, her betrayal forgiven but not forgotten.

For the media's critics, it was proof that the industry didn't regulate itself adequately. And Munusamy proved them right: in 2019 she was accused of having had the State Security Agency (SSA), the government's intelligence arm, pay secretly for her flashy car. Although it had been done in the period when she was out of journalism, and she adamantly denied the allegations, the *Sunday Times* quietly paid her to go away.

In the case of Wa Afrika, the paper's forgiveness was to haunt them.

*

Stephan Hofstatter had had a stellar career. His first notable job in journalism was in 2003 as a specialist reporter in land reform at *This Day* newspaper, which ceased publication after around a year. He then spent six years writing about the same subject for *Business Day, Financial Mail* and *Farmer's Weekly*, establishing a reputation and winning categories in the Sanlam Financial Journalism awards, the Mondi Shanduka Newspaper Journalism awards and others.

The list of significant stories he had a hand in breaking is long, varied and impressive. Between 2006 and 2010 he focused on the causes of underdevelopment in the Wild Coast region and this led to a number of exposés, such as the looting of a state-funded food-production programme, and pro-mining lobbyists who were using the identity documents of dead people to bolster their case. In 2008 he exposed the Land Bank, whose mandate is to support agriculture and land reform, funding an exclusive polo estate in KwaZulu-Natal. For *Business Day* and the *Sunday Times* in 2009, he broke a story about how banks were financing the illegal conversion of panelvans into minibus taxis, despite warnings that these would be death traps.

Hofstatter was brought in to the *Sunday Times* investigations unit in 2010 and that year, working with Wa Afrika, exposed a corrupt real-estate deal involving the then Commissioner of Police, Bheki Cele, leading to his dismissal. The following year the duo published the contract that showed how French arms company Thales had secretly paid the wife of Zuma's spokesperson, ANC leader Mac Maharaj.

The prominent and radical self-proclaimed spokesperson for the poor, Julius Malema, was also a target in 2011, when Hofstatter, Wa Afrika and Rob Rose showed the money trail linking Malema to the granting of lucrative contracts in his home province of Limpopo. And Hofstatter had a hand in the exposé of Durban businessman Thoshan Panday's crooked deals which were to become part of the Cato Manor story.

In the critical period of the *Sunday Times's* controversial stories, though, Hofstatter's personal life was in a shambles and his marriage under stress. In a radio interview in 2017 he said there was a lot he couldn't recall, having been in a fog of emotional turmoil for much of this time. He sometimes came to work after a sleepless night with his mind in a haze, he claimed, and cited this from time to time in disavowing responsibility for stories that appeared under his name.

Piet Rampedi was another key unit member. He was emerging as a star reporter on the *Mail & Guardian* in the early 2000s when Wa Afrika pushed hard for him to be brought into the *Sunday Times* investigations unit. Rampedi was known to be a complicated character so there was some reluctance but Wa Afrika insisted he was the right man for the team, and his voice prevailed.

Rampedi turned out to have excellent sources, and was brilliant at bringing in information. But he was proprietary about his sources. He often wouldn't share their identities with his colleagues and became indignant when they asked routine questions about where information and documentation had come from. That should have been a warning sign for any editor, as it broke the rules of newsroom accountability, but Rampedi consistently came up with good and useful material – and the temptation to use it was great.

Rampedi appeared to be motivated as much by ideology as journalism, backing those who said they were challenging white supremacy or ridding state institutions of a recalcitrant old guard. This put some distance between him and some of the others in the team, particularly since he didn't easily trust the white members.

Former *Sunday Times* subeditor Jeremy Gordin told me in 2019 that one Saturday he'd heard on the radio a report that contradicted a story Piet Rampedi had filed. He suggested the radio report needed to be checked out, but Rampedi wouldn't do it. 'He went around mumbling that his work was being questioned by this white man. Nobody would challenge him.'

While the investigations unit generally saw themselves as going after anyone who they could show was crooked, Rampedi increasingly identified with one political faction. This became even clearer after he left the *Sunday Times* in 2018 and started his own publication, *African Times*. On its launch, Minister of Communications Faith Muthambi, who was personally and deeply implicated in the Zuma project, took the extraordinary step of congratulating Rampedi on the launch of the publication and promising 'community newspaper owners such as Rampedi' government assistance and support. The paper itself became a voice for this faction, and Rampedi would never clarify who funded the shortlived venture.

Rendering the facts

The phonecall came to the *Sunday Times* reception in mid-2011 and was put through to the investigations unit. Rob Rose answered it.

The caller had quite a story to tell. Police were undertaking illegal renditions of Zimbabweans wanted for crimes back home, he said. They were cutting corners, and not going through normal extradition processes, the source claimed, taking these Zimbabweans to the border and handing them over illegally. Some of them were then being tortured and killed.

That's interesting, Rose told him, very interesting. But we'll need evidence, hard evidence, like documentation and eyewitnesses.

Rose's colleague, Mzilikazi Wa Afrika, met this source at least twice to gather the evidence and try to assess his credibility. Few sources are impeccable and seldom are their motives pure, so a reporter has to get to know them to evaluate their evidence and trustworthiness. If their motives are self-serving or they have a record of dishonesty, that doesn't invalidate the story; it just means the journalist has to tread more carefully to make sure the public interest, and not only the source's, is being served.

'Deon Basson [a legendary financial investigative reporter] taught me that if you have the paper trail, the documents and other evidence that shows what happened, then the source becomes much less important,' Rose told me in informal discussions in 2019. And he's right: if you treat the source just as a tip-off pointing you in the right direction, then you're on safer ground. You have to have supporting evidence for whatever they tell you, anyway.

This source went further, however, giving the team – Rose, Wa Afrika and the third member, Stephan Hofstatter – a dossier of much of the evidence they needed, such as paperwork that showed the men being signed in and out of holding cells on the way back to Zimbabwe. And the source convinced them that he was doing it because he didn't like what he was seeing, that he was concerned about police misconduct.

The team checked out the paperwork, and it seemed authentic. They did their own independent fact-checking, such as of police-station records, over some months. Wa Afrika was taken to meet some of the men who'd been handed over to the Zimbabwe authorities and had returned to South Africa, and the families of men who'd died or disappeared after being returned to Zimbabwe. He heard their stories first hand, and the stories held together.

But much would depend on what the police said when they were asked about it by the reporters: a firm denial would mean the investigations unit had to be absolutely sure of every element of the story.

To get a response, the three men did something unusual: rather than phone a spokesperson, they went right to the top, phoning Lieutenant-General Anwa Dramat, head of the crack police unit, the Hawks, the division that appeared to have managed the so-called renditions. They were in luck. Dramat confirmed to them that the Zimbabweans had been arrested and handed over to Zimbabwean authorities. But it was a proper and legal extradition, he said.

The *Sunday Times* reporters asked him for the paperwork that would show that it had gone through the proper processes. Dramat was unable to give it at short notice.

So they had their story. It was a human-rights story that had a number of the keywords that made for an attention-grabbing front-page headline: criminals, illegal migrants, murder, torture, high-profile senior police officers and Zimbabwe. They had the response that confirmed that it had happened, and all that was in dispute was its legality.

*

Across town, at the rival *City Press*, the renditions tip-off had also come to one of South Africa's best-known investigative reporters, Jacques Pauw. He says it took him just a few days of probing to come to the conclusion that this story 'was utter bullshit'. He cast it aside.

*

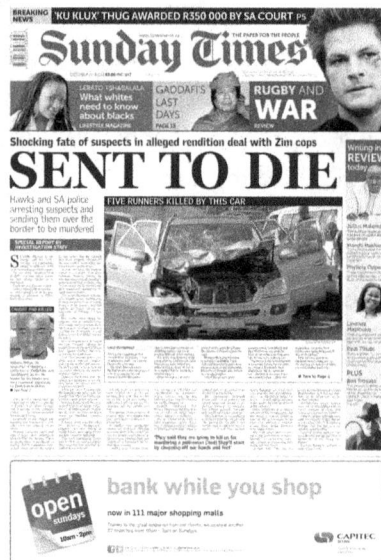

The *Sunday Times* headline on 23 October 2011 was in massive capital letters across the front page: 'SENT TO DIE'. Across the top of the page was a strapline: 'Shocking fate of suspects in alleged rendition deal with Zim cops' and the subhead was 'Hawks and SA police arresting suspects and sending them over the border to be murdered'.

> Senior officials in the Hawks and SA police Service are conducting illegal 'renditions' with their Zimbabwean counterparts – by arresting 'suspects' and illegally sending

60

them across the Beit Bridge border to be murdered.

Explosive intelligence reports – listing at least three deaths – are understood to be in the possession of Minister of Police Nathi Mthethwa.

They detail a 'renditions' operation led by officers re-porting to Hawks boss Anwa Dramat and Gauteng police commissioner Lieutenant-General Mzwandile Petros.

The newspaper had judged the actions illegal. It didn't say there were accusations that the policemen were breaking the law, nor that there was evidence to suggest it, but stated it as fact. The denial by Dramat was pushed down the page. Quote marks were put around the word 'suspects', raising a question of whether they were even criminals, but not around the word 'illegal'. It is in these small details that nuances were crafted and conveyed.

The story was credited as a 'special report by investigation staff'. Unusually, it ran with no byline, no individuals claiming credit for the 'scoop', and consequently no clear responsibility.

*

Something odd happened in IPID's probe into this story: it quickly became focused on two senior policemen, Hawks boss Anwa Dramat and Hawks Gauteng regional head Shadrack Sibiya.

Thirteen affidavits from members of the police Crime Intelligence division appeared in the IPID docket, describing Sibiya as having been present at many of the events, and Dramat as having come personally to congratulate the team on the operation and instruct them not to tell anyone about it.

What was odder still was that these affidavits had been collected and submitted by Crime Intelligence officers, even though this division didn't do investigations and shouldn't have had a hand in IPID investigations, which were meant to be independent. IPID investigator Humbulani

Khuba later said in an affidavit that he was instructed that the Crime Intelligence officer would help the investigation but this would not be in the report. They were trying to keep secret the fact that they had a hand in it, and this was 'unusual and problematic'.

IPID recommended that Dramat, Sibiya and four others be charged with defeating the ends of justice and kidnapping. This was leaked to the *Sunday Times,* whose coverage also shifted to focus on these two men.

On 13 October 2013 the headline ran, 'Hawks boss fingered in rendition scandal'. 'Damning new documents,' the investigative team said, 'put Hawks boss Lieutenant-General Anwa Dramat at the centre of a rendition scandal.' Sibiya was accused alongside him. Their report was based, they said, on 'internal police memos and a sworn statement by a senior border police official'. The word 'rendition' was no longer in quote marks.

'I don't know anything about this thing. I was not involved and I have never been involved,' Sibiya insisted in the same issue of the *Sunday Times.* 'Crime Intelligence is behind this whole thing – I don't know why.'

The heavy hand of the police Crime Intelligence division in the investigation raised a flag that should have been recognised by journalists. Crime Intelligence was headed by Lieutenant-General Richard Mdluli, a dubious figure caught up in a range of political and professional battles who was known to use his position to protect himself and his allies, and target his enemies.

In 2007 Mdluli, an old apartheid policeman, had been involved in a massive personal battle with a well-known and respected prosecutor, advocate Gerrie Nel, whom he had investigated and arrested for corruption. The charges against Nel had been thrown out of court for lack of evidence.

In March 2011 Mdluli had been arrested and charged for the 1999 murder of his ex-girlfriend's husband, while in September that year he'd been held for fraud and corruption. The repeated dropping of charges against him was to become a mammoth political battle and one of the acts that corrupted and discredited the NPA, where a number of officials were accused of improperly letting Mdluli walk free.

It emerged later that Mdluli had sent a personal letter to Jacob Zuma shortly before Zuma became president, promising him service and personal loyalty of the sort that were to epitomise the corruption of the police for political ends. And in appointing Mdluli, Zuma did what he often did: pluck someone – preferably someone with a tainted history – from obscurity and, regardless of their competence, promote them into a position of authority, so that they owed their position to him. In this way Zuma was assured of their loyalty to him personally, even above their oath of office.

Zuma was himself facing serious potential charges and he needed to have in place key policemen and prosecutors who were dependent and loyal. Mdluli was one of those.

One has to wonder: if Sibiya was correct that Mdluli was the cause of his troubles, was the original source who'd called the media with the tip-off on the rendition story planted by Mdluli, with the artful pretence that he was concerned about police wrongdoing? Why had this source taken it to the media and not directly to IPID? The *Sunday Times* team members I've spoken to don't know enough about the source to be sure. But they certainly believed at the time that their source was a genuinely concerned whistleblower.

More likely, though, was that Mdluli had spotted the rendition accusations and pounced on the opportunity to go for his enemies.

The *Sunday Times*, meanwhile, ploughed on, seemingly oblivious to these shenanigans, even when other media began to suggest that all wasn't what it seemed with this story.

*

The story took another turn with the appointment of Robert McBride to head IPID in 2014. On his arrival, McBride called for a review of all outstanding cases. When he found this one, he immediately said there was something amiss in the way it had been handled.

The IPID report, which recommended that Dramat and Sibiya be charged with kidnapping and defeating the ends of justice, hadn't been done according to standard operating procedures. Rather, the investigation had been carried out by Crime Intelligence and they had simply handed over their file – with affidavits from their own members – implicating Dramat and Sibiya.

'[Crime Intelligence] do not have an investigative function,' McBride said in his Zondo Commission affidavit, 'and this smacked of an attempt by [Crime Intelligence] to present their work as the work of an independent IPID investigation ... I was not satisfied that the evidence ... was fair and credible.'

Indeed, the IPID investigator, Humbulani Khuba, indicated to McBride that he was uncomfortable with how he'd been pressured to bend the rules in this case, to finish it quickly and submit it, even when he was aware that it wasn't complete. And he was told to submit it directly to the NPA without having it signed off by the head of IPID, yet another break with standard procedure.

Khuba told of a pattern of unusual interference. He'd been ordered to work closely with someone in Crime Intelligence, even though it was Crime Intelligence people who'd conducted the controversial arrests and border handovers. And he'd been told to keep this collaboration secret. Communication had been through a special, irregular email address, and Khuba was asked to go to a hotel to send emails rather than send them from his own desk. He was told not to brief the IPID head of investigations, an extraordinary bending of the rules. He received numerous calls from the Minister of Police, Nathi Mthethwa, asking to meet him on the matter, including offers to fly him to Cape Town for the meeting.

And Khuba made another allegation that went to the heart of the story: he said he found that as he gathered evidence and briefed Crime Intelligence and IPID, the material would appear in the *Sunday Times*.

Although he complained to his superiors and asked them to investigate this, they did not.

This shows how extensive the state-capture activity was and how state structures were divided between those who were part of the project, and those who were resisting it – and how the latter were themselves targeted. And it makes clear how the media was used for this purpose, being leaked selective, half-baked allegations as soon as they could serve a purpose.

One of the evidence items not yet gathered, and not in Khuba's report, was an analysis of the cellphone records of those who were purported to have been part of the renditions, which would place them at the scene or not. When McBride looked into this, he found that Dramat and Sibiya's phone records suggested that they had not been present.

*

It helps to know something about the extraordinary character that is Robert McBride.

He has a chubby face that makes him look at least ten years younger than his 56 years, and a gentle, soft-spoken demeanour. But behind this self-deprecating softness lies a man with an extraordinary record of courage and commitment, a maverick with a propensity for finding trouble.

As a young man, McBride was part of an underground unit in the ANC's military wing, Umkhonto we Sizwe (MK), which became legendary for its bravado. When in May 1986 one of its cadres was wounded and arrested, handcuffed to his bed in Pietermaritzburg's Edendale Hospital under police guard, McBride led his unit in a dramatic daylight rescue.

McBride became infamous for the 1986 planting of a 60-kilogram car bomb outside a packed Durban bar, Magoo's, in which three women died horribly and scores were maimed. McBride said that they'd been ordered to target the bar because it was a security-police hangout. Since the ANC didn't generally target civilians, the bomb

65

was deeply shocking and hugely controversial, especially since none of those killed were police.

When McBride was caught and sentenced to death, he was a man hated by some and admired by others – a symbol of the terrible violence that seemed to be spiralling out of control at that time.

His sentence was commuted and he was released as part of the 1990–1994 negotiations, and he was later granted amnesty by the Truth and Reconciliation Commission, although they found the bomb to have been a 'gross human-rights violation'.

I know of one particular incident that demonstrates both McBride's courage and his soldier's loyalty to the ANC. In 1993, when right-wingers drove a vehicle into a conference centre near Johannesburg where constitutional negotiations were taking place, and threatened ANC leaders, McBride dashed back home, grabbed an AK-47 he had kept hidden, put it in his car boot and drove off to defend his leaders. It wasn't needed in the end, but I have little doubt that McBride would have used it if he'd found it necessary.

He received the Merit Medal in Silver and the Conspicuous Leadership Star from the South African National Defence Force when MK guerrillas were integrated into the national army. But McBride still had a long walk to respectability.

He was employed in the Department of Foreign Affairs, but was repeatedly caught up in dubious intelligence work. He was arrested in 1998 in Mozambique and charged with gun-running. He maintained he was investigating arms smuggling, and was released after a few weeks in a Maputo prison. He faced an assault charge the following year following an incident with a notorious Cape Town gangster, Cyril Beeka, in an escort agency.

There was some outcry when in 2003 he was appointed chief of the Metro Police for Ekurhuleni, an area adjacent to Johannesburg, and it blew up when he crashed his car and was accused of drunken driving and then of obstructing justice.

This wasn't a man who played by the rules. He couldn't stay out of the public eye, nor out of trouble, but through it all he proclaimed and demonstrated his commitment to the ANC and to public service, although he had his own rather flexible definition of what this meant. He also had his fair share of enemies, and was a lightning rod for conservatives who distrusted the ANC, so it was often difficult to discern the extent to which he was being targeted in these incidents.

IPID seemed like a good place for him: there, he could use his investigative and intelligence skills, and his mix of ANC loyalty and maverick independence.

As always, he found trouble early: in his first round of briefings, he homed in on the 'renditions case' and the threat to charge his longstanding cadres, Dramat and Sibiya, both of whom had ANC backgrounds.

*

In an interview in a Pretoria café in 2019, in a steady voice, Robert McBride relayed his story to me in careful detail. But as he talked, he looked sideways or down or into the distance or at his phone – everywhere but at me.

He was suspicious of the Crime Intelligence input into the IPID report and he told me that telephone records, not fully analysed in the first report, indicated that the evidence against Dramat and Sibiya was dodgy.

The IPID report was amended, clearing Dramat and Sibiya, and McBride signed it off and submitted it to the prosecutors and the Minister of Police. In McBride's view, this was now the valid IPID report. The Minister, though, preferred the first, unsigned, report he'd received, so he stuck with it and raised questions about why McBride had changed the report.

Minister Mthethwa was not a man known for his political independence. He'd shown a willingness to go along with whatever demands were made of him by the Zuma presidency, in order to keep his position.

A great deal often hangs on a word or a definition. In this case, it was whether the first iteration of the report was a 'final' report or an 'interim' report, and whether the second was a 'new' report or just the 'final' report. McBride argued that he'd completed the report properly and that the first version should have been discarded as interim; for the Minister, it was convenient to ignore the second version, stick with the first, and suggest that McBride was doing something wrong in amending a report before signing it.

You might think that IPID would've had the authority to determine which version was its own report, but that version didn't suit Mthethwa.

Not one to hold back, McBride spoke out. Mthethwa instituted disciplinary action against him for altering the report and obstructing justice, and suspended McBride from office.

Mthethwa was replaced in the midst of all this, and the baton was picked up by the new Minister of Police, Nathi Nhleko. Nhleko's dedication to President Zuma was such that he was willing to make a fool of himself in his defence. He would be the one to call Zuma's controversial state-funded swimming pool a 'firepool' and make a much-mocked video to show how it was used for this purpose. He appeared in Parliament in 2016 and used the first report to gun for Dramat and Sibiya; he didn't even mention that there was a later report that contradicted the one he'd presented.

*

Nathi Nhleko commissioned a firm of private lawyers, Werksmans, to compare the two IPID reports. The brief was narrow: they had to look at how and why the report had been amended, and whether there was a prima facie case against Dramat, Sibiya and others for the 'renditions'.

Werksmans' report, compiled by attorney Sandile July, pointed out that the second report had excluded evidence that implicated Dramat and Sibiya. As we know, McBride had questioned the validity of this evidence, and it had then disappeared from the report, though McBride denied removing it himself. Werksmans didn't accept the reasons for the removal of the evidence and doubted McBride's version that he hadn't done it.

Werksmans concluded that the second report introduced no new evidence, yet reached the opposite conclusion, clearing Dramat and Sibiya. The removal of evidence and the changed conclusion weren't justified, they said. In fact, 'the only logical conclusion' was that the second report had been created for the purpose of exonerating Dramat and Sibiya. The deletion of evidence, the report said, was a criminal offence.

The Werksmans report laid out the evidence that Dramat was fully aware of the 'renditions' and that Sibiya was actively involved and present at key moments. That evidence all came from police Crime Intelligence, Mdluli's unit, though Sandile July, the report's author, was likely unaware of the internal rivalries that lay behind Mdluli's involvement.

The Werksmans report recommended that Dramat, Sibiya, McBride and others be charged. July had never spoken to Dramat or Sibiya, so had never heard their side of the story, which seems to be a fundamental shortcoming of a report making such far-reaching recommendations. The report had taken Mdluli's officers' affidavits at face value.

When the report was later challenged before the Zondo Commission of Inquiry, Werksmans declined to appear to defend it. They argued that they'd done what they were commissioned to do and wanted to avoid being pulled into the dispute. But it was hard to give credibility to a report when its author wouldn't defend it in public.

In the interim, though, the Minister had what he wanted: an independent legal report that nailed McBride, Dramat and Sibiya. The report was quickly leaked to the *Sunday Times*.

*

Anwa Dramat and Shadrack Sibiya were suspended from their posts in 2014 and 2015, respectively, pending an investigation. They contested their suspensions in court and won, but agreed to go on leave when they and others were charged in court for the 'renditions'.

In 2015 Sibiya was fired and Dramat signed a deal to leave the police with a golden handshake. The charges against them were dropped.

McBride challenged his suspension in court. He eventually won and was reinstated. But while he was on suspension, he said, 'competent members of IPID were transferred from the organisation and replaced with persons of mediocre calibre, thus effectively hollowing out the organisation and leaving it with a much-reduced capacity'.

While Dramat, Sibiya and McBride all eventually cleared their names, for a few years their lives were torn apart. And once they were out of office, the charges and accusations against them disappeared.

Meanwhile, the Hawks had had their claws pulled, as had IPID. Zuma's team was riding high, having got rid of three men who were an impediment to them and their allies.

What had started for the *Sunday Times* as a human-rights story had become weaponised in intra-party and intra-state political battles.

*

When I visited Shadrack Sibiya in his large City of Johannesburg office in 2019, where he was heading the anti-corruption unit, papers and files were sprawled across the floor. He was preparing to give evidence before the Zondo Commission of Inquiry into Allegations of State Capture and he was sorting all the evidence accumulated over the years into these unruly piles.

When I asked him why he thought he'd been targeted, he stood up, walked across the room and took off one of the piles the autobiography of journalist Mzilikazi Wa Afrika, one of those who'd written the *Sunday Times* 'renditions' story. On the cover was a picture of a moment in 2010 when Wa Afrika had been arrested.

It was a brief but high-profile arrest understood to be an attempt by elements of the Mpumalanga regional police to intimidate Wa Afrika into stopping his investigation into corruption in that province. It drew national attention as the first time in the new order that a journalist had been arrested for his work.

In the picture, Sibiya was standing behind Wa Afrika as he was marched off to the cells.

'I was only there because when police came from Mpumalanga to make an arrest, and it was protocol for local police to give them support, Dramat asked me to be there,' Sibiya said. 'From that day, Mzilikazi targeted me.'

I was surprised, because my question really was why he believed Mdluli had targeted him and Dramat. The answer to this, though, was obvious: it had been Sibiya, under Dramat's orders, who'd led the earlier investigation into accusations that Mdluli had killed his ex-girlfriend's husband in 1999.

Sibiya meticulously laid out his case for me, to show that he'd never been present at the renditions, and that they'd been executed by Crime Intelligence itself. He'd done this for many journalists – anyone who asked, actually – but he was patient in running through it again and able quickly to find supporting documents from the dozens of piles spread out on his office floor.

Crime Intelligence officers had carried out and been formally commended for the renditions, he showed, but suddenly Crime Intelligence themselves started investigating the renditions, produced evidence from their own people that Dramat and Sibiya were present and responsible, and this information had been fed to IPID. And it had been leaked to the *Sunday Times*. Pictures of the handover of alleged criminals to Zimbabwean police did not include Sibiya or Dramat, but mostly Crime Intelligence officers.

As he gave me his detailed account, I realised that this narrative wasn't something I'd seen in the *Sunday Times* in the many years since it had run the story, nor in any of its many follow-up stories. It was a version the paper never carried, until 2018, when it retracted the story and gave space to Dramat.

For six years, on a complicated and contested story laden with political importance, the *Sunday Times* had only summarised Sibiya or Dramat's accounts in a few minimal lines popped in at the end. In line with the *Sunday Times*'s traditional 'treatment', the newspaper had taken a position on the story and stuck with it. It had not seen a need to give any weight or substance to the counter-narrative, even though this had been spelt out for them.

The story had been heavily contested, notably as part of a wider political contestation, but the *Sunday Times* had not presented it this way, had not conveyed the disputed versions. That would have been messy and not lent itself to firm, unequivocal headlines.

*

Some journalists take the view that their role is simply to mirror what's happening in the world: gather all sides of the story, check the facts, and convey them as neutrally as possible, suspending any bias, prejudice or personal opinion, balancing different viewpoints. These are the techniques taught to beginners as a formula to cope with contested facts and heated narratives under pressure of deadlines. It's the approach loved by most risk-averse media lawyers.

More seasoned journalists, as opposed to just reporters, embrace the choices they have to make and see their job as making those decisions in the best way to convey the stories, nuances, contradictions and conflicts. Their job is not just to report, but to explain, to take the reader on a narrative journey, to enable the audience not just to know the facts but to understand, to empathise, to identify, even to care.

When we report, it's a pretence that we can offer just the facts. Collectively, we can't avoid an infinite series of choices, from what stories to cover and what not to, who to interview and which of their words to use, and how to describe a scene or a character, to how to convey whether you trust someone or are sceptical. Do we call it a rendition, or an illegal extradition; do we describe it as illegal, or a human-rights violation; do we put quotation marks around these words, or use qualifiers such as alleged, seemingly and appear to; what do we put at the top of the story and what do we drop down to the final paragraphs that seldom get read; do we say the source is senior, official, in-the-know, or elderly, short-sighted or peripheral?

We try and make these decisions with self-awareness and care, but sometimes they are also instinctual, habitual or just unconscious. They are never neutral. In the words of *Washington Post* writer David Broder, 'The process of selecting what the reader reads involves not just objective facts but subjective judgments, personal values and, yes, prejudices.'

And then these decisions are filtered by editors, lawyers and other colleagues, with their own concerns, duties and prejudices, sometimes for the better and sometimes for the worse. An editor might have an eye on a certain audience, or knowledge that someone is particularly litigious; a lawyer's job is to keep you out of court. Sometimes we fight for our decisions, and other times we let them go. Many times we have little choice. Often the final decision is determined by purely practical considerations, such as space and deadlines.

'The newspaper that drops on your doorstep,' Broder wrote, 'is a partial, hasty, incomplete, inevitably somewhat flawed and inaccurate rendering of some of the things we have heard about in the past 24 hours.'

The critical fact, though, is respect for the story and the audience. If the story is contested, the audience wants to know that. They want to know that you're choosing facts not to suit your purpose, but because they're important to the story and to their understanding of it. It's fine, if skilfully done, to convey which version of a story you give more weight to, but not if you do it by hiding the alternative version. Your service is to the story and the audience, not to an outside influence; you're not expected to be neutral, but you're also not expected to be partisan.

At the *Sunday Times*, though, they took a view on a contested story and stuck with that view. They saw their obligation as sorting out the messiness for the reader, preventing any confusion or un-certainty, offering clarity in a confusing world. They had a technical obligation to give a right of reply to those who contested their version, but it was no more than technical, no more than doing the minimum to meet an obligation. Professionalism was a box-ticking practice, no more than that.

*

McIntosh Polela was the Hawks' spokesman when the *Sunday Times* first phoned, in 2011, to ask about the 'renditions' story. When the *Sunday Times* phoned Dramat, he called in Polela and Sibiya, and they sat round a table and crafted their response, setting out why there was no truth in the allegations.

'I assisted the *Sunday Times* … with the correct information. But when I read the front-page article a day later, I was dismayed to discover that they had ignored the information I had given them,' Polela wrote later in an opinion piece in the *Mail & Guardian*. 'I called [investigative team member Rob] Rose to point this out, and I was immediately dismissed.'

Maybe Polela's information wasn't correct, and maybe Dramat and Sibiya's version wasn't credible. It's hard to know because the *Sunday Times* never reported it. They needed a strong narrative, and that didn't allow for a competing one.

Polela suggested that members of the *Sunday Times* team were in the pocket of Crime Intelligence, part of the bid to bring down Dramat and Sibiya. Polela also charged that he knew of three journalists who'd taken payment to write stories, although he didn't name them and he didn't link them to this story.

When I contacted Polela to ask about this, he said he was too busy to meet. After a few email exchanges and postponed meetings, he stopped responding. He was demanding accountability from the newspaper for things it had said in print, but wasn't prepared to offer it himself.

*

Colonel Kobus Roelofse worked for a special inter-governmental structure, the Anti-Corruption Task Team, which had investigated Crime Intelligence in 2012. He swore in an affidavit in March that year that a member of Crime Intelligence had told him that in October 2011 he'd heard senior officers talk of the placement of a newspaper article relating to Anwa Dramat and Shadrack Sibiya which would divert attention away from themselves. A journalist who was on the Crime Intelligence payroll was writing the story.

Roelofse said that the newspaper article 'was published in the *Sunday Times* on 23 October 2011'. It was the 'Sent to Die' story – the one not attributed to individual journalists, just to 'investigative staff'.

This was hearsay, twice over. Roelofse had been told it by an unnamed officer who'd overheard it. It wasn't hard evidence, although it's hard to ignore the fact that the article appeared in the newspaper as allegedly promised. And it's often cited as evidence that at least one of the *Sunday Times* reporters was paid by Crime Intelligence, which ran a secret and notoriously abused slush fund.

*

As I dug into this story, I discovered that the extralegal handing over of wanted criminals between neighbouring countries in this region had been happening for some time. It wasn't allowed for in law, but it was done quickly and quietly. If Zimbabwe or Swaziland were hunting for someone accused of a serious crime – particularly one involving something like the death of a policeman – and that person had fled to South Africa, they asked their counterparts to find and return that person. And vice versa, if a serious criminal had fled from South Africa to a neighbouring country.

Normal extradition processes, which are long and costly, were circumvented and the person was taken to the border and handed over in a show of cooperation. What happened once they'd been handed over was the business of the country where the crime had happened.

It wasn't routine that they assisted each other in this way, but it was established police practice. 'It didn't happen all the time,' one knowledgeable former senior policeman told me. 'It happened when it had to happen.'

So the *Sunday Times* was onto a story, and to stick on it the fashionable label of 'renditions' made it sexy, as did the names of top cops. But were these cops responsible? It's classic spycraft to take a story with a kernel of truth and insert something into it, to change the angle, to spin it, to divert it. It's more effective than making up an entire story from scratch.

Much later, I interviewed a senior member of the Office of the Inspector General of Intelligence, the SSA watchdog, who was looking into the role that SSA agents had played in the state-capture project. He was tight-lipped, determined not to break his oath of secrecy, so I had to ask him general questions. 'This was the way they operated, am I right? When someone was targeted for political reasons, the SSA would put them under surveillance, intercept their communications, infiltrate their organisations and look for some dirt, some controversy, anything. Then they pinned it on their target person, put together a dossier and leaked it to the media. Is that right?'

He hesitated, then narrowed his eyes. 'What makes you think they bothered to find the dirt? They usually just made it up.'

I wasn't convinced. 'Take the renditions story,' I said. 'They found a story and pinned it on Dramat and Sibiya. But there was a story there, there was a rendition. The *Sunday Times* were on to something.'

He looked away. 'Are you sure? I don't think that there was a rendition.'

'But there was a paper trail. There were photographs. There was evidence.'

'That's what they do,' he said. 'That's what they do.'

Love, tax and spies

This is about a story that wasn't worth publishing. Then it was. And about what happened in the six months between when it wasn't and when it was.

The spokesperson for the South African Revenue Service (SARS), Adrian Lackay, came to the *Sunday Times* for an informal briefing early on 3 February 2014. He told them that a cigarette dealer who was in the taxman's sights, Adriano Mazzotti, was spreading stories about being spied on illegally by the SSA, the Hawks and police Crime Intelligence working with British American Tobacco (BAT), and was alleging an improper relationship between senior SARS investigator Johann van Loggerenberg and a tobacco-industry attorney named Belinda Walter.

It was typical of Lackay to pre-empt an emerging and potentially damaging story by briefing journalists himself, and warning them against taking Mazzotti's stories at face value. Lackay had solid relationships with the journalists and he was happy to take them into his confidence. And he was concerned that journalist Malcolm Rees was talking to Mazzotti and Walter, and appeared to be close to them. Be careful, he warned the *Sunday Times* reporters: Mazzotti will try to use this story, and your newspaper, to undermine SARS's action to stop his illegal tobacco activity.

'There was no public-interest element in what Lackay told us,' a senior *Sunday Times* editor informed me in an off-the-record interview, 'so we didn't do the story'. But the briefing was important, because it meant the *Sunday Times* team knew early on about attempts by tax dodgers to spread disinformation and undermine SARS.

Rees was a young and talented journalist, a former student of mine, who was making his name at the *Sunday Times* for probing investigations into business and financial matters, and in particular the murky world of the tobacco industry. SARS had moved in on illicit tobacco sales and was exposing the shady and overlapping areas between the legal (tax-paying) industry and its illegitimate cousin, the burgeoning illicit (non-taxpaying) industry. Having become one of the most effective tax-collectors in the world, SARS was stirring many pots, and the multibillion-rand tobacco trade was a big one.

The tobacco industry had been on SARS's radar for some time. Since cigarettes were heavily taxed, there had been a massive growth in the illegal sale of tax-free cigarettes. Some companies were smuggling these into the country; others were smuggling in raw tobacco and running a dual business, with a legal cigarette factory during the day, on which tax was paid, and an illegal one at night, to avoid the tax.

In 2005 SARS had teamed up with the police and national intelligence in two projects aimed at tobacco smuggling: Project Cheetah and Project Coerce. In 2008 they carried out their biggest-ever bust, confiscating 45 million illegal cigarettes from a company called Masters International, owned by the notorious one-time arms dealer John Bredenkamp.

*

Around 2010 an inter-agency Illicit Tobacco Task Team was set up to coordinate the campaign against illicit tobacco. Although it had been SARS that had proposed that such a body be established, when it was done, it excluded SARS but included representatives of BAT, its investigations company Forensic Security Services (FSS), and the SSA.

This alliance brought together, with big tobacco, some of the most corrupt elements of state security and police.

Its main target at first appeared to be BAT's commercial rivals, its second SARS itself. When the small tobacco dealers formed the Fair Trade Independent Tobacco Association (FITA) in 2012, its first meeting was, according to *amaBhungane*, bugged by the SSA with assistance from FFS.

By 2013, Van Loggerenberg wrote in his book *Tobacco Wars*, cigarette smuggling had attained 'epidemic proportions', estimated to have reached 40–50% of the market. SARS had a number of different investigations, audits and inspections taking place, and they decided to bring these together into one project called Honey Badger.

In November 2013 SARS wrote to the two tobacco-industry bodies, the Tobacco Institute of South Africa (TISA) and FITA, telling them that fifteen local companies were going to be prosecuted for smuggling and tax evasion. This included not just the small operations, but some of the major, mainstream players as well. Van Loggerenberg warned them of plans to increase monitoring 'where the general levels of compliance appear to be undesirable and which, in SARS's view, require special attention and intervention'.

Watch out, SARS was saying to the tobacco industry, we're coming after you. They were probably hoping to draw out some whistleblowers. 'What we didn't realise at the time,' Van Loggerenberg wrote, 'was that we were up against interests and people with influence and power way beyond our imagination.'

And as another journalist, Pearlie Joubert, put it: 'That was the letter that lit the keg, that made Zuma and his son go for them, that put SARS on the radar of the state-capture mob. It said, we are on to you. And it involved millions of rands.'

A few months later, Belinda Walter contacted the *Sunday Times* to tell them about her affair with Johann van Loggerenberg.

*

Malcolm Rees had sources in all three armies in this battle: the tax investigators, the legal tobacco industry and the illegal tobacco industry.

Each was ready to rat on the others, and dedicated their substantial resources to try and lead Rees and other journalists down their own path. This gave Rees insight into a rough, tough, dirty world where business and gangsterism overlapped and much was at stake.

Tobacco-industry lawyer Walter in particular had been cultivating Rees during 2013, taking him to meetings with traders and pushing stories on him, although Rees had published little of it. But in January 2014 she gave him documents, notes, recordings and other evidence showing, she said, how elements of the police, SSA and SARS were allegedly in the pockets of BAT and the larger tobacco companies, and that they were working together in a dirty war against the smaller players. She said the time had come to 'expose them', and she sought redemption for the role she'd played.

Rees published 'BAT's smoke and mirrors war on rivals' in the *Sunday Times* on 30 March 2014.

Then the Van Loggerenberg-Walter relationship blew up and the couple split. Walter told Rees that Van Loggerenberg had leaked confidential SARS information to her and admitted to using illegal surveillance. She showed text messages from him that appeared to support her story. Suddenly, there was public interest in the story, since it was now about a SARS official's alleged abuse of the powers of the tax office.

It was messy, though. Walter had worked for FITA, which represented the smaller firms, many of which were locked in combat with both SARS and their bigger rivals such as BAT, and were being investigated by Van Loggerenberg and his team. She was also the lawyer for cigarette firm Carnilinx and, it emerged later, on the payroll of BAT.

When the *Sunday Times* approached SARS for comment, spokesman Adrian Lackay told the paper that they had 'significant and credible evidence' of Walter's involvement in 'incidents of spying, double-agents, dirty tricks, leaking false allegations and discrediting SARS officials ... as far back as 2010'.

Walter had also admitted to being an agent of the SSA, so she was a triple-timer, if not a quadruple-timer, juggling multiple hats as a spook, lawyer and lover. And the *Sunday Times* knew it.

It looked, frankly, like she was a honeypot who'd set out to compromise a key SARS investigator, wearing at least one of her many hats. At her and Van Loggerenberg's first meeting she'd worn a recording device provided by the SSA.

Van Loggerenberg, though, is adamant that there was genuine love: 'One cannot predict that one will fall in love or not. In this case, I did. I consider this to be intensely private and I abhor being forced to explain,' he said to me in a 2019 email. Van Loggerenberg is also adamant that he took the appropriate steps to declare and manage the conflict of interest.

Love, tax and spies – it was a perfect *Sunday Times* mix, a dream front-page splash, and they were gearing up to run it.

Then Walter suddenly withdrew her allegations against Van Loggerenberg in a long, rambling series of emails to the *Sunday Times* in the first week of February 2014. What she'd told Rees was a bunch of lies, she said. Made 'under duress, in an extreme emotional state of fear and distress', her statements were 'untrue and defamatory' and would 'cause harm to the defamed, innocent third parties'. She retracted her claims 'in their entirety' and said her word couldn't be relied on 'in any form or manner whatsoever'. She even threatened legal action if the paper carried the story she'd given them.

She and Van Loggerenberg had made up.

And Walter went further, accusing the paper's reporters of corruption. The illicit tobacco companies had made 'offers of money ... in the form of cash, holidays and cocaine' to Malcolm Rees and there was an understanding that he 'would not report negatively on them', she charged. Another reporter, Loni Prinsloo, had received sponsorship for a sports team from these 'sources'.

The *Sunday Times* investigated. Their lawyers told them they couldn't do a staff lifestyle audit, so editor Phylicia Oppelt and legal editor Sue Smuts questioned Rees and Prinsloo. The offers had indeed been made to

Rees; he denied taking them, but had failed to report the matter properly to his superiors. Prinsloo's team had received the sponsorship, but she viewed it as a private matter that didn't impinge on her work.

The *Sunday Times* could've rewritten the story, making Walter's turnaround just another twist in an intriguing saga that showed up tobacco-industry attempts to subvert the tax office. But, sensing what damage it could do, Lackay and other senior SARS officials met with and appealed to the editor to tread carefully, as did the influential Minister of Finance, Pravin Gordhan, himself a former tax chief. Don't damage the institution; it's too important, too vital to the country's economy, they argued.

SARS was much respected, standing out as a triumph of successful government management, an institution that had vastly improved since the new government had taken power in 1994, and one much feared by taxpayers.

And SARS officials had long cultivated a healthy relationship with the media. All the reporters knew Lackay as a helpful friend of the press; he and Van Loggerenberg, along with acting chief executive Ivan Pillay, had briefed them on various matters, often taking them into their confidence. They often passed on tip-offs and stories, as it boosted their work in pursuit of tax dodgers and spread fear among the culprits. And as individuals they were liked and respected.

In February 2014 the *Sunday Times* shelved the story.

*

Six months later, the story was suddenly taken off the shelf and brushed off. Editor Phylicia Oppelt was hell-bent on running it.

Belinda Walter had revived her allegations and claimed to have made a formal complaint against Johann van Loggerenberg, and she'd thrown in a few more claims for good measure. He was mentally ill, unstable, an alcoholic, corrupt, a pathological liar, a sociopath and 'likened to a paedophile', she now complained. She said she'd been lying when she'd said she was lying, and that in fact she was telling the truth the first time around. There was no longer any mention of the duress, fear or distress that apparently had led her to lie.

There was suddenly a great rush to finish the story at the *Sunday Times* and get it into print.

*

'Love affair rocks SARS' was the headline on 10 August 2014. 'An ill-advised love tryst gone sour has turned the heat on SARS enforcement head Johann van Loggerenberg,' the article said. His relationship with Belinda Walter, described as 'a Pretoria-based tobacco lawyer', had 'ended "acrimoniously" and the sensational accusations emerging in the fallout appear to have sparked inquiries from the Hawks crime-fighting unit, state intelligence and the police'.

That was one way to tell the story.

Another, based on the same facts in the hands of the reporters, could have been headlined 'State spies and tobacco tax dodgers in campaign to smear SARS' and 'SARS charges that illicit cigarette sellers using honeypots, subterfuge and smears in war against tax collector'.

This is a stark example of how journalists can frame a story to mean something quite different, how the choice of angle, headline, wording and quotation can be used to have an entirely different impact. It's in those choices that journalists exercise their power and influence. When you're looking for a nifty description, do you call the tobacco industry a 'giant taxpayer' or a 'shady tax evader', as both are true? Do you label the tax office as one of the world's most effective, or a powerful institution overreaching and abusing that power, as there was evidence for both of these claims?

Do you call Walter a lawyer, an industry lobbyist, a spy, a serial fantasist or a honeypot, as she appeared to be all these and more? Do you portray Van Loggerenberg as a highly effective investigator, an obsessive workaholic who pushed the boundaries of legality, or a hapless romantic who fell in love with the wrong woman? Do you highlight the love affair, or the bid to undermine the tax office?

Which sources do you give credibility to, and which do you downplay? Do you put this story on the front page, indicating that it's a major national scandal, or inside, where it's treated as a juicy and intriguing tale of shenanigans in an institution we all love to hate?

There was no mention in the *Sunday Times* story that Walter had previously admitted to lying to the paper or that she'd twice changed her story. The story did, however, carry warnings from Van Loggerenberg and SARS itself that the newspaper was being used by those who were threatened by SARS's investigations. Van Loggerenberg called it a campaign 'driven by people who would benefit from him being sidelined at the tax authority'. SARS itself was more explicit: this was part of an '"attack" on the tax authority – driven by key players in the highly lucrative world of illicit tobacco smuggling'.

At the end of the report, the *Sunday Times* threw in, as if in afterthought: 'The saga threatens to blow the lid on far deeper networks of misinformation and dirty dealings that have been established to prop up and protect one of South Africa's largest criminal industries.' This was a semi-concealed, down-story admission that they were aware of a meta-story of misinformation behind the raw sex saga. They stated clearly as a fact, not as allegation or speculation, that the tobacco industry was full of crooks involved in a dirty campaign against SARS – but the reader had to turn to page five and the end of the story to see just a hint that the story shouldn't be taken at face value. It was as if, under pressure to produce a good headline, the journalists had managed to sneak in recognition that they knew there was more to this story, that it wasn't just a steamy love affair gone wrong.

Each of these elements of the story was the result of one of the many small decisions a journalist has to make at every stage of the news-gathering process to shape the narrative and what impact it will have. The good journalist makes these choices consciously, aware of the responsibility of each of these decisions. We do what we can to find an appropriate balance between impact and nuance, accuracy and simplicity, readability and complexity, and usually have to stack the commercial interest of our outlets against the public interest served by getting the information out. We often have to balance our personal values against those of the institutions that pay us to do the work. And we balance the ethical and the legal against the public's hunger for voyeurism. We crave an audience as big as possible, but we want also to be believed and trusted. And we do it under considerable deadline pressure.

In reality, our task most of the time is to find a workable balance between these conflicting demands. We work within the bounds of the possible based on what information we can get, what we can do with it, and how we can get it into the public arena – and this involves compromises and tough decisions all along the way.

Certainly, we work within a commercial newsroom framework that determines some fundamentals: our choices may be overridden by those

85

with more power, so the individual journalist might have less control over the use of their story than they would like; the format requires an 800-word piece with a pithy eye-grabbing headline, so nuance and complexity can quickly get pushed aside. And we've already identified the *Sunday Times* culture and practice that favoured unequivocal assertions, one single firm narrative, and gave the minimum of space and prominence to any contestation of that narrative.

The reporter's priority might have been, at best, to capture the story as fully and accurately as possible, but the editor's was to make the story easy to understand and attention-grabbing. Editors in particular also have to keep an eye out for potential blowback from lawyers, readers, subjects or advertisers. The substance of the editor's role is to balance these conflicting pressures in a way that still produces an interesting – and, hopefully, accurate – product.

All journalism in an open society is about finding a balance between good reporting and popular journalism. The good editor is the one who can achieve both. The genius editor is the one who can achieve both at the same time.

Editing is a tough job done under pressure, and few are those who do it well.

*

What had happened in those six months for the *Sunday Times* to suddenly trust Walter and revive the story?

Another narrative that had been developing in other media – and which had gone surprisingly unheralded – pointed to major corruption in the tobacco industry. Sam Sole and Lionel Faull of *amaBhungane* reported in March 2014 that an *amaBhungane* investigation had shown how 'two major multinational companies used their considerable resources to influence South African state security agencies to protect their commercial interests'. The dominant BAT had 'parlayed its support for law enforcement into preferential access to state security structures –

and, with that, the alleged capacity to spy on its competitors'. The major multinational Lonrho, infamous for its dirty dealings in Africa, 'was able to sidetrack a criminal investigation' of a subsidiary that had been caught red-handed smuggling truckloads of illegal cigarettes from Zimbabwe.

In July 2014 Angelique Serrao at *The Star* newspaper had stated it baldly: 'SARS target of tobacco industry backlash'; the taxman's clampdown on the tobacco industry had made SARS a 'target of spies, double agents, dirty tricks and the leaking of false allegations to discredit them', she said.

Malcolm Rees himself wrote in the *Sunday Times* in March 2014 that a 'year-long ... investigation' had revealed that BAT appeared to be committing 'industrial espionage' on a grand scale, running a network of 'agents' placed to spy inside rival organisations and paid through travel debit cards in fake names.

But it was Jacques Pauw's story in *City Press* in August 2014 that brought things to a head, probably because it showed Pauw had an inside track on the workings of the SSA and had much more damaging information. Pauw's angle was that the SARS love affair had uncovered an SSA special-operations unit, of which Walter was an agent, that used 'state resources to conduct dirty tricks campaigns, smuggle cigarettes and disgrace top civil servants'. '*City Press* is in possession of hundreds of [SSA] SMSes, emails and tape recordings that date from 2001 to 2014 ... The unit works from a house in Pretoria's eastern suburbs, and its members have access to the most sophisticated listening and tracking devices – including a so-called grabber, which can pinpoint the location of a cellphone.'

Pauw had put his story to the SSA for comment during the week prior to publication, as well as a set of questions for Walter with a dead-line to respond by Friday 8 August. The questions made it clear that she was about to be exposed as the triple agent she was.

She met her handlers at the SSA immediately after they received Pauw's questions and they jumped into action to pre-empt Pauw and *City Press*. They knew that if they kicked up enough dust around

Pauw's story, it would lessen its impact. They could divert attention by putting a different spin on the story in the *Sunday Times*.

This is what some call 'censorship by noise'. Old-style censorship was to stop people saying things you wanted to keep secret; spin is designed to put the best possible angle on a story when you can't stop it emerging; and noise is about creating confusion and uncertainty through disinformation, with the effect that the public can't differentiate between truth and fiction, and become sceptical of all accounts.

As political theorist Hannah Arendt wrote, 'The result of a consistent and total substitution of lies for factual truth is not that the lies will now be accepted as truth, and the truth be defamed as lies, but that the sense by which we take our bearings in the real world – and the category of truth versus falsehood is among the mental means to this end – is being destroyed.'

The SSA knew that what would trigger the *Sunday Times* – particularly the fiercely competitive editor Phylicia Oppelt – was the knowledge that *City Press* might beat them to the story. This was when Walter suddenly made contact with Rees at the *Sunday Times* again, with her revived allegations against Van Loggerenberg, and also let the *Sunday Times* reporters know that their key rivals *City Press* were about to scoop them.

This created panic in the newsroom and a big push to revive the story they'd put aside six months previously. And even though Oppelt and her colleagues were fully aware of Walter's duplicity and unreliability, the editor revived the story. Oppelt spoke that same Friday with Lackay on the phone, berating him because her rivals had the story; when he pointed out that it was *City Press's* own investigation and that he had little influence on them, she slammed the phone down on him.

Rees was later to say that he'd never felt so much pressure to do a story – as a junior, he'd had little choice in the matter. Operating under this pressure, he made a foolish error in the run-up to the story, one that would haunt him. He asked to meet Van Loggerenberg the day before the story was going to run, giving him, in *Sunday Times* fashion, only an hour, even though Van Loggerenberg had insisted he needed longer to put his case. They met hurriedly in a fast-food restaurant, and Rees told Van Loggerenberg that his editor was now insistent the story was going to run that week.

When Rees rushed off, he left on the table a copy of an email he'd been reading from during the interview. He'd attempted to black out Walter's name as the source of the email, but it was still legible. It appeared to be a set of suggestions as to what he should ask Van Loggerenberg, with a promise that Walter would give a response only after Van Loggerenberg had given his side of the story.

It looked like Rees was relying on a person he knew to be unreliable. And he was giving her the last right of reply.

He was being played.

*

This is how the same story got entirely different treatments from two credible newspapers on the same day. For anyone who read both stories, there was no way of knowing whether it was SARS that was rogue, or the SSA, or both, or if indeed it was *City Press* or the *Sunday Times*. For the Taco Kuiper Award for Investigative Journalism that year we received four entries with entirely different versions of the same story; we had to cast them all aside because there was no clarity on the facts.

It was a triumph for the professional disinformation agents, the noise-makers.

Another side of the story

The *Sunday Times* had treated the SARS story as a tale of sexual intrigue gone wrong. But there was a background to the story that changed how the whole thing came across, and it was one that the SARS officials told to anyone who would listen, again and again.

The project to fix and modernise SARS had been extraordinarily successful. The tax net had grown from 1,7 million South Africans in 1994 to 2,6 million in 1999, to more than 6 million in 2009/10, and to 13,7 million in 2011, and revenue had risen steadily at an average of 11,6% per year since 1994. SARS had moved into a new strategic phase, homing in on 'the illicit economy' – activities such as drug dealing, smuggling, poaching and corruption, where organised crime was intentionally working to escape the tax net. This was a huge part of SARS's 'tax gap' – the chasm between what they should have been collecting and what they were succeeding in collecting. Targeting this money was complicated and risky, but promised more significant results than chasing the individual taxpayer who was late with his returns or who'd skipped a year or who was exaggerating his expenses.

This shift in priorities was a key step in turning SARS from a routine administrative operation into a proactive enforcer that was meeting and beating increasing annual targets for revenue collection.

The institution went on a public-relations drive: we're chasing the crooks so that the state can fix our education, health and housing problems, they told South Africans. The taxman became a hero of the new democracy, and was looked on with the mix of fear and respect that would encourage individuals to pay up.

In 2005 SARS drafted an Illicit Economy Strategy, and by 2007 it had been approved and was being implemented. It became central to the taxman's activities. SARS set about drawing up agreements with the police, state security, the NPA, the border and maritime authorities, and the Asset Forfeiture Unit, which had overlapping responsibilities – not an easy task because many of them were operating at a much less effective level than SARS.

And, inevitably, there was rivalry and turf wars. The deputy head of SARS, Ivan Pillay, set it out in his official submission in October 2014 to the Sikhakhane committee inquiring into the Van Loggerenberg/Walter affair. He told of a 'fragmented and weakened criminal justice system ... lack of alignment ... disjointed handing of cases ... institutions weakened over the years'.

Nonetheless, SARS worked hand in glove with its justice-system colleagues, even training and covering the costs of special tax units within the NPA and agreeing to second tax experts to what was then the National Intelligence Agency (NIA, later the State Security Agency, SSA).

At the same time, SARS strengthened its capacity to fight internal corruption, introducing a 'no gifts' rule, for example, and increasing internal monitoring. It put in place a systematic framework for case selection that ensured that an individual taxpayer couldn't be arbitrarily targeted. This tightening up, Pillay wrote in his submission, had two negative effects over time: a growing number of former employees with a grudge, and organised crime shifting from offering bribes to making physical threats against SARS officials. 'SARS officials were shot at, received death threats, [were] assaulted, had their homes broken into, laptops with key evidence stolen ...'

And then there were the inevitable 'dossiers'.

*

Dossiers have a special place in recent South African political history. They can hold just one page of information or they can be a thick wedge of documentation, but they are used to package intelligence to give it impact, credibility and authority. When a source slides a dossier over the table to a journalist, or slips it to him in a crowded train station, it isn't just an allegation, or a titbit of data, or gossip. It's a dossier. It has weight. Even if it doesn't.

'Dossiers have become a feature in how disaffected elements and intelligence sources try to manipulate the media,' Pillay, a former ANC intelligence man, underground and in exile, who himself has been the target of such dossiers, told me in a 2019 interview. He's a carefully spoken, self-effacing man, thoughtful and deliberate with the few words he offers in conversation. 'It is probably because of where we came from, in the early 1990s. It starts with the old intelligence services. A lot of them were around trying to sell information – and tailoring and packaging it to interest a potential buyer.'

This was a time when old-guard intelligence officials were uncertain of their future and trying to get in with the new government, and ANC intelligence people were trying to find their feet in the state structures. The ANC intelligence people were competing with each other and the old guard, trust was low and the stakes – essentially position, power and resources in the new order – were high. The currency of the new order was a dossier, a compendium of information, some probably true, some half-true, some suspected, some embellished, presented to make a case for or against someone.

There are numerous examples of such dossiers, and they've taken different forms. Most emerged from divisions and power struggles within the governing party, and some showed that a well-constructed dossier of information could be used and abused to great effect – no matter how spurious the content. In 2002 a dubious character called James Nkambule purported to have a dossier alleging that three prominent ANC people were plotting the overthrow of President Thabo Mbeki, for example, and there was the Browse Mole report in 2007, which made allegations of covert support from some of the continent's more corrupt dictators for Jacob Zuma's presidential bid.

Here's another example of how the game was played. A laptop was stolen from the house of a SARS official in February 2010; it contained minutes of a meeting that included one of many budget wish lists for the investigative unit. None of these had been passed or approved, and the budget remained at a paltry R12 million. But the minutes from the stolen laptop appeared years later in a dossier given to the *Sunday Times*, quoting R546 million to be allocated for 'informant fees'. SARS no longer had the original minutes to verify or challenge this number, because the minutes had been on the stolen laptop, but believed it at the very least to be a typing mistake from the wish list budget of R54,6 million, and this was apparent once the subtotals were added up; and the official who'd typed the original document later provided an affidavit confirming that it was a typing error. But the *Sunday Times* used the erroneous number, and it kept cropping up as 'evidence' that SARS was running a secret informant budget.

In the period after Jacob Zuma became president and took hold of the SSA, the trickle of dossiers to journalists turned into a flood. This was what happened when state-intelligence structures were politicised and open to use for partisan or factional purposes. It was a dossier that the SSA gave to President Zuma in 2017 that led to the highly contested recall of Finance Minister Pravin Gordhan.

In newspaper newsrooms, dossiers came so frequently and piled up so high that they became a source of humour. One day during this period journalist and sometime member of the *Sunday Times* investigations unit Pearlie Joubert was walking past the desk of her colleague, Archie Henderson, in the large and crowded *Sunday Times* open-plan office, and she pretended to trip.

Henderson looked up sharply. 'Are you okay?'

'Just tripping over another dossier,' she grinned.

There was a consistent pattern: when someone in police, prosecuting or tax offices investigated those close to or around President Zuma or his allies, a dossier would soon turn up at a newspaper's offices.

Ivan Pillay confirmed this. 'There has been for some time a willingness by journalists to be fed leaked documents. I can recall about ten such dossiers. For many years, we have spent considerable resources managing the impact of these dossiers,' he said.

One of these was 'Project Snowman', from former SARS undercover agent Mike Peega, who was the first to charge that there was a secret SARS investigations unit that was out of control, operating as a law unto itself and targeting friends and allies of President Zuma. It was repeatedly pointed out that Peega, a former special-forces soldier, had been booted out of SARS after having been arrested for rhino poaching while on holiday from his SARS job.

The first time his allegations against SARS emerged was when two of his colleagues opened a case of extortion against him and he threatened to make public his allegations about the secret SARS unit unless he received a large payout. He took the allegations to politician Julius Malema, who was himself in trouble with SARS, and so lapped it up. But the dossier contained little real evidence and was riddled with unprovable claims and obvious untruths.

It did contain a kernel of truth, though: a unit had been formed in SARS and there were questions raised about its modus operandi and its secrecy, and some of its targets could be linked to President Zuma. To try to show there was nothing covert or illegal about what they were doing, SARS in 2009 and 2010 went on a wide campaign to brief all media houses, many politicians, parliamentary committees and even President Zuma with a detailed document refuting the Snowman charges line-by-line.

Peega's allegations that this unit was behaving illegally nonetheless kept coming back like a cold sore on the face of SARS. Peega's credibility was zero on a good day, but Operation Snowman or a version of it would turn up every few months, cited by someone else with an axe to grind. And there was no shortage of axe-grinders when it came to the national tax office.

Elements of Peega's story turned up in another dossier, this time rebranded 'Broken Arrow', which went through several iterations and added allegations of racism within SARS. As late as 2019, Peega's dossier appeared to play a part when the Public Protector re-launched the accusation of a SARS 'rogue unit'.

In the period leading up to *the Sunday Times* 'SARS love affair' story in late 2014, the distribution of 'intelligence reports' containing all sorts of allegations against SARS officials, produced by disgruntled ex-staffers or tax dodgers and distributed to political parties, journalists, parliamentarians and others under SARS investigation, became, according to Van Loggerenberg, 'a veritable cottage industry'.

'SARS is confronted by a set of adversaries acting singly or in concert whose interests are to weaken its enforcement capacity,' Pillay wrote in his 2014 Sikhakhane submission. 'These include, but are not limited to, former disgruntled employees who can no longer access employment opportunities within the public sector ... delinquent taxpayers for whom it is in their interest ... to weaken SARS's capabilities ... [and] other state institutions [with] a sense of rivalry.'

In 2012 alone, SARS had dismissed 398 employees, including 23 senior managers, and many of the allegations that appeared in the media originated from among them. Their insider knowledge often rang true, and many had documents and other material to back them up.

Although these dossiers varied, there was a pattern to the allegations: SARS was exceeding its mandate, breaking the law or intercepting communications illegally. And then the most insidious and damaging accusation of all: racial discrimination was rife in the organisation, where black African employees were not getting the same treatment and promotion possibilities as others.

Central to these allegations was always the smallest of several groups that targeted organised crime: SARS's High-Risk Investigations Unit (HRIU), in its various iterations over time. And the names that came to the fore every time were Pravin Gordhan, the SARS chief who'd led the reform of the organisation and moved on to be Minister of Finance; Ivan Pillay, his deputy and longstanding cadre, who'd led the investigative and compliance strategy; and Johann van Loggerenberg, who oversaw investigations.

95

From about 2005, a new accusation started to do the rounds: that these three were targeting Jacob Zuma and those around him, that they were caught in the political battles of that period between the presidential aspirant and his detractors.

SARS officials had to constantly counter this kind of misinformation.

*

At the same time, the SARS investigations arms were honing their skills and experience, and their investigative units were growing in impact. They began to notch up significant successes against high-profile figures.

KwaZulu-Natal crime boss Michael Barnabas was convicted for tax evasion, as was Western Cape crime boss Colin Stansfield. There was also action against crooked mining magnate Brett Kebble's estate, as well as those of his killers, Glenn Agliotti, one of the most notorious of Johannesburg's underworld operators, and another, Lolly Jackson. SARS played a key role in the jailing of Serbian gangster Radovan Krejcir. They recovered over R700 million from businessman Dave King and went after soccer supremo Irvin Khoza and shady dealmaker Billy Rautenbach. They nabbed a major JSE-listed retailer, Metcash, for fake invoicing, with penalties totalling R265 million. They also targeted the electronics import industry, where a number of individuals and companies were convicted and over R67 million recovered.

SARS was also confronting prominent politicians, in the ruling party and its opposition. Jacques Pauw reported in his book *The President's Keepers* that Zuma hadn't filed tax returns during the early years of his presidency, and had also not declared suspicious income from a private company for his first few months in office. And Zuma's tax matters came up again when the Public Protector, Thuli Madonsela, said he was liable for fringe-benefit tax for the state-sponsored improvements on his private house at Nkandla. In 2014, Pillay, as acting SARS commissioner, confirmed that Zuma was being investigated for the Nkandla matter.

In the same year, outspoken politician Julius Malema struck a deal with SARS to get out of his R20-million tax hole.

*

From 2007, as Zuma became president of the ANC, SARS officials identified a noticeable change in the attitudes to SARS of the NPA and police Crime Intelligence. Inter-agency cooperation started to fall apart.

SARS had planned to set up a special-projects unit with the NIA to lead their charge on organised crime. As the NIA was absorbed into Zuma's SSA, however, this plan fell away. Van Loggerenberg met with police Crime Intelligence to see if they could accommodate such a unit, but nothing came of this initiative.

That was when SARS had to make a plan to do what they could with their own resources.

When, in 2009, Peega alleged that SARS was running an illegal 'covert unit', and treading in SSA territory, SARS thought it tactical to call in the SSA to investigate whether there was truth in this. The SSA looked into it on three occasions, and told Pillay that all was fine, but would never formally give SARS the outcome. SARS asked every year for at least five years for a report, and did not get it. They suspected that the SSA had indeed found nothing amiss in SARS activities, but weren't prepared to say so in writing.

In 2013, according to Van Loggerenberg, SARS was getting multiple reports about SARS people being put under surveillance 'but our attitude was that we were doing nothing wrong, so it [did] not matter', he said.

In 2014 there was a series of threats to SARS officials. Some had break-ins at their houses where valuables weren't taken but hard drives and laptops were. SARS's HRIU also had a break-in during which a hard drive disappeared, but R500 000-worth of other equipment wasn't touched. 'I can't say who it was, but it was odd,' Van Loggerenberg said.

And they began to hear things. A senior police Crime Intelligence man questioned someone who'd once worked with SARS, asking for dirt on Van Loggerenberg. Another was recorded saying that he knew 'big heads are going to roll at SARS'. Party officials at ANC head-quarters were saying that there were ANC bigwigs who wanted to replace the leadership at SARS and remove the Minister of Finance. Public Enterprises Minister Lynne Brown told a journalist to tell Ivan Pillay that he was 'going to be pushed out from SARS, humiliated, and never allowed to work again'.

In July 2014, another well-placed journalist told Van Loggerenberg that SSA people were saying he was corrupt and would be fired soon. 'All of this I put in an email to Ivan [Pillay]. All these red flags, something [was] afoot ... But Ivan was on sabbatical so didn't see it until he got back. And by then Tom Moyane had been appointed [as Zuma's man to run SARS].'

When, in 2013, a recording emerged of SARS's respected head, Oupa Magashula, having an inappropriate conversation about a potential female employee, Magashula resigned. But who was listening to his phone conversations and who had leaked it? The prime candidates were the SSA and police Crime Intelligence, the two bodies that had the capacity to tap phones and were known to be abusing it.

SARS wrote to the Inspector General of Intelligence, the SSA and police Crime Intelligence to ask if any of their people were responsible for it. They got no reply from any of them – an ominous sign of what was to come.

Van Loggerenberg's trial by media

It's crisis control 101: if you're facing a media exposé and you can't knock it down, or just hide until it passes, then you create doubt and confusion and diversion. That's what the SSA and its tobacco allies were doing.

In the *Sunday Times*'s first story, Johann van Loggerenberg was described as 'a former apartheid undercover police agent'. It's one of the most damning things to say about a South African, short only of calling someone a murderer, a rapist or a paedophile. Like all of those epithets, it leads to immediate isolation and condemnation.

There's a visceral fear among many that the new order is riddled with former apartheid agents who are sleepers within the bureaucracy, waiting for an opportunity to undermine the new democratic order. Many would have seen that and nodded with a sense of knowing, of confirmation of these fears, and of the story.

The day after the article appeared, Van Loggerenberg wrote to Rob Rose and Malcolm Rees about this description and asked to meet them in his personal capacity. They met at SARS and, Van Loggerenberg says, they were 'rather arrogant'. He told them, 'I take great exception to the label you have attributed to me. You did not ask me about my career and you clearly have no idea what I did in [that] period.' They refused to retract it, nor did they distance themselves from it.

Rees later said he knew nothing about this line and saw it for the first time on the printed page. He didn't believe it to be true when he saw it, and still doesn't, he said in a 2019 statement. Those words had been 'edited into' the story after it had left his section editor, Rob Rose.

A number of people told me it had been inserted by the editor-in-chief, Phylicia Oppelt, and two told me that she had admitted privately to it. Another staff member said he'd traced the versions of the story through the *Sunday Times* computer system and that the addition had been made when it was in Oppelt's hands.

To me, though, she said, 'Perhaps I did. I don't remember.' And in a written statement she gave me in 2019, in the same breath as she distanced herself from it, she restated the slur: 'What was clear from leaked correspondence was that Van Loggerenberg had an "RS" [secret police] number when he did his military service ... I will apologise to Van Loggerenberg once he hands over the records of his entire military service.'

Van Loggerenberg did, in fact, join the police after school as part of his national service in the 1980s. He says he underwent training, worked in a police charge office for six months, then spent time as a gate guard, administrative official, cook, dishwasher, mobile police-station manager and driver. In October 1993 he joined a secretive police unit known as Organised Crime Intelligence, and worked until 1998 as a 'deep-cover long-term agent'.

He's adamant that he did no political work, and that his role was to infiltrate crime syndicates, mostly those dealing in drugs. He won't talk details because he says it was dangerous work and his life could still be at risk, but he showed me internal reports of him working under-cover in Durban to infiltrate mandrax rings. Like all good smears, the 'secret police' allegation had some loose basis in truth – but it had been deliberately tainted with an apartheid link to smear him.

How would Oppelt have known about this? It turns out that her ex-husband, Rudolf Mastenbroek, who'd held a senior position in SARS, had fallen out with deputy director Ivan Pillay after Pillay had appointed Van Loggerenberg above him. Mastenbroek had refused to answer to Van Loggerenberg, and had left soon afterwards, bringing to an end his ambitions to hold a senior public-service post.

Mastenbroek, who built up the criminal-investigations department in SARS until his resignation in 2013, presented himself as a stickler for the rules and the law. He viewed Pillay and Van Loggerenberg as cowboys who pushed the limits – not for personal gain, granted, but to pressurise errant taxpayers – and he would have no truck with this.

Mastenbroek and Oppelt had had a messy divorce, but they shared two children and were co-parenting at the time of the SARS stories. While Mastenbroek has adamantly denied being the *Sunday Times* source on the story, he shares with Oppelt a near-obsession about Van Loggerenberg's past. It's possible he was bolstering the story of Van Loggerenberg's background and his view that these SARS officials had gone 'rogue'.

Mastenbroek was the original source that led his university friend and *Sunday Times* journalist Pearlie Joubert into the story. Joubert said Mastenbroek tried as early as 2013 to get her to write the 'rogue unit' story for the *Sunday Times*.

'Adv Mastenbroek has been actively soliciting the media with information of a particular hue and slant regarding SARS since 2013, after he left the employ of SARS,' Joubert wrote in a June 2015 letter to Judge Frank Kroon, Minister of Finance Nhlanhla Nene, and his deputy Mcebisi Jonas. 'It was clearly his intention to discredit certain persons by way of the media as early as April 2013.

'I am of the firm opinion that Mastenbroek has played an active and decisive role in "influencing" the very particular and devastating bias my former employer [Oppelt] has shown on the stories relating to the so-called rogue spy unit within SARS. Mastenbroek briefed me in April 2013 on various SARS stories he thought we (the *Sunday Times* investigations unit) should pursue. I shared Mastenbroek's information, as an anonymous source, with my colleagues (and later the editor) at the beginning of May 2013.'

One of the allegations Mastenbroek made to Joubert was that Van Loggerenberg was 'an old security policeman' and 'an apartheid spy'.

But why had Phylicia Oppelt chosen to insert the slander against

Van Loggerenberg into the story, then refused to retract it, then forgotten about it, then raised it again at every opportunity?

*

Johann van Loggerenberg is a character worth getting to know better, in order to understand how this saga played out over many years.

My first personal encounter with him came when I made a passing mention in a 2017 newspaper column of his 'affair' with Walter. He waited five months before writing me an 1 800-word, tortuously argued, pedantically detailed email challenging my choice of the word 'affair'.

The letter was scrupulously polite in an old-fashioned way, with the first five paragraphs begging my forgiveness for his directness in approaching me and flattering me as 'a well-known media person with a mighty pen' and a sense of 'good manners and decency'. Then he got down to business. He found my views of him 'offensive, disparaging and highly contestable' and questioned how I could mention him without ever speaking to him.

I'd written an article for the *Daily Maverick* in praise of the best journalism of the time, but with a warning that we should also pay attention to the shoddy reporting – such as that of the *Sunday Times* – that did such harm. My misstep had been to say that the *Sunday Times* story had begun 'with a legitimate tale of sex and power': Van Loggerenberg's 'affair' with Walter.

My use of the word 'affair', he argued, was to 'sex up the story ... to sell news'. 'In my world,' he wrote, 'an "affair" is suggestive of an adulterous kind of romantic relationship ... something sneaky and dishonest ... If you knew me, and the lady, during the time of our relationship, you would not have considered it an "affair". At best, we were dating.'

He ended the email by suggesting that we could have 'a dialogue to see if there is any purpose to discuss it further at all'. When I took up his offer and went to meet him in 2019, he told me that he knew he could be obsessive and that some people found him difficult to work with. This was an understatement: those who worked with him usually admired his dedication, hard work and attention to detail, but also described the nightmare of dealing with a demanding workaholic who had little private life, often slept in his office, and drove himself and his staff relentlessly.

In his book, *Rogue: The Inside Story of SARS's Elite Crime-Busting Unit,* he was quite honest about himself: 'My private life was dull, if not downright unbalanced … I had virtually no friends … I was estranged from my family … I worked virtually every day of the week, sometimes even sleeping in my office and showering at the local gym … I didn't socialise much and couldn't even make small talk with people. I was also rather intolerant towards colleagues who had families and social lives … [I realised] how disassociated I had become from the things that should matter to ordinary people. All I thought of, and busied myself with, was work. I came across as aloof and unapproachable, and I know my colleagues found me difficult at times.'

It was easy to see why he was such a successful tax investigator, a job for which pedantry is an asset.

When I started to ask him questions, he gave detailed and meticulous answers, citing paragraph and page numbers on affidavits from years before, quoting verbatim, with dates and places, and doing it all with the patience of a man who'd done it many times before for journalists and was content to do it as many times more as required to make his case.

Once I engaged with him, he was relentless. He would send long, complicated WhatsApp messages up to a dozen times a day, including copies of and detailed responses to any relevant media coverage of documentation. Every message reflected his anger, frustration and obsessiveness. If I asked him a question, his answers would require hours of reading. He let nothing go. He never omitted a detail. His case was always argued meticulously and completely.

He set a personal record on 4 July 2019, when I asked him casually if he knew someone. Starting at 10.26am, he sent me 74 messages and about a dozen pictures of documents, some of them hundreds of words long and many with links to online material. At 9.46pm, he wrote, 'Okay, will stop now.' Within a minute I got another WhatsApp: 'Last words ...', followed by five more messages. 'Just delete these if they irritate you,' he threw in.

This singular man's life and career had been turned upside down in the long battle in which he'd been treated with gross unfairness by SARS and the media. He'd been humiliated in public, repeatedly and relentlessly. He'd been accused of the vilest things, and when he'd spoken out about it, he'd often been ignored. He'd had to rebuild his life, his career and his reputation from scratch.

While I got to know Van Loggerenberg quite well, I had to depend on second-hand views – mostly from people who now despise her – to try and get past the newspaper stereotype of Belinda Walter as a 'Pretoria Mata Hari' (as *City Press* called her). On the evidence, she was erratic, fickle and unreliable – but there were those who'd wanted, for their own purposes, to believe and use her story. It gave SARS's enemies – and these were not in short supply – a wedge to drive into the organisation.

I tried to find and talk to Walter, but without success. She'd dropped out of sight, with no social media, no internet presence and no visible legal practice. Her phone numbers and email addresses no longer worked.

*

In the weeks after the first 'Love affair rocks SARS' report, the *Sunday Times* investigations unit moved in and took over the story from Rees. They were fed a constant flow of material about SARS and, ignoring the flak and conflicting reports by their rivals, they ramped up their coverage.

On 12 October 2014, the headline was 'SARS bugged Zuma'. On 9 November, it was 'Taxman's rogue unit ran brothel'. This was no longer a racy tabloid love-affair saga; it was a suggestion that the unit had gone completely wild, was contemptuous of the law and was interfering in national politics, way beyond its brief. According to the reports, the SARS officials had broken into and planted listening devices in Zuma's home when he was running for ANC president; they were involved in illegal surveillance and 'house infiltrations' to spy on taxpayers; they had set up their own brothel, and posed as bodyguards for prominent politicians in order to eavesdrop on them; the unit had become 'a law unto itself', issuing its agents with fake identities.

It was breathtaking stuff, often stated, in keeping with the *Sunday Times*'s traditional 'treatment', as fact. In the first story, SARS was allowed a token three-line 'vehement denial', with a fuller statement hidden on the bottom of page two. In the second story, you had to go to the last few sentences on page five to find SARS's two-paragraph denials.

The first story had the names of Rampedi, Wa Afrika, Hofstatter and Rees on it. The order of the names was determined by each person's relative contributions to the story, so this implied that Rampedi was the lead writer while Rees had made the least contribution.

The second story was attributed to Wa Afrika, Rampedi and Hofstatter. Now Wa Afrika was the lead, and Rees had dropped out. It wasn't long before Rees, unhappy with the direction the story was taking, resigned.

The key descriptor for the SARS unit had now become 'rogue'. The word had first appeared in the earlier 'renditions' stories and Pauw had used it in his very first 2014 SSA exposé to describe the agents who he'd said were framing the SARS officials. It was a useful journalists' tool, a conveniently vague label that could be thrown around with abandon, one that the lawyers could live with. You had to be careful about saying they broke the law, or exceeded their mandate, or even that they made mistakes, as they could sue for that. It was safer to say they'd gone rogue.

There was a total of 36 stories over the next two years that reinforced this picture of SARS. But there was a vagueness in the reporting – a lack of names, dates and other specifics – that should have worried any editor, and the stories were riddled with unproven claims and naked falsities.

The paper sourced the stories to documents its reporters had 'seen' (but didn't have in their possession) and 'SARS officials who spoke on condition of anonymity'.

One source of proof that was presented was that in leaked emails Van Loggerenberg had been asked where he'd got details of some conversations and he'd said, simply, 'Intercepted' – not who'd done the interception or whether it was legal or not, just a claim that it had come from an intercepted conversation. The report also cited as evidence a memo from the unit that outlined 'rules of play' that included 'group is not known' and 'cost centre is not known'. The reporters didn't explain what this meant or how it supported their case.

The evidence for the brothel was a memo from one person: 'Members were told to establish businesses as a "cover". One of these was the brothel. "I was very much unhappy about the brothel as a SARS employee was also pimping young women," a member wrote.' There was no indication of where this brothel was in Durban, no photograph, no details of the 'pimping', and no substantiation or verification at all. It was just a second-hand claim.

The spying allegation was supported by an 'intelligence official [who] confirmed … that the cabinet security cluster had independently established that a bug had been planted in Zuma's house'. Note it wasn't SARS that had planted it, just that one had been planted. It wasn't clear what it meant to 'establish' this fact, or to do so 'independently'. And in the 'SARS bugged Zuma' story, it was stated that the SARS unit had carried out the bugging in 2005, as well as intercepting one of Zuma's meetings in 2007 – but the unit didn't even come into existence until some years later.

The man at the centre of the 'Zuma bugging' story sent an email denying it three days before the story appeared. '[We] were never involved in any bugging operation on President Zuma's house or him as an individual and, for that matter, any other surveillance operations or the interception of communication of any citizens. This would have been illegal and during the period of my employment at SARS we never engaged in any illegal activities,' he wrote. Not a word of this appeared in the *Sunday Times* report.

Another example is on 9 November 2014 the paper reported that Van Loggerenberg had admitted in a letter to SARS Commissioner Tom Moyane that they had run a rogue unit, calling it a 'confession'; I've seen the letter and there's nothing in it that amounts to such an admission.

And on 12 April 2015 the *Sunday Times* reported that Van Loggerenberg was 'a CV cheat' who'd 'exaggerated [his] qualifications by passing himself off to a journalist as an MBA graduate' – a claim for which no evidence has been provided to this day.

SARS sent the *Sunday Times* a long and detailed email pointing out that much of the information appeared to be a repeat of allegations from the dossier put together by the discredited former official, SSA and tobacco-industry agent, Mike Peega. This wasn't mentioned in the *Sunday Times* story.

Where was the *Sunday Times* getting its information? Piet Rampedi later told the Press Council that it came from a combination of former SARS officials, current SARS officials and 'intelligence officials'. He refused to name them, but he was confirming what *City Press* was saying: the SSA and/or police Crime Intelligence had a hand in it.

Jumping the gun

The first *Sunday Times* tweet went out at 7.16pm on Saturday 27 May 2017:

> GuptaEmails: They reveal Gupta plans
> to resettle President Zuma and his family
> in Dubai > Details in #SundayTimesZA
> tomorrow.

A flurry followed:

7.30pm: #GuptaEmails: They handpicked Mosebenzi Zwane after screening his CV >
Details in #SundayTimesZA tomorrow

7.45pm: #GuptaEmails: They show Van Rooyen
lied as Guptas paid for his Dubai trip. He
had a companion > In #SundayTimesZA
tomorrow

8pm: #GuptaEmails: How they treated ministers and CEOs to luxury in Dubai – chauffeured Jaguars, BMW7s and 5 star hotels >
In #SundayTimesZA 8pm

8.15pm: #GuptaEmails: Reveal how a minister
reported government plans to Guptas, even
before cabinet meetings > In #Sunday-
TimesZA

8.41pm: #Exposed: Proof the Guptas run South
Africa.

*

'HERE'S PROOF, MR PRESIDENT!' was the screaming *Sunday Times* headline the next morning, 28 May 2017. And the intro could not have been plainer and more hard-hitting: 'A series of explosive emails show the extent of the Gupta family's control over cabinet ministers, and state-owned companies and their CEOs and boards.'

The report went on to reveal that the CEO of the Guptas' company Oakbay Investments, Nazeem Howa, had prepared notes for ANC Youth League president Collen Maine advising him how to respond to media questions; that the Guptas had been sent Mosebenzi Zwane's CV a month before he was appointed Minister of Mineral Resources, and had flown him to Dubai and paid for his accommodation there; that they had arranged for Dan Mantsha, director of state arms-procurement company Denel, to be chauffeured around Dubai, and for Matshela Koko, soon-to-be CEO of the giant state power monopoly Eskom, to be put up in a deluxe hotel suite; and that they'd arranged for Zuma and his family to acquire residency in Dubai.

It seemed that finally the media had the proof to back up what was widely suspected about the Gupta-Zuma relationship, and could no longer be denied.

The material had been offered to them, Andrew Trench, who led the *Sunday Times* team at the time, told me in 2019. 'I'd heard rumours that *Daily Maverick* was on to something big, but we didn't solicit it. It came to us. We authenticated it based on the knowledge of where it came from. We did some basic verification and the feedback was that it was legitimate. Also, the size of it was such that no-one could have invented it.'

In a boardroom at Tiso Blackstar, the *Sunday Times*'s parent company, reporters from all four of the group's newspapers (the *Sunday Times*, the *Sowetan*, *Business Day* and the *Financial Mail*) were pulled together, and they worked together in what was dubbed the 'Cvofefe Room'. (No-one can now explain this reference to Donald Trump's obscure tweeting, though it seems oddly inappropriate.) One cluster of reporters drew up lists of names of individuals and entities, to do searches on them in the emails; one or two reporters did the searches – thousands of them. A second group read emails at random in the hope of spotting interesting leads; on a whiteboard, they listed possible stories. Every morning they would choose a few of those and reporters would get on the phone to follow up and find collaboration.

It was quite a feat to process the information and generate a bunch of stories within a few days, especially for a newspaper where the rush for a splash headline had got them into trouble before. But they faced deadlines and contemplated the glory of beating their arch-rivals, *City Press* and the *Daily Maverick*.

This was rushed journalism.

What the *Sunday Times* published were hastily found, juicy bits and pieces from the emails that pointed to how far the Guptas' tentacles had spread and how poisonous they were. But the newspaper *hadn't* taken the time to delve into the depths of the emails and pull together the various strands. And the rush to publish meant that the story about Dubai residency for Zuma and his family was off-kilter. It was followed up by a report that the Guptas had bought a huge mansion for Zuma in Dubai, but this turned out also to be a dubious assertion.

Still, this time the *Sunday Times* was lucky. The source material was authentic.

PART II

SLOW JOURNALISM

A remarkable find

John (not his real name) picked up one of the 10 000 or so hard drives lying around the workshop.

He could've picked up the one next to it. If he'd taken any other drive, his life – and those of numerous others – would have turned out differently. It's hard to say whether it would have been better or worse, but it would certainly have followed another trajectory. There would be moments to come when he would regret that his eye had fallen on that particular hard drive.

I can't say how John came to be in this workshop, or how the hard drive came to be there, to protect him and his colleague Stan (also not his real name). But John, at a loose end that day in late 2016, picked up the discarded drive and started to work with it.

A short while later, John told Stan that he'd retrieved the contents of the drive, and it was downloading onto another drive. When about ninety percent of it had been copied across, the original drive collapsed.

He gave the hard drive containing the retrieved data to Stan. Stan looked at whose drive it was. 'And *voilà!*' he said.

It belonged to Ashu Chawla, an executive at Sahara Computers, one of the many companies controlled by the infamous three Gupta brothers, Rajesh, Ajay and Atul. John and Stan were not particularly political, but they followed the news and everyone was talking about the Guptas. Their name had become synonymous with corruption of a special kind.

Their mansion in the Johannesburg suburb of Saxonwold had become notorious as a palace of nefarious deals. To say 'I ate curry in

Saxonwold' was to say that you were important enough for the Guptas to want to solicit your favour; there was immediate suspicion that you'd done an underhand deal with them. The racial undertone of the curry reference was a true South Africanism, not accidental.

Working closely with one of the president's sons, Duduzane Zuma, the Guptas were said to be manipulating government tenders and contracts for their own multibillion-rand gain. They weren't alone in such activity, but the Guptas were accused of taking corruption to a different level – what became known as state capture.

They were accused of having such a hold on President Jacob Zuma that they were influencing the appointment of cabinet ministers and other key state officials to the benefit of their own businesses. The Guptas would get the president to appoint their cronies to boards such as that of the national electricity provider, Eskom. Eskom would suddenly cancel a longstanding contract with a major coal mine, saying their coal was substandard. When that mine went into liquidation, the Guptas would buy it cheaply and sign a new, massively overpriced contract with Eskom which, in the hands of their allies, suddenly had less concern about the quality of the coal.

When the Minister of Mineral Resources got in their way, they had Zuma replace him. When the Minister of Finance raised objections, he was moved sideways. When the NPA took an interest, those who ran that office were driven out. When police investigated, they were shafted. When tax officials looked too closely, they were targeted.

The Guptas were rampant, with an extraordinary capacity to influence decisions of state and turn them to their own benefit.

It wasn't unusual or a new thing for special minority interests – particularly industrial and mining interests – to have undue influence on the South African state. The country had been shaped by a confluence of mining, industrial, class and racial influences, and apartheid had been the product of these forces working together for the benefit of the few who'd held the state in their grasp. And there'd certainly been earlier periods when barons of the economy had had a say in the

116

appointment of parastatal boards and even cabinet ministers, or had been able to do special deals with the tax office or public prosecutor.

But never had this been done so brazenly, so extensively, and at such cost to the operations of state institutions. And now it was being done in a constitutional democracy, under a government that said it was there to serve the poor, to fight corruption, to right the wrongs of the past.

The institutions that were there to prevent such corruption were being systematically undermined, and it was being done at a massive cost to the economy.

It was justified in the name of black empowerment. President Zuma and the Guptas were adept at exploiting the ANC's policies to correct the injustices of the past by favouring black businesses and professionals, which in turn favoured them. They were taking contracts away from the white-minority owners who'd always dominated industries such as mining, their supporters argued, and they were sharing the opportunities among black people who until recently had been blocked from such enterprises. They were righting historical wrongs, driving the economic transformation that had been so elusive since the political change of 1994.

Their cynical justification for what they were doing, and for those who assisted and enabled them, was that they were pushing the change the ANC government hadn't brought to the country, tackling the 'white monopoly capital' (WMC) that continued to dominate the economy and which had the most to lose from the Guptas' success. WMC was a useful phrase employed by their public-relations agency, British experts Bell Pottinger, which had laid out a strategy of how to divert attention by pointing fingers at white capital.

It helped, of course, that the Guptas shared the benefits with those who backed them in this endeavour: where they earned billions, they handed out millions. Since President Zuma had a chronic financial problem, and displayed a remarkable incapacity to live within his not-insubstantial means, assistance for him and his family was welcomed.

It was a relationship perhaps best depicted – as is so often the case – in a Zapiro cartoon, one of the drawings of the country's leading satirist, Jonathan Shapiro. He showed Ajay Gupta shaking hands with President Zuma, handing over a bag of money, while Zuma has a map of South Africa under his arm, ready to make the exchange.

It was, of course, rampant destruction, as state entities were looted and institutions – such as the tax office – denuded of capacity. The beneficiaries of this form of empowerment were few. But those who opposed the Guptas were casually labelled as WMC lackeys.

The Guptas were flamboyant, and their every step and misstep was followed by the media. The country became largely divided between the few who were in on the game and those who saw them as corrupt and dangerous. There were also those with a foot in both these categories.

*

The hard drive John had picked up contained a few years of emails – hundreds of thousands of them – to and from Sahara Computers executive Ashu Chawla. He'd taken the broken disk drive to a computer-repair company, but it was a difficult case and it would have cost about R10 000 to fix. Chawla had declined to pay.

It was probably the most costly R10 000 he never spent.

The damaged drive had been put onto a discard pile, and went on a roundabout journey for some months before landing in a pile intended for spare parts, where on that quiet afternoon in 2016 John went in search of a drive to work with.

When Stan realised whose drive it was that John had picked up, he immediately told John to make two copies of the data. He wanted to take a look at the emails, but he wasn't in a hurry and the data needed some work to make it readable.

A few days later, when he had some spare time, Stan sat down and read a few of the emails, and then a few more. Then he put them aside for a while because he was busy, and came back later and read some more.

He slowly began to realise that he had in his hands information that could throw the whole issue wide open. 'I realised,' he told me in a 2019 interview, 'that Zuma wasn't running the state. The Guptas were.'

The sources' quandary

At first Stan didn't do much with the material. Over the next few months he occasionally took a look and learnt a bit more. 'I didn't know the names I found there, but I would hear a name in the news and would search for it.'

In early 2017 he saw a news report on trouble at Eskom, and the Guptas were mentioned because they'd taken control of the mine that was making billions from selling coal to the state power company. He went to the emails and did a search on Eskom, and could see the correspondence between the Guptas and Eskom management.

One day he was watching a parliamentary inquiry on television when one of the MPs asked for a key document. 'We've got that document!' Stan shouted at the TV. He gradually began to copy and put aside some of the most interesting material he found.

One particular trail of emails he found dealt with Mosebenzi Zwane. The trail started with the drawing up of his CV when he was still a relatively obscure local politician, passing through various hands and ending up with President Zuma's son, Duduzane. A few months later Zwane was a surprise appointment as Minister of Mineral Resources, a key office for the Guptas and their mining interest. The email trail showed their hand in Zwane's unexpected promotion.

The political battles around the Guptas heated up, and he realised the weight of what had fallen into his hands, Stan became nervous. He didn't know what to do with the drive, and discussed it with his wife.

In early 2017 Stan watched a televised broadcast of President

Zuma answering questions in Parliament. Zuma strutted and giggled and treated his critics with contempt. He had the swagger of immunity. Stan thought, No, Mr President, you shouldn't be doing that. Presidents don't behave like that. People must see what's behind the laughter.

He was irritated enough to think again about what he should do with the emails. 'We're not political in any way, shape or form,' Stan said later, referring to himself and his wife. 'It's a matter of right and wrong. The fall of a president wasn't in our minds at all at any time. We're just regular South Africans.'

*

Stan wanted to get the information into the public domain, but didn't know how to. He didn't know whom he could trust. He didn't know anyone in the media he could talk to about it. But he knew about a small newspaper with a reputation for hell-raising investigative work, the *Mail & Guardian*. He looked up its address and one Saturday morning in November 2016 he drove to its office in Rosebank, central Johannesburg.

What Stan didn't know was the sad state of the *Mail & Guardian* at that time. The paper was a shadow of its former self, living on its history and reputation.

I was one of the founders of the paper – then *The Weekly Mail* – as an alternative anti-apartheid voice in the 1980s, when it developed a reputation for covering security-force repression and the struggle against minority rule with a cheeky, defiant attitude towards the censorship of the time. The heart of the paper had been its investigative team and its reputation for fearless, uncompromising muckraking, dating back to the apartheid era. In 2010 that team had set itself up as *amaBhungane*, a semi-independent *Mail & Guardian* partner.

By the end of 2016, when Stan drove to the Rosebank offices, the newspaper belonged to Trevor Ncube, a successful Zimbabwean newspaper publisher who'd developed a lifestyle and ambition beyond what the paper could sustain, especially when the economy took a downward plunge. He'd rifled the assets to buy himself a luxury house and car, but owed money to printers, staff and freelancers.

When relations with Ncube broke down, *amaBhungane* – which had made its name on exposing such shenanigans – broke away and set itself up as an independent, grant-funded operation.

When Stan came knocking at the *Mail & Guardian*'s door that Saturday afternoon he was carrying a piece of paper showing the Zwane email trail. He had the biggest story of the decade and was in search of the paper's investigative reporters, but everything was locked up, and nobody – not even a security guard – was present.

Stan was at a loss for what to do.

*

Fortunately, Stan was persistent. In December 2016 he phoned the offices of the opposition Democratic Alliance and was told to speak to a particular MP. They arranged to meet the next morning at 9am in a Benmore coffee shop.

Stan got there early. The MP never turned up. 'I had a couple of cups of coffee, and then left. He never phoned back.' It was probably just as well, as the data wouldn't have had the same credibility if it had emerged from the parliamentary opposition.

'There was a lot of conscience-wrestling,' Stan told me. 'I didn't want to have regrets. I said to myself that if I don't do something with this, in five years I'm going to regret it.'

That is when he spoke to another acquaintance – let's call him Mr M – who had connections in the media world. Stan showed Mr M what he called the 'Zwane trail' – the emails that showed how the Guptas had pushed a little-known local politician named Mosebenzi Zwane for Minister of Mineral Resources. 'I said I had a lot more, but would only reveal it on a risk-reward basis,' Stan said. 'I would only take the risk for the right reward – not necessarily money, but we had to have protection.'

Mr M told Stan that media wouldn't pay for the information, as this would undermine their credibility if it ever came out. They left it at that.

The next morning Mr M called. He'd arranged for Stan and himself to have a drink with a well-known newspaper editor. At the meeting this editor, who had no idea that it was anything more than a drink with a friend, had a few too many, and Mr M felt he couldn't ask Stan to hand over the material.

So Stan was adrift. While the country was hungry for the evidence to expose what was going on, while most journalists would've done anything for what he had, and while he wanted to get the information into the right hands, he couldn't find anyone to give it to.

Mr M, though, didn't give up.

*

'I need some advice,' Mr M said. 'I have a friend who has a computer hard drive with emails on it that show the relationship between the Gupta family and senior politicians. He doesn't know what to do with them.'

Mr M had phoned Brian Currin, a former human-rights lawyer who'd handled this kind of hot information before. Back in 1989, Currin had worked with one of the best-known whistleblowers, Dirk Coetzee, a former police commander who'd revealed the existence of the apartheid police's Vlakplaas death squad.

Still, Stan was jittery when he and Mr M met Currin in February 2017: he was 'visibly nervous, shocked and deeply concerned', Currin said in a 2019 interview in his Sandton office.

Stan had brought with him the paper trail of the Zwane emails, as a taste of what he had, and he told Currin how he'd come to have it. 'It sounded dinkum,' Currin said, but there wasn't much he could do until Stan trusted him enough to show him the material.

Currin had a long chat with Stan to help him relax and to start winning his confidence.

'I asked Currin why he was doing this,' Stan recalled later. 'It is my life, he said, it's what I do. That was great. I had seen his CV and there was no better man for this.'

It took a while, and a few meetings, before Stan gave the sample CDs to Currin and Mr M to look at over a weekend.

'We both came to the conclusion that there was certainly stuff of interest on the CDs,' Currin said.

High stakes

The Guptas seemed to control the president, and the president controlled the machinery of state.

President Zuma had been head of security for the ANC in exile and his *modus operandi* was that of an intelligence operative: he said little and listened a lot. He knew the power of information and of having loyal intelligence agents to do his bidding.

One of the first things he'd done on coming to power was to consolidate the internal and external national spy agencies into one giant unit. He changed the name from the National Intelligence Agency to the State Security Agency – a significant change in emphasis – and put his closest, and most ruthless and corrupt, allies in charge.

Those who stood in his or the Guptas' way and who could not be bought were systematically sidelined. Where people were protected by the law or the constitution, Zuma's agents would set out to smear them and make their jobs and their lives miserable, until they took a golden handshake to stand aside and be replaced by more compliant officials. They did this even to old comrades, loyal veterans of the ANC and Zuma's close struggle cadres.

There had been a series of mysterious break-ins at the offices of critics of Zuma and the Guptas where nothing was taken except files and computers – information. News24 reported that there were nine such 'ominous burglaries' in homes and offices between 2010 and 2017. A robbery at the Chief Justice's office, for example, came the day after a highly contentious political decision, and another at the Pretoria High

Court just after a key judgment against the government; and armed robbers who targeted the Helen Suzman Foundation, which had initiated the legal action, went straight for key computers and ignored everything else in the building.

Fake social-media profiles and internet bots were used to troll journalists who wrote about them in ways they didn't like. Suggestive pictures of these journalists were circulated and fake internet sites popped up with material designed to upset their families and damage their reputations. It included some of the country's most respected editors, like Ferial Haffajee, who'd led the *Mail & Guardian* and *City Press*, and Peter Bruce, editor-in-chief of *Business Day* and the *Financial Mail*.

There was a lot at stake, and these were people who'd shown they were prepared to do whatever it took to hold on to that stake.

The two whistleblowers had reason to be fearful. As, now, did Brian Currin.

*

Stan and John wanted to get enough compensation for the material to enable them to be safe and secure. They were risking their own and their families' lives and businesses, and they needed to look after themselves. And they wanted help to get the material into the right hands to ensure that the corrupt were held to account.

Stan had sealed the the original material and a mirror copy in a safe, and was reluctant to give the full set to Currin until he'd secured his own position.

Currin, for his part, didn't yet know how valuable the information was. He didn't know whether these guys were genuine and if they actually had all they claimed to have. There isn't money in this, he told them. Nobody is going to pay you for it, because that would eventually come out and it would be used to discredit your motives: if you did it for money, would you be prepared to jazz up the data for more money?

It was an ethical balancing act for Currin: he needed to look after the whistleblowers, but he didn't want any suggestion that they were doing this for personal gain. And he didn't know enough about Stan and John to be certain of their motives.

'Mr M and Currin suggested we leave the country, and asked me to provide a cost for abandoning the country and leaving,' Stan says. 'I said I would think about it. The next day I came back and said we wanted to leave the country for a year or two. He said, fine.'

Stan understood that they might not be able to come back to South Africa, but thought that if they had enough money for two years, they could re-establish themselves elsewhere. Currin proposed that he would raise money to get Stan and John and their families out of the country until things had settled down.

They discussed an amount, but before Currin could raise the money he had to authenticate the material, and he could only do this if he had a full copy. He had to win Stan's trust enough for him to share sight of his treasure. He arranged a first tranche of R200 000.

They then discussed how best to handle the material. Currin, Stan and Mr M worked through the options until they were clear: they couldn't trust any law-enforcement agencies or political leadership enough to pass it on to them, so they agreed the emails would need to be made public. What was the best way to do this?

Should they put the raw data on an international site where everyone could have access to it and make of it what they will? Should they approach the Washington-based International Consortium of Investigative Journalists (ICIJ), which had handled and coordinated previous data dumps?

The first such major data dump was LuxLeaks in 2014, when 86 journalists in twenty countries had worked together on a treasure chest of documents to show how Luxembourg had enabled tax avoidance by giving preferential treatment to large companies channelling their profit through that country without having to pay much tax. This was coordinated by the ICIJ, pioneers of cross-border collaboration, and it demonstrated the power of this kind of work to explore every local and global angle of a story, and give it impact in each affected country.

The 2016 Panama Papers came next: they contained 11,5 million documents of client-attorney records from a company in the central-American country that specialised in providing offshore havens for the rich – some legitimate but some involving tax dodgers, fraudsters, sanction busters and money launderers. The data dump included the records of 214 488 entities dating back to the 1970s. More than 350 journalists from 80 countries, again coordinated by the ICIJ, had worked on it for a year before publishing simultaneously in 2016.

A year later the Paradise Papers, a trove of 13,4 million documents, blew open the use of many small island countries as tax havens by the rich and powerful. It exposed the secret dealings of more than 120 politicians from around the world, in an investigation involving more than 380 journalists in 67 countries. This was a new era in using huge quantities of digital data to unravel the secret world of global finance.

Another option for Stan, Currin and Mr M was Julian Assange's WikiLeaks, the radical transparency operation that had made its name enabling anonymous data leaks, but which controversially published the material unredacted and unprocessed. Assange had pioneered the use of the internet for massive, untraceable leaks to protect whistleblowers and disseminate raw material, opening up the world of secrecy but at the same time offering little protection to those implicated in unfiltered material which may or may not have been accurate.

Eventually the three agreed they had to give the data to someone who had the skills and contacts to verify and process it. The reams of raw info had limited value without those who could make sense of it, turning it into something that told a story.

*

A couple of weeks later, Stan gave Currin two copies of the material, password-protected so he didn't have access to the content. One was to be sent to a friend of Currin's in London as a backup; the other was given to a well-known activist, Mark Heywood, in Johannesburg, so that there would be a safe version close at hand. Stan said he would hand over the passwords when his position was secure.

Heywood was one of the leaders of the Save South Africa campaign, which was fighting against state capture and the Zuma presidency, and he had access to funds. More importantly, Currin had known him for a long time and trusted him.

Heywood introduced Currin to Branko Brkic, the editor of the *Daily Maverick*, who jumped in a plane and flew from Cape Town to Johannesburg the same day.

'This is too big for us'

'I thought I had a rocket in my head. This was the silver bullet. I immediately said this was bigger than *Daily Maverick*, this was an industry-wide thing.'

The date was 7 April 2017. Branko Brkic had just heard about the Gupta email trove. He sent a WhatsApp message to his ever-patient chief executive Styli Charalambous: 'We have a game-changer.'

Charalambous was the man who juggled the cashflow against all the odds to keep Brkic doing what he did. He dreamt of the breakthrough that would turn the business around, so it was natural that Brkic would tell him first that they had the story that had the potential to give them a national profile and the credibility as a news source that every editor works to build.

Then Brkic called Stefaans Brümmer of the investigative unit *amaBhungane*. 'We need to meet,' he said.

It was to Brkic's credit that he saw immediately that his outfit was too small to handle such a mass of data alone and that he needed partners on the project.

Brkic's *Daily Maverick* had fought its way into the Johannesburg media landscape as a small but important outlet to watch because you were never quite sure what would be in it. For a long time Brkic himself was never quite sure what would be in his own publication because he never knew from day to day who would call him up to offer a piece of writing. (More recently, though, he's built up a core staff of journalists.)

His wasn't among the biggest of the South African news sites, but it was influential beyond its numbers. Brkic, a visionary and idealistic publisher-editor, had launched and closed a string of bright, spunky and ambitious publications, always interesting, always beautifully designed, and always on the brink of both a financial breakthrough and imminent collapse.

He'd started in what was then Yugoslavia, back in 1984, and had grown that country's biggest privately owned publishing house. He'd come to South African in 1991, started in the reproduction business and then moved into magazines. *Maverick* and *Empire* were two notable examples, but both had failed.

In 2009 Brkic turned the website *Daily Maverick* into a news site.

Brkic was (and is) the editor's equivalent of the perpetual-motion machine, able to keep going on the power of his own ideas and energy alone. He was always sleep-deprived and stressed, but widely admired for his passion for the craft of journalism, for his willingness to take risks and for his eagerness to stand out in an otherwise placid media landscape.

Brümmer's operation, *amaBhungane*, was the polar opposite: an independent, donor-funded, non-profit investigative unit he ran with his colleague of long standing, Sam Sole. Breaking away from the *Mail & Guardian* a few years previously had given them a degree of freedom from deadlines and editorial demands, and the ability to set their own standards.

AmaBhungane's strength was, and remains, persistent, steady, rock-solid work – slow journalism, in contrast with the speed of the social-media-driven instant news cycle and the frenzied rush for scoops and screaming headlines.

AmaBhungane is the isiZulu word for dung beetles, creatures that slowly and steadily gather the dung of cows and other animals, and roll it into balls in which to lay their eggs. They're notably strong, able to gather up to 250 times their weight in dung in a night. *AmaB*, as the unit was often known, was the best at the slow and patient gathering of the muck of South African politics, and laying journalistic eggs in it. It had built a strong reputation for repeatedly exposing corruption and poor governance in long, complex, detailed, sometimes painfully difficult to read – but meticulous and important – pieces.

AmaB's work was steered by a solid sense of journalistic ethics, such as looking after and respecting sources and the careful verification of details. This was what had built its reputation for reliability, but in this case it was also to make the outfit vulnerable to the fierce competitiveness of fast-breaking news.

When Brkic called, Brümmer assumed he wanted one of their occasional catch-ups over coffee. The relationship was important to both of them: *amaB* needed good, friendly outlets to get their work out, and Brkic valued their investigations, especially because he didn't have to pay for them.

Brümmer suggested they could meet in about ten days. No, Brkic said firmly, it has to be sooner. What I have to tell you is a game-changer. For all of us. For the whole country.

*

Was it vodka or tequila? That was the one point Brümmer and Brkic couldn't agree on when they told me about the meeting. Brümmer said that when he heard what Brkic had to tell him, he ordered a shot of vodka. It was lunchtime, but he was off coffee, so a vodka was called for. Brkic is adamant that it was tequila. Whom to believe? This account has to be precise, accurate, worthy of the subject matter.

They'd met at Clarke's Bar and Dining Room in Long Street, Cape Town, Brkic's regular hang-out. It's a casual, noisy place with long wooden benches, serving simple fresh food for mostly young clients.

On this day, Brkic had the kind of story to tell Brümmer that journalists dream about, the kind that keeps us going, that justifies those long hauls of gathering information and cultivating sources that we hope one day we might be able to use, that takes us out from behind our computer and puts us in front of the television cameras, that thrusts small websites into the national spotlight, that brings down the powerful – the kind where every detail is seared into our memory.

Brkic told Brümmer how Currin had come to him to tell him about the two men who had a windfall of potentially valuable information in their hands. It was massive, Brkic said; there were thousands and thousands of emails.

This story is bigger than me, it's bigger than us, it's bigger than all of us, he said. Brkic had only had a quick look at the sample material, but he wasn't a man for understatement. He was a man of enthusiasm and energy, of passion for a great story. I don't have the people and skills to handle it, he said. We need to work together on this.

Brümmer, ever cautious, insisted they talk first about security measures. They would never discuss the matter on the phone – only in face-to-face meetings. The sources should probably be taken out of the country and given what was needed to start a new life. That would take a lot of money. Could they find that money?

Brkic thought he had the person who would back them, a super-wealthy businesswoman who wrote an occasional column for him, usually a fierce attack on corruption and bad governance.

They discussed putting a team together to work on the material. But if it got out that they were working on something big, they would be vulnerable to a raid or theft or malicious disruption of some sort. They had to get a copy of the material out of the country.

But the journalists would still be vulnerable. Maybe they had to work out of the country, in a neutral place where South African security agents or the Guptas' goons couldn't get to them easily. But even if they did this, once they started publishing, steps could be taken to stop them, to keep the revelations out of the public eye, or to discredit them or the material.

Did anyone already know about this? Were they already in danger? Brümmer's mind was racing. Were they being set up? Who were these whistleblowers and how could the reporters know if they were genuine? Did they need to meet them themselves?

Be careful. Be careful.

The data would have to be assessed and authenticated. How would they do that? If it held up under scrutiny, they would need to drop the other stuff they were working on and throw everything at this, Brümmer thought.

It would take a while, and many discussions, but they realised they had to get their team and the material to a safe place. And they couldn't rush it. They had to get it right and maximise the impact. As exciting as it was, patience was required. Once it was all written and ready, and they started releasing it, they couldn't be stopped.

They set up a protocol to continue the discussion. If they needed to talk, they would include a panda emoji in a message. Thirty minutes later they would meet in a Cape Town park, leaving their cellphones in the office, and take a stroll.

Brümmer had been an investigative journalist for around twenty years, and had broken many big stories. But this was of another order. The importance of the story and the possibility of inside information made this potentially a once-in-a-lifetime breakthrough. His heart was pumping.

So Brümmer ordered a shot, and downed it.

The president's keepers

The Guptas had first appeared in the South African media in the social pages in the late 1990s, a few years after arriving from India. They were pictured at political functions hanging around cabinet ministers, and at cricket matches they sponsored. They were introduced into these circles by Essop Pahad, President Thabo Mbeki's bag-carrier and political hitman, who later served on a number of Gupta corporate boards.

It wasn't long before the Guptas were linked to their first scandal. *The Star* newspaper and specialist publication *IT Web* reported in 2001 that Sahara Computers had won part of the Gauteng Online contract to put computers and connectivity in all the province's schools, a grand multibillion-rand project that would leapfrog these schools into the internet age.

In the event, Sahara Computers dumped hardware in the schools without the software it had promised. It was 'a giant sham', journalist Pieter-Louis Myburgh wrote in his 2017 book, *Republic of Gupta*, and an audit revealed that the schools never went online and the hardware wasn't maintained. In what became 'one of the province's most costly failures', Gauteng spent R1 billion before Sahara was fired.

Looking back now, it's surprising how little coverage this received, or that the Guptas won more government business after this.

Martin Welz's *Noseweek* picked up the Guptas story next. *Noseweek* is essentially a one-man operation and Welz sometimes veers off in pursuit of an idiosyncratic obsession, so when in 2008 he hinted in a story about the Guptas' attempts to elbow their way into an Angolan mining deal, it was a typical *Noseweek* story – complicated, hard to follow, with as much innuendo as hard fact. Still, it was another early sign that the three brothers were worth keeping an eye on.

*

Reporter Mandy Rossouw liked to get out of the office. When she offered to drive to the rural area of Nkandla in KwaZulu-Natal in late 2009 to do a light feature for the *Mail & Guardian* on how President Zuma's rise to power had affected his home region, it sounded like a good end-of-year feature. And a fun trip.

Her colleague Chris Roper offered to go along as her photographer and driver, since he was the only one in the office with a decent 4x4.

At the president's home, they noticed some building going on. Rossouw talked her way into the site office and saw plans taped to the wall: what was going up was a sprawling complex, a large-scale development.

Now she had a different story.

Back at the office she made some calls to find out more. When he heard what she had, editor Nic Dawes moved it to that week's front page: 'Zuma's R65m Nkandla splurge' was the splash on 4 December 2009. And the punchline: 'The taxpayer is footing the largest chunk of the bill.'

The story, it must be said, wasn't entirely accurate. The amount of R65 million was grossly underestimated, as it later turned out that Zuma's house cost the taxpayer at least three times that. Despite this, or maybe even because of it, the story was to dominate political conversation for a long time as a stark exhibition of Zuma's attitude to state power and assets. It kicked off a long legal and political battle over who was responsible for this abuse of public money and how to hold Zuma to account.

Again, it was one of those journalistic moments to be treasured.

Despite all the state machinery for controlling procurement and tenders, and a constitution that has the highest guarantees of transparency and accountability, it had taken a nosy and intrepid reporter on the ground to spot something odd and ask the right questions, and an editor with an instinct for a good story to publish it.

'When the #GuptaLeaks emails were released later, and the numbers in play escalated from hundreds of millions to hundreds of billions, what they revealed was what Mandy had already found, at the far end of a shattered road on a warm November day: the truth about Jacob Zuma, in broad daylight, if we would only look at it,' Dawes wrote in a 2018 anthology of investigative journalism.

*

AmaB had been tracking the Guptas since shortly after Zuma became president in 2009, when the investigative unit was still part of the *Mail & Guardian*. They published their first big splash on 19 March 2010: 'Zuma Inc – How Jacob Zuma's family fortunes have literally taken a turn for the better since his presidency.'

It was the first hint of the Zuma-Gupta network – quickly labelled 'the Zuptas' – and the first evidence that the Guptas were more than run-of-the-mill carpetbaggers.

'An investigation [by the *Mail & Guardian*] suggests Jacob Zuma's women and children are bidding for private benefit from their presidential connections,' the *amaB* story said. It showed a massive graphic of the company registrations and interests of Zuma's large family, giving 'a disturbing picture of the Zuma family's push into business, especially in the period since Zuma's ascension to the ANC presidency'.

It listed sixteen adults – wives, lovers and offspring – linked to Zuma, of whom fifteen were in business, holding a collective 134 company directorships or close-corporation memberships. Two-thirds of these had been registered since Zuma's ousting of Thabo Mbeki from the ruling party leadership in 2007, and they sprawled across property, resources, trade, mining, telecoms and IT.

It was a detailed exposé of Zuma and his family's booming capacity to leverage off his position, drawn largely from meticulous examination of public records of companies and property. It was prescient, though the language used to describe what Zuma and the Guptas were doing was still tentative. The *amaB* team raised four 'worrying issues': Zuma's habit of relying on others to support his huge family; the emergence of 'political entrepreneurs' who worked through Zuma's children; controversial business connections and practices among the family members; and gaps in Zuma's official declaration of interests.

The *dramatis personae* were listed in three groupings: 'The Wives', 'The Nephews' and 'The Guptas'. The Guptas had been close to Mbeki's right-hand man, Essop Pahad. When Zuma had ousted Mbeki from the party leadership, they had moved fast to get someone close to Zuma on board: Zuma's most prominent son, 26-year-old Duduzane Zuma, had joined a number of their company boards over the next few months.

The *Mail & Guardian* wove together bits and pieces of the public record, with an early instinct for what would emerge as important. The report didn't say much more about the Guptas, but it had tagged them.

It was just the beginning, Brümmer told me in 2017, of 'an unhealthy fascination with the Guptas ... People started telling us of them giving instructions to cabinet ministers. These were just allegations and rumours at that stage, but it told us they were worth focusing on.'

A little later, *amaB* assigned young reporter Lionel Faull to work through all the public information on directorships and properties to develop a 'comprehensive compendium' on the family. It was the kind of decision that makes investigative journalists what they are: following a gut instinct that it's going to be useful to know all you can about your subjects, and putting resources and energy into stockpiling data on them, knowing the hours of dull work could pay off in the long run. *AmaB's* non-profit, deadline-free status gave it the space to do this.

Still, Brümmer recalls his colleague Drew Forrest asking repeatedly at weekly news conferences, 'All this work? When are we going to get a story?'

Stories did flow, a total of 68 by *amaB* between 2010 and 2017. They came with increasing frequency – there were 28 in 2016 alone – but most of them were brushed aside by those named in them. Some showed loans and bonds from dubious sources to Zuma's wives and children.

The first mention of the Vrede Dairy Farm, which was to become one of the most gripping stories of the diversion of state money for private gain, came on 31 May 2013. The dairy, in the Free State, was established as a public-private partnership with the aim to empower black farmers; bank statements later showed that no payments were made to the beneficiaries, and that the farm was just a shell through which money was sent to India.

The year 2014 saw stories about how state enterprises were diverting advertising spend to support the Gupta newspaper, *The New Age*, and increasing evidence of the brothers getting sizeable kickbacks for steering government tenders to allies.

These stories painted a picture, but it was still sketchy. The stories were often too complicated and carefully worded to have immediate impact.

It was the Guptas' ostentation and arrogance that finally trapped them.

The wedding of the year

When Eyewitness News reporter Barry Bateman checked his Twitter timeline on the evening of 20 April 2013, there was a puzzling tweet. It said guests for the huge Gupta wedding at the Sun City resort would be landing in a private plane at the Waterkloof Air Force base near Pretoria the following morning.

'It cannot be, I thought. That's an Air Force base, never used for private planes,' Bateman told me in 2018.

He tweeted his doubt, and raised his eyebrows when Moegsien Williams, editor-in-chief of the Gupta newspaper *The New Age,* liked and retweeted it.

Williams was a respected journalist who'd decided to throw in his lot with the Guptas, and often said they were poorly treated by the rest of the media. He seemed to appreciate the fact that Bateman had questioned what appeared to be an outrageous story.

Bateman put the matter aside. But the next morning, as he was driving from his Pretoria home to the Eyewitness News Joburg headquarters for a news conference, he saw a cavalcade of cars with flashing blue lights turning on to the R21 highway towards Sun City. 'I phoned the office and said I was going to be late. I had to check this out.'

At the Air Force base he found dozens of people milling around, climbing into transport and heading off with police escorts. 'There was a hierarchy of people: some flew off in helicopters, some stepped into large SUVs, others in[to] Mercedes sedans, and then the riffraff got into buses.'

At the front, directing everyone, was Atul Gupta, one of the three brothers. Bateman approached him and was warmly greeted until he asked on what authority they were using the Air Force base. Atul brushed him off, saying he would talk later.

When Bateman tried later, Atul was in a hurry, stopping only to say, 'We must chat another day. I am about to open a TV station.'

The offer was typical Gupta, Bateman said: 'Report nicely about us and there would be a job for you.'

It was an early taste of how the Guptas operated, what investigative journalist Pieter-Louis Myburgh would label in his book, *Republic of Gupta*, 'an unapologetic assertion of might and money'.

Bateman didn't immediately realise the significance of what he was witnessing. He wanted to hold the story to do later that day, but again it was an editor who spotted its importance. Eyewitness News editor Katy Katapodis told him he had to go live on air immediately.

At 8.26am Bateman tweeted:

> #GuptaWedding dozens of Gupta family members are arriving at Waterkloof Airforce Base from India on chartered flights.

He filed at 9am for the group's network of radio stations, notably two leading talk stations, Radio 702 and CapeTalk, and by 10am it had been picked up by other news outlets.

This time Gupta editor Moegsien Williams didn't like or retweet it.

'It was the first real evidence of the influence this group of people had over government. There were so many elements to it – not just the Air Force base, but the police escorts and the VIP protection … I didn't appreciate that fully at the time,' Bateman said.

In fiscal terms it was a relatively minor abuse of state resources, but it caught the media and public imagination. Why this story? For one thing, it shed light on what was already an intriguing story: the 'wedding of the year', the ostentatious show of money, influence and hubris that framed the Gupta family and was already irritating many. Add political scandal to gossip, throw in a bunch of well-known names, mix in a garish venue like Sun City, and you had the magic media formula.

'The brazenness of this act of entitlement – transforming a military air base into a red carpet for the friends and relatives of the president's benefactors – was the ultimate act of chintzy parvenu one-upmanship. And yet the implications were massive. *Nothing* was sacred in the land of the profaned,' Richard Poplak wrote in the *Daily Maverick*.

Another factor in the spread of a story is always how those implicated in it react to it. Do they dampen it down or do they feed it?

Just two hours after Bateman's first report, the Department of Defence (DoD) said it had no knowledge of any private plane getting permission to use the base.

The Guptas issued a statement saying they had got permission because the flight included 'foreign dignitaries, including ministers'. But the Department of International Relations and Cooperation (DIRCO), which handled foreign-ministerial visits, said this had nothing to do with them and it would have happened through the Defence Force. Later the same day, DIRCO, in the words of Myburgh, 'shook off the apparent bout of temporary amnesia ... and ... indicated that the flight had indeed received official permission to land at the base'.

Then the DoD distanced itself from the earlier statement of its official spokesperson, implying permission had been granted, but not by them.

DIRCO lashed back, saying the DoD had to take responsibility. And then the ruling party, the ANC, stepped in to mix things up even more, with secretary-general Gwede Mantashe issuing a statement demanding clear explanations from its own people in government: 'The ANC will never rest where there is any indication that all and sundry may be permitted to undermine the Republic, its citizens and its borders.'

With this statement, the ruling party itself had now escalated this from the abuse of state resources to an attack on the country's sovereignty. It was a textbook case of how to turn a small event into a national story.

Nothing fuels a story like government officials pointing fingers at each other, particularly when they can't even do it consistently. Nothing fires up journalists more than the sense that the ruling party is divided on an issue.

When the media was alone in reporting these matters, they had often been dismissed. But when the media reports were picked up by political and civil-society organisations that spoke out, took legal action, and mobilised interest in the matter, more stories were generated and the story gained momentum.

The opposition parties brought up the Waterkloof Air Force base story in Parliament and used it as campaign fodder. The Economic Freedom Fighters (EFF) disrupted Parliament repeatedly to torment Zuma about it, calling him President Zupta. Others went to court, some for more information, some to force accountability, some just to keep the issue alive.

It helped that South Africa had an active and well-funded civil society – organisations such as Freedom Under Law, Corruption Watch and the Helen Suzman and Ahmed Kathrada foundations, which turned to the courts to pursue these cases; and a judiciary prepared not just to assert its independence, but to push the limits of its reach when it saw it as important. In their 2017 book on state capture, *Enemy of the People*, Adriaan Basson and Pieter du Toit listed ten court cases that were critical in putting the brakes on the Zupta escapades.

New organisations sprang up to take up these issues, such as Save South Africa and the National Foundations Dialogue, which brought together the foundations of former presidents Thabo Mbeki and FW de Klerk, very different political figures united by their distrust of Zuma.

There was also the growing power of social media to make certain stories viral, to amplify certain voices and views, and to influence the mainstream media – put to use by many political and civil-society organisations. Gone were the days when agendas could be set or manipulated by the traditional media: the media were now only one cog in the machinery of accountability.

Journalists closely monitored who was at the wedding, partly for social gossip, partly out of fascination for the Guptas' outlandishly garish and ostentatious style. There were reports that the family tried to insist on having only white staff serve them and their guests.

There was also a growing sense that the event was providing insight into who was hanging out with the Guptas. It included the president, ministers and businesspeople in the public and private sectors.

Impervious Zuma, arrogant Guptas

In the months that followed, there were a series of cabinet reshuffles that reinforced talk that the Guptas' influence over Zuma extended to top-level appointments. Unknown middle-ranking Free State politician Mosebenzi Zwane was suddenly elevated to Minister of Mineral Resources in September 2015, where he actively furthered Gupta family interests.

In December that year Nhlanhla Nene was suddenly axed as Finance Minister and replaced by little-known Gupta ally Des van Rooyen in what was seen as a swoop on the final bastion against the Guptas' capacity to influence government and its spending, the Treasury. Under massive public pressure – including from his own party – Zuma was forced to back down, bringing back Pravin Gordhan as Minister; but when Gordhan proved recalcitrant, Zuma fired him too, in March 2017.

A key moment came when some senior government players broke ranks to talk of how the Guptas had offered them cabinet positions and bribes to entice them into their circle of control. In March 2016 Deputy Finance Minister Mcebisi Jonas said the Guptas had offered him a R600-million bribe and the job of Finance Minister if he played along with them.

Eccentric ANC MP Vytjie Mentor claimed the Guptas, in the presence of President Zuma, had offered her the post of Minister of Public Enterprises if she agreed to cancel the South African Airways route to India, as they had lined up an Indian airway company to take it over, with themselves as middlemen.

Another ANC member, Themba Maseko, who'd headed government communications, told of President Zuma calling him to say he must help the Guptas, and then being asked by the brothers to put all government advertising in their newspaper, *The New Age*.

All of this was covered by the media with a growing sense of shock and awe, but the Zuptas appeared unstoppable. Many of the institutions of accountability that might have put the brakes on this were themselves compromised: the Hawks, the NPA, the SSA. All had been put into the hands of Zuma acolytes who were turning a blind eye and going after those impeding the project. The system of checks and balances on the abuse of presidential power was failing.

Two constitutional institutions stood out in contrast to this: the Public Protector and the judiciary, particularly the Constitutional Court, both of which were led by individuals appointed by Zuma but who'd turned out to be more principled and independent than he'd anticipated.

Public Protector Thuli Madonsela published her *State of Capture* report in October 2016 in response to a series of complaints about the appointment of cabinet ministers and directors of state-owned companies and the awarding of state contracts to Gupta-linked companies. The complaints were all based on media reports. Madonsela laid bare the available information that pointed to something very wrong in the Gupta-Zuma relationship, and said the president should institute a judicial inquiry into state capture. It was a strategic and smart intervention, as she even took the power to appoint the head of such an inquiry out of the hands of the president and gave it to the Chief Justice.

Zuma's response to the growing pressure was labelled a 'Stalingrad strategy': to dig in, defend tenaciously and wear down the opponent by whatever means possible. Zuma appeared impervious, increasingly resorting to an ethnic and racial populism to characterise his critics as opponents of his belated and opportunistic claim to a policy of radical economic transformation.

Scholars climbed in. *The Betrayal of the Promise* report of May 2017 from a group of leading academics didn't add much information, but it offered a systematic interpretation, suggesting that this was more than routine corruption. There was a coherent strategy behind it: 'South Africa has experienced a silent coup that has removed the ANC from its place as the primary force for transformation in society,' they wrote.

This report said that the media were caricaturing Zuma. 'They conceive of Zuma and his allies as a criminal network that has captured the state. This approach, which is unfortunately dominant, obscures the existence of a political project at work to repurpose state institutions to suit a constellation of rent-seeking networks that have been constructed and now span the symbiotic relationship between the constitutional and shadow state.' The talk of radical economic transformation was no more than an attempt to give this project 'a cover of legitimacy', the academics noted.

Church leaders followed, when the South African Council of Churches announced its own investigation, including an 'unburdening panel', a confessional for those who wanted to come clean.

The Organisation Undoing Tax Abuse (Outa), a suburban organisation formed to fight road tolls, produced charge sheets for Zuma and others to be prosecuted.

There were public marches expressing a growing middle-class outrage – 'the largest since the advent of democracy', according to the *Betrayal of the Promise* report.

Zuma, though, appeared invulnerable. He still had too strong a patronage base in the ANC for his growing group of critics to take him on in the party. He had control of key institutions, the ANC top six office bearers and the ANC national executive. He and his allies were threatening the judiciary and the media, two institutions of accountability over which he didn't have control. They had the power to make his life difficult but – it seemed – not to stop him.

He geared up to fight back at the ANC leadership election in late 2017. He was reaching his term limit, but he moved to put into office someone on whom he could depend for continuity, his former wife Dr Nkosazana Dlamini-Zuma. Brazenly hypocritical, the notorious patriarch began to argue that it was time for the country to have a woman president.

There was a growing sense of helplessness in the face of this. It appeared that despite everything, Zuma would have his ex-wife elected to replace him and help him avoid prosecution. The Guptas might be on the defensive, but there were others who would step into the gap.

Then came the #GuptaLeaks.

*

Brkic got a sample of the material on a memory stick just before the 2017 Easter weekend and arranged to drop it off with Brümmer, for him to look at the contents. Brümmer waited up for Brkic. He came after midnight. 'Let me know what you think,' he said.

Brümmer sat through the night going through the sample. The most striking thing about the material was its size: nobody could have created such a database from scratch; making such a vast trove look and sound authentic would take years of work.

Brümmer recalled a fake-email spy scandal of a few years previously, when a bunch of emails had surfaced that cast suspicion on key people in ANC circles who'd appeared to be plotting against the party leadership. Because the emails played into political suspicions of the time, many people – even intelligent people – fell for them, but a closer look had raised doubts. The people who'd supposedly written the emails had misspelt their own names and titles, and used language they wouldn't normally use. The emails had been fabricated.

There was one big difference, though. Those emails had come as printouts, so the dates, format and other metadata couldn't be checked. This lot came as raw data, so they would be able to check whether the metadata was consistent and what changes had been made.

The metadata is the information that sits in the background of every digital document: its identity, structure, context and other administrative information. It reveals when and on what computer the document was created, what type of document it is, and if and when it was amended. In a trove of emails, the metadata would include information such as the date the emails were sent, who sent them and the subject matter. So if you access the metadata, you can learn a great deal about a document, and this is where Brümmer would need to go to authenticate the material.

But he had only a sample of the emails, and he couldn't do this most important check until he had it all. Also, even if this stash of emails was too large to have been totally manufactured, someone might have taken an existing trove of emails and inserted fakes among them. That was classic spycraft: planting fake material among authentic stuff. (Later, they would bring in an expert to check the metadata, and it would show that the emails had all been created in sequence, which was hard to fake.)

Brümmer's main task at this stage was to see if the information matched what he'd learnt from years of research into the Guptas. Did the characters, the events and the narratives tally with what he knew? Were they real? By the time the sun came up on Good Friday, he was confident that the material was genuine and that it was rich with Gupta insider information.

He sent Brkic their agreed signal: a smiley-face emoji.

The billionaire

Magda Wierzycka doesn't smile for the camera. In the many pictures of her in the media, she looks straight back at the lens, stern, expressionless and cold. This is how one of the country's best-known and most successful businesswomen chooses to be seen.

I could find only one exception: the *Sunday Times* must have insisted that a profile of her include their own photographer's portrait, not a hand-out. On their pages, she's relaxed, smiling, looking into the distance, a warmth creeping into her image.

The grandchild of a Jewish holocaust survivor, and the child of Polish refugees of the 1980s who spent some time in a refugee camp on their way from Central Europe to southern Africa, Wierzycka is notoriously tough and determined. She came to South Africa as a teenager, her doctor parents recruited by the apartheid government looking for whites with skills. She speaks passionately about the need for political engagement to get things right in this country.

She's had a stellar career in her climb to the top of the business pyramid – and her position as the sole woman on the country's rich list. Trained in actuarial science – because that's the scholarship she could get – she was CEO of an emerging empowerment investment company, African Harvest, in her 30s, and now, in her 40s, she headed her own, massively successful Sygnia fund managers.

Sygnia was shaking up the market with a low-fee passive-investment management model, and Wierzycka herself was its strongest marketing tool. She wrote columns for the *Daily Maverick* that were unusually outspoken and passionate for a business leader, particularly about issues of corporate governance and corruption. At first, she wrote about excessive fund managers' fees, and in praise of her own successful model.

It was unusual to find a fund manager writing a newspaper column in which she was taking on her competitors, but she didn't hold back. She wrote extensively around companies that were enriching themselves – apparently corruptly – from the state grant system, lambasting rival fund manager Allan Gray for 'fleecing the poor' because of its involvement with one of these companies. She raised tough questions about the responsibilities of investors and the behaviour of her rivals.

At the height of Zuma's presidency in October 2017 she wrote '10 steps that business can take to make South Africa work again'. She'd quickly become a leading voice for business opposition to the Zuma government and its corruption.

She scouted around for ways of using her money to fight corruption. She teamed up with the Helen Suzman Foundation to take to court 'everyone and anyone' linked to corruption at Eskom, and they initiated some important interventions. When a whistleblower was fired from the state power utility, Wierzycka hired that person without ever meeting her.

'Yes, I can emigrate and buy a nice property outside London. But I reached a Rubicon. I could have walked away, I knew the consequences, but what do you do? I am not that person who walks away,' she told the *Sunday Times* in January 2018. 'I don't want to emigrate again. Having gone through what I did in childhood, possessions mean nothing to me. I had to leave my dolls and teddy bear as a child in Poland, so nothing material is important to me.'

On Twitter she showed none of the caution and diplomacy typical of business leaders. 'We have thieves running Eskom,' she broadcast. She was active, vocal and effective.

Sometimes her passion got the better of her – a dangerous thing on Twitter. She tweeted that she was devoting time to finding the solution

SO, FOR THE RECORD

to Cape Town's water crisis, and told us to watch her timeline. She didn't solve it.

One day Wierzycka tweeted that South Africans could contribute to the unemployment problem by each employing another domestic worker. It's a common syndrome: rich people who think that because they can make money, they're all-smart and all-wise, full of billionaires' bombast.

'Black Twitter' lambasted her, while Twitter bots – automated user accounts that generate posts without any human oversight – said she'd started out as a stripper, putting out manipulated photographs of her as a bondage artist. She withdrew from social media for some time and hired security for her family.

Later, she took on the Public Investment Corporation (PIC), a state-owned entity that manages government employees' pension funds, for its dubious investments in the companies of notorious business shark and ANC hobnobber Iqbal Survé, and her voice was loud and sharp enough to have the Johannesburg Stock Exchange (JSE) block his company's listing. Her capacity to analyse these companies' financials and her willingness to call on them was shaking up the market.

Wierzycka tried to buy back the one percent of her company that Survé's companies owned and offered him a below-market price. In her letter to Survé, revealed by Survé in December 2018, she slipped in, 'If we part company now, I will move on from [the] Ayo, Vunani, Sekunjalo [all Survé companies] stories. It would be, in both parties' best interests, a once-off offer.' It seemed she was offering to lay off them if they paid the right price.

Survé charged her with attempted extortion. She called it 'negotiation'. Now she admits that letter was foolish, and she continues to pursue Survé, and the JSE for its reluctance to deal with his shenanigans.

Wierzycka was the person Brkic approached to fund the #GuptaLeaks project.

*

When Brian Currin met Magda Wierzycka, she immediately put a R200 note on the table and said, 'I'm hiring you.' That would bind him to client privilege, and everything that passed between them would be secret. But Currin hadn't practised as a lawyer for years, and he wasn't for hire. Wierzycka's was the action of a master of the universe: someone who thought she could buy anyone's loyalty, who presumed money was all that was needed to buy the discretion of a person like Currin.

Currin thought she would be a good ally – she was smart and shared their aims. 'My impression is that she was hard-core, ruthless, a good person to have on your side.'

She quickly agreed to fund the operation and give Currin a first tranche of R200 000 for the sources and R50 000 for his own travel expenses. She asked to meet the sources and Currin facilitated this.

*

Stefaans Brümmer flew from Cape Town to Johannesburg to meet with Brkic and the sources, and Magda Wierzycka gave him the use of her boardroom for this purpose. On his way, Brümmer stopped at a computer shop in Dunkeld to buy two hard drives. 'I know that whistleblowers often get cold feet. We had to be ready to get the material there and then.'

They hit it off in that first meeting and agreed on the terms. Stan would hand over the full trove, and Brümmer and Brkic would be responsible for the funding to get Stan, John and their families out of the country.

Stan took a leap of faith. On a handshake, and before the R200 000 down payment had been made, he agreed to copy the material onto the hard drives overnight.

The next morning, Currin gave Brümmer the two hard drives and a password on a scrap of paper.

Brümmer then flew to Durban to brief his *amaBhungane* partner,

Sam Sole, who hadn't yet been told about the scoop. 'I was paranoid about communication,' Brümmer said.

Then he went back to Cape Town, nursing the hard drive in his hand luggage, to take his first close look at all the material.

This was the critical moment. He sat down at his desk and connected the hard drive to his laptop to find out how valuable were its contents.

The password didn't work.

He tried it again and again, without success.

His first response was to panic. Had they been set up? Was this all a trick? Or had something gone wrong with the material? Would they be able to retrieve it?

Wierzycka said she had an expert who could take a look at the hard drive. She happened to be in Cape Town at the time and was going back to Joburg, so she volunteered to carry it up with her.

They were relieved to discover the problem was only a lower-case letter in the password that had to be capitalised, and the hard drive was returned to them. But that period when the material was in Wierzycka's hands turned out to be critical.

*

Over the next while, Stefaans Brümmer, Branko Brkic and Sam Sole discussed their options. They considered basing the team in Amsterdam and were offered a house in Brussels. Brkic wanted the team to go work on the Croatian island of Corcula, which he knew well, but that idea fell apart when they realised they would all need visas – a requirement that would take paperwork and time, and could alert the authorities that something was going on.

They settled on Ireland, which had no visa requirements and good pubs, and identified a farmhouse they could rent. About twenty of them would travel there, separately, using different routes and modes of transport, to avoid suspicion.

To leave enough time to absorb all the material, and to allow the whistleblowers to sell up and leave, they set September 2017 – four months away – as their rough publication date.

On Friday 26 May Brkic went online to rent the farmhouse in the Irish countryside.

*

A later meeting with Wierzycka at her apartment didn't go well. 'We need a legal, a political and a media strategy,' the CEO told the *amaB* team, and laid out what she had in mind.

No, they said: we're journalists. We have to play it that way. We research, we verify, we write … That's all.

It was, for them, a fundamental principle: they would put the information into the public arena in the most effective way, and then the politicians, prosecutors and lawyers could do with it as they saw fit.

But Magda Wierzycka didn't work that way. She was used to giving orders. She'd set up a meeting with the former Minister of Finance, Pravin Gordhan, a political insider who was leading the internal ANC charge against the Zuptas.

Brümmer and Brkic said no, you must leave us to do our work. Conspiring with politicians would taint the journalism.

The dung collectors

To understand *amaBhungane*, you have to understand what set them apart among South African journalists.

From around 2000 South Africa's political journalism had been dominated by a small group of ANC insiders, many of whom flip-flopped as the fortunes of their sources and allies changed from time to time. A number actively campaigned for the dismissal of President Thabo Mbeki and for Jacob Zuma to replace him, and then turned on Zuma, as if surprised by the longstanding evidence of his corruption, and backed Cyril Ramaphosa.

This grouping showed remarkable versatility in moving with the political tide in the organisation, often working as intra-party factional partisans rather than journalists. When they backed Zuma, they could find little wrong with him; and the same applied when they backed Ramaphosa. They thrived on internal leaks from whichever faction they were with at any one time about those on the other side, and their insider knowledge often trumped that of more independent reporters. Readers had to accept their stories with this knowledge and with scepticism.

By contrast, *amaB* is fervently non-partisan, in an almost old-fashioned way. It has strict rules about who it takes money from. 'We do not sell advertising. We do not take funding from governments or corporates. And we do not take funding to investigate specific stories or themes,' its website states. That's a lot of exclusions.

AmaB does take money from individual businesspeople and their personal foundations, and publishes details of all donations it receives above R10 000. Magda Wierzycka's large contribution in this case was going straight to the sources, but she did also give R100 000 later in 2017 directly to *amaB*, although she did it personally to avoid the restriction on corporate donations.

AmaB doesn't sell its stories: it gives them to partners on the sole condition that the outlet takes responsibility for any legal comeback.

And *amaB* doesn't conspire with politicians about when and how to publish its material. The reporters' job is to do the research, produce the stories and get them out. They are journalists, and that's all.

*

AmaBhungane comes from a long tradition in South African journalism: small groups of journalists who broke away from the restrictions and limitations of the mainstream media to start operations that struggled financially but made a long-lasting impact on the country's political evolution. Free of the financial responsibilities of commercial media, these journalists could do and say things others couldn't. They broke the rules and conventions of mainstream journalism.

This tradition goes back to the very first independent newspaper in the Cape Colony in the early 19th century, when the first printing presses were allowed into the country. Thomas Pringle and John Fairbairn couldn't get permission from an autocratic colonial governor to publish a journal that rivalled his own official one, so they joined with a printer who had permission to put out a newsletter, *The South African Commercial Advertiser*. When the governor insisted on vetting their work before publication, they decided to close down in protest, and began a long fight for their right to publish. Fairbairn went to London to pursue it, came back to start the paper, and was closed again. It was only in 1859 that Fairbairn, by that time an MP, helped pass a law to remove the restrictions on publication. (By then Pringle had gone back to the London to play a key role in the fight against slavery.)

Pringle and Fairbairn established a pattern of defiant upstarts taking on authority and the mainstream media to say things that needed to be said.

When black national political organisation began to emerge in the late 19th century, the momentum came from a group of editors who started and ran their own small publications. Their voices and languages were barely heard in the white newspapers of the time, so they created their own, at first working with missionary publications and then breaking away to launch their own. Their publications were small and struggled to survive, but it was these owner-editors – John Tengo Jabavu, Sol Plaatje, John Dube and others – who first brought black voices into the broader political arena, articulated opposition to the race policies of the time, and provided the core leadership that came together in 1912 to launch the South African Native National Congress – the organisation that would become the ANC.

Key founder Pixley ka Seme started the multilingual *Abantu-Batho – The People,* an important alternative voice aligned to the early movement until 1931. It was the first attempt to create a national voice.

In the 1950s, when then-ANC Youth League figures Nelson Mandela and Walter Sisulu started to turn the ANC into a more radical mass movement, a critical element was its kindred newspaper, the small, struggling *Guardian/New Age* (it changed its name every time it was banned, re-emerging under a new title). It was closed in the early 1960s, along with the banning of the ANC and the Pan Africanist Congress.

When political opposition began to re-emerge in the early 1970s, alternative publications played a role, providing a very different view of the country's politics than a mainstream media that had largely hunkered down to survive a decade of repression. As the uprising spread in the 1980s, so did a network of alternative publications. I was involved with one of them, *The Weekly Mail,* but there was also *New Nation, South, Grassroots, Saamstaan, The Indicator* and – significantly – the first Afrikaans one, *Vrye Weekblad.*

These papers covered township and factory-floor uprisings, and exile politics, in a way that distinguished them from the more cautious, centrist commercial newspapers. They confronted censorship more aggressively. And they continued another tradition: that of publishing hard-hitting investigative reporting.

It was from this tradition of small breakaway groups, fiercely independent and willing to push the boundaries of accountability reporting – often in the face of censorship and repression – that *amaB* came, as did two other publications that feature in this narrative, the *Daily Maverick* and *Noseweek*.

*

Magda Wierzycka tried to talk Brian Currin into ditching *amaB* and the *Daily Maverick*. They were too slow, she said, contemptuously. She didn't like their plan to go out of the country, prepare all the stories and then manage a stepped release over time. She wanted the information spread widely and quickly.

Currin said no, they were working with *amaB* and the *Daily Maverick* as their partners, and that was the way Stan wanted it. He trusted them. They were out not for short-term political gain but for the long-term impact of careful exposé. The story needed to be woven together from the data to ensure it had the most impact, and *amaB* were the people to do this.

At one point, Wicrzycka said she'd spoken to her lawyers, and that it was important that she draw up a contract with Stan. She needed to protect herself, she said.

That's not how it works, Currin told her. She couldn't buy their material or their loyalty.

Wierzycka asked for a copy of the affidavit Currin was working on with Stan to show the chain of evidence. The affidavit, though, was not complete, and Currin, aware that it would back up the authenticity of the email material and that he needed to keep it close, said no.

Wierzycka asked to meet Stan again before making a final decision on whether or not to give the rest of her financial support to the project.

Currin set it up, but he was in Cape Town so he didn't attend the meeting. In that discussion, Wierzycka tried to prise Stan away from Currin, *amaBhungane* and the *Daily Maverick*. Stan didn't go along with her.

Wierzycka was due to meet Currin to give a final decision on her backing but she suddenly decided that the *amaB* team was taking too long. On 4 May 2017 she sent Currin a WhatsApp that was typically curt and cold: 'Brian, no need for a meeting. Please communicate with Branko. Based on what I now know, I am out.' And then, without explanation, straight to the matter of money: 'As per the invoice you sent me, as I am not proceeding with the issue, please ensure that my money is refunded. … Certainly, I expect R50k you helped yourself to for travelling to London …'

Currin was worried that all his delicate work getting people to cooperate with and trust each other was falling apart, and was livid at the insinuation that he'd helped himself to money. He returned the R50 000 for his travel expenses.

Now, how would they proceed without the money? Where would they find other finances?

Brümmer spoke to someone well connected to grantmaking organisations, who introduced him to the principal of a foundation who quickly agreed to help. It wasn't the full amount needed, but it was enough of a building block for a solution. He flew to Johannesburg, where he met Currin to tell him they had other backers.

Things were back on track and they started preparing to go to Ireland.

*

On the evening of Saturday 27 May 2017, the flurry of teasers about the #GuptaEmails scoop that was to appear in the *Sunday Times* the next morning went out on Twitter.

More haste, less speed

'We were in a race from day one. We thought *City Press* had it as well.'

Andrew Trench, who led the *Sunday Times* team that broke the #GuptaLeaks story, justified their decision to publish immediately in order to scoop their closest rivals. *City Press* had, in fact, received a copy of the emails, but, more cautious about the contents, were unable to process it for that weekend.

Trench only got his hands on the full collection of emails after the *Sunday Times* had published its first stories. Then 'we did seventy stories that first week – before *amaB/Daily Maverick* got their first one out,' he told me in our 2019 interview.

Branko Brkic and Stefaans Brümmer had to change gear quickly. The *AmaB* team dropped their plans to go to Ireland, and journalists set out, working day and night, to process the material.

Brkic and Brümmer urged Stan and John to leave the country quickly for their own safety, but they had personal matters to sort out and couldn't just jump on a plane. Stan gave the original hard drive and a clone to Currin, who lodged them with an attorney friend, as they would then be protected by attorney-client privilege. Brkic put someone on a plane to take a copy of the material out of the country but when that person got to Dubai, they phoned to say that in the rush they'd left it behind, and someone else had to fly out the next night.

Brkic didn't tell Brümmer about this blunder for some time – only when they were ready to laugh about it, some time later, and take another shot of vodka. Or was it tequila?

*

The first stories from the *amaB/Daily Maverick* team came out four days after the *Sunday Times*, on Thursday 1 June 2017, in the *Daily Maverick*. The piece headlined 'Guptas and associates score R5,3bn in locomotive kickbacks' showed how the president's friends and their associates were diverting billions of rands from Transnet's purchase of locomotives to their offshore accounts.

> In a scheme so audacious and lucrative that it puts the notorious arms deal to shame, they:
> - Entered kickback agreements totalling R5,3 billion with the Chinese manufacturer that became [state rail and port company] Transnet's favourite locomotive supplier;
> - Influenced procurement processes through their associates at Transnet;
> - Are pocketing R10 million from each R50 million locomotive that Transnet is buying.

On the same day, the *Daily Maverick* published '#GuptaLeaks: Duduzane Zuma, kept and captured':

> The 35-year-old son of President Jacob Zuma emerges from the #GuptaLeaks as kept and captured by the Gupta family, serving as a key channel for influence on official decision-making, including his father's.

The following week presented a new angle: 'How Bell Pottinger sought to package SA economic message'. The *amaB* team had discovered who was behind the trolls, the bots, the fake websites, the threatening thugs, the emergence of the new rhetoric of radical economic transformation: it was a British public-relations firm that had mastered the dark arts of PR and shown a preparedness to use them for some of the world's most corrupt and tyrannical leaders.

> In January last year Victoria Geoghegan, British-based PR firm Bell Pottinger's financial and corporate partner, met with President Jacob Zuma's son Duduzane to strategise a campaign aimed at marketing 'a narrative that grabs the attention of the grassroots population who must identify with it, connect with it and feel united by it'. In so doing, the firm undermined the ANC's capacity to communicate its own policies and programmes to South Africans and hijacked the ruling party's message, seemingly to benefit the image of the Gupta family.

This internationalised, deepened and widened the story. The Guptas and their allies weren't just corrupt; they had attacked the very fabric of South African society.

Stung by losing the first round to the *Sunday Times*, *amaB/Daily Maverick* wrote a defensive covering note with the first stories: 'Why did we not publish before? Why did we let ourselves be "scooped"?'

> The answer is in what we shall call a story of heroes and the misguided.
>
> The heroes are whistleblowers who may be risking their lives to expose the truth, and others who assisted in the process. For now, for their safety, they shall remain unsung.
>
> The misguided are people whom we had trusted and let into the process, but who took a copy and without our knowledge caused a selection to be leaked to the two newspapers last week. Their motive was short-term political gain.

AmaB/Daily Maverick took a different approach, the note explained, based on journalistic values: 'We ... held back in the interests of in-depth inquiry and the safety of the whistleblowers.' Those who'd leaked the information 'appear[ed] to have put expediency above the whistleblowers' safety'.

Angry and frustrated, the *amaB* team wagged their fingers at their rivals and the unnamed allies who'd let them down. But their accusations were misplaced. As they themselves later admitted, the *Sunday Times* did what any newspaper would have done, given these stories; they would have been foolish to hold back. The Sunday paper may have been somewhat reckless, but that's part of the *Sunday Times's* make-up.

And *AmaB/Daily Maverick* had been naïve in their handling of the story, too trusting of those they'd thought were reliable allies and too optimistic that they could take their time and keep control.

*

News24, the country's biggest news outlet by a long way, had been left out, so editor Adriaan Basson – himself an accomplished investigative reporter – phoned Stefaans Brümmer. I'll give you a couple of my best investigative reporters and run all your material if we can have access, he offered.

For *amaB*, this meant a much bigger audience, as News24, part of the giant Media24 group, had a massive online readership, and access to its sister newspaper, *City Press*, which competed directly with the *Sunday Times*. But the *Daily Maverick* was his partner, so Brümmer had to get Brkic's assent.

Brkic agreed to partner with News24, an act of exceptional generosity. 'This story belonged to the whole country. Nobody could keep it for themselves,' he said.

They formed a formidable *amaB/Daily Maverick/*News24 alliance, bringing together *amaB*'s investigative skills, the *Daily Maverick*'s credibility and News24's huge reach.

Brkic, meanwhile, had used the opportunity to raise money to form his own investigative unit, and cheekily named it Scorpio – a reference to the Scorpions, the specialist anti-crime unit that had been dismantled by the ANC a few years previously when some of the party's leadership became uncomfortable with the unit's successes in targeting corruption.

They also brought in Cape Town-based open-data specialists OpenUp, London-based specialist investigators Finance Uncovered, where their original researcher Lionel Faull now worked, and a freelance expert in tracking corporate finance.

*

In the years leading up to the #GuptaLeaks, investigative journalists around the world had had to deal with the new digital phenomenon of massive dumps of data that required large, collaborative teams to deal with them. They often had to work across borders, and with secure communication. Gone was the figure of the lone investigative reporter meeting sources in dark alleys and soldiering through whisky-laden nights to break a story. This was a digital era that required new skills and techniques. And patient, slow journalism.

What was unusual in the #GuptaLeaks was the combination of this new kind of team collaboration and the element of intense competition, with two large teams racing to generate stories from the material. It was the best of both worlds: the power of collaboration and the incentive of rivalry.

And the two institutions couldn't have been more different. The traditional-media *Sunday Times* was South Africa's biggest newspaper, long its most influential, and was driven by screaming headlines, hard deadlines, and a sense of its own power and influence. The paper was coming out of a bad period, with a reputation damaged by some stories it had got wrong, and was eager to show its journalistic mettle.

AmaB, on the other hand, represented a new force in journalism: a philanthropy-funded non-profit operating outside of conventional newsrooms with their pressures and deadlines. They didn't have to fill the next day's front page; if their story was incomplete, they could work on it for longer. They didn't need to cut everything back to 800 words, since they could put online as much as they thought the story merited – sometimes indulgently – as well as dossiers of their evidence and interviews.

They didn't have the baggage of traditional media, weighed down by their pre-digital legacies, and depended much more on their individual reputations. What kept them in line was that they had to convince outlets like the *Daily Maverick* and occasionally even the *Sunday Times* to run their material, and for this the accuracy of their stories and the strength of their reputation was everything.

Some would sneer at *amaB's* position of relative privilege. But it gave them space and time to work in a different way, the luxury of a different set of values and priorities. It gave them relative immunity to the economic pressures that were taking a toll on publications like the *Sunday Times*.

Slow and steady wins the race

AmaBhungane and the *Daily Maverick* and their enlarged team won out, their journalists doing what they did best: ploughing through the material, drawing on the information they had accumulated and piecing it together to give a full picture.

Both *amaB* and the *Sunday Times* continued to run stories for some weeks, but it was *amaB's* slower journalism that gained ascendancy. This was borne out by their winning most of the journalism prizes that year, despite having been beaten to the first punch.

AmaB published 92 #GuptaLeaks stories in the year that followed, and what emerged was an impossible-to-deny, unusually detailed and documented picture of the Gupta family influencing state decisions, placing their cronies in key state and parastatal positions, and manipulating tenders from the massive state-owned enterprises to the benefit of themselves, their friends and the Zuma family. While much of this had been apparent, the scale and brazenness of it was beyond what had been imagined, and now there was hard evidence.

As *The Wall Street Journal* put it:

> Many South Africans believe the country's real seat of power is a suburban, 140,000-square-foot compound [the Guptas' Saxonwold home] shielded by concrete walls and sometimes guarded by an armored personnel carrier ... [The Guptas'] riches and close ties to President Jacob Zuma have plunged the country

into its gravest political crisis since the overthrow of white-minority rule.

Even ANC spokesman Zizi Kodwa, whose professional life had been dedicated to dodging serious allegations on the organisation's behalf, took to Twitter in September 2017 to say that 'the evidence against the Guptas can no longer be ignored'.

It wasn't all smooth sailing, though. Groups of political thugs – like Black First Land First – started to harass journalists, even going to their homes to protest noisily and aggressively. Meetings of journalists were violently broken up. They labelled anyone who went up against Zuma as agents of white monopoly capital and positioned themselves and Zuma as populists whose attempts to seize control of the economy on behalf of the black majority was blocked by those who opposed change. It was overladen with racial slurs and threats of violence and destruction.

The story took on an international dimension as it emerged how global firms had facilitated the Guptas' work. The emails exposed the complicity of auditing firms – notably KPMG – in helping hide the manipulation and deception; of consultancy firms – notably McKinsey – in inflating contracts with state-owned enterprises to allow for massive kickbacks to Gupta allies; of service providers – such as international software giant SAP – which paid kickbacks; of lawyers – such as Hogan Lovells of London, accused by Lord Peter Hain and Treasury deputy director-general Ismail Momoniat of facilitating state capture; and of PR firm Bell Pottinger in trying to divert attention from its clients, using race and dirty tricks to accuse others (those they labelled 'white monopoly capital') of being the real culprits in state capture. These firms showed a startling willingness to bend their practices, rules and procedures – and sometimes even the law – in order to get lucrative work from the Guptas and their friends, and they enabled much of the fraud and theft.

This was important, since it's sometimes alleged that private media target a black government more than they do the white private sector. The *amaB/Daily Maverick team*, for example, published a devastating series called The McKinsey Dossier, as well as stories on Bell Pottinger and KPMG.

The impact rolled out in waves. Bell Pottinger closed down in disgrace. KPMG's South African heads Trevor Hoole and Steven Louw and five other senior executives stepped down; they also agreed to pay back R23 million in fees earned from SARS, and to donate to education and anti-corruption causes R40 million in fees earned from Gupta-related entities. McKinsey suspended South African director Vikas Sagar and agreed to pay back the astounding amount of R902 million it had earned from Eskom in consultancy fees. SAP at first denied paying a R100-million kickback to a Gupta company to secure a Transnet contract, but had to back down, place its management team on 'administrative leave' and start a major investigation.

And, of course, Jacob Zuma failed in his bid to have Nkosazana Dlamini-Zuma replace him as head of the party in December 2017. Shortly afterwards, Zuma was ousted as president and replaced with Cyril Ramaphosa, who promised a clean-up.

On the day of Ramaphosa's ascension, Styli Charalambous, the *Daily Maverick* CEO, sent Brkic's text back to him: 'We have a game-changer,' he said.

Betrayal

It took a while for Stefaans Brümmer and Branko Brkic to piece together how the *Sunday Times* had got its hands on the material.

At first they feared that Stan had acted behind their backs, and relations with him became tense. Then they tried to piece together who else might have leaked it. Their own team was a close and committed bunch, and they didn't believe there was a traitor within. They trusted Currin. But who else had had access to the material?

The realisation dawned that the one person who'd had access to the hard drive, who'd said she had an expert who could crack it when they couldn't get into it, was Magda Wierzycka. And she'd broken with them shortly afterwards.

Brkic was sure it was her, but Brümmer and Sam Sole were less so. They texted her to ask, and she stated firmly that she hadn't given the material to the *Sunday Times,* nor had she kept a copy.

Then they heard that the newspaper had got it from some of the people around Pravin Gordhan. Since they knew Wierzycka had been in touch with Gordhan, this strengthened their suspicions of her. After all, she was the one who'd wanted a political strategy to deal with the story; she was the one who'd wanted it out quickly. Perhaps she hadn't given it directly to the newspaper, but had given it to Gordhan and he'd passed it on.

Brkic was so livid he wouldn't say her name. He called her Lady Macbeth. He regarded the betrayal as a triumph of short-term political point-scoring over ethical journalism and the safety of the sources, the act of someone who thought she knew journalism better than journalists, but who had no idea what it took to do a story properly and ensure it was watertight. 'It was the thinking of an 8- or 9-year-old with no understanding of politics, or the capabilities of the Sunday papers, and their position or influence,' he said.

At the time, Pravin Gordhan had been preparing for an ANC executive meeting where they were to confront Zuma about his relationship with the Guptas, and wanted the information out before then. 'They thought the *Sunday Times* would swing the ANC meeting,' says Brkic. 'It didn't. Of course it didn't.'

Wierzycka hadn't only withdrawn her support, Brkic said, but had actively undermined their strategy. And she'd allowed the material to come out before the whistleblowers were safe.

Brümmer and Sole, though, kept saying they suspected it was her, but they didn't have the evidence.

*

A journalist can tell a great deal from how a person reacts when asked questions. When someone tries to avoid talking to you, and puts their lawyer on to you, it touches a journalistic nerve: this person is too defensive, they have something to hide, they have something they don't want to talk about.

Brian Currin was eager to talk to me, relaxed about going over the story a few times to check details, and willing to show me documentation and cellphone messages. When I met Stan, he talked quite freely while making it clear when there were things he didn't want to share.

My first email to Magda Wierzycka in April 2019 asking her to meet me to tell her side of the story drew no response. It took some prompting through a patient personal assistant to get her answer:

> You will be well aware that making statements with
> regard to the Gupta leaks are not without risks to

one's own safety and that of your family, as well as to third parties. I am accordingly not prepared to be interviewed on this topic. However, I am prepared to consider questions you may wish to put to me in writing in this regard and to reply thereto in writing.

Since this was two years after the original leaks, and she was a prominent CEO surrounded by as much security as she desired, it was hard to see that the risk was still so great. I replied:

You have shown yourself to be admirably outspoken and unafraid to express your strong views, more so than most people in your position. I am mystified then what it is about a conversation with me that presents a risk to you or others. I assure you I do not intend to write anything that endangers anyone's life.

I put to her the one overriding question I wanted to ask: 'How did you get involved in #GuptaLeaks, and how did it unfold from your point of view?'

She would have none of it. 'The safety of my family, third parties and my own are at stake', she said, asking me to put the version I had to her in full and she would consider responding. I said that if I were to follow this approach, I would need to do it later, when I'd amassed all the relevant information, but urged her to see that a one-on-one conversation would work better for both of us.

When I went back to her in January 2020 to ask to meet with her, the reply – and a threat – came from her lawyer, Rael Gootkin of Werksmans: 'Our client instructs that she is not prepared to engage with you regarding the contents of your book and should you intend mentioning our client in your forthcoming book, you do so at your own risk.'

But she had second thoughts, and shortly afterwards another missive arrived on a Werksmans letterhead, along with an unusual – perhaps unheard-of – request: 'Our client is willing to talk to you in person, to ensure that your narrative from her perspective is correct, but only under the condition that a non-disclosure agreement is concluded between you and our client.'

I replied: 'I am bewildered why your client is treating me like an enemy. It seems to be contrary to her support for independent journalism.' But I bent over backwards, as I felt obliged to at least hear her explanation of what had happened: 'If I speak to her, she is entitled to say things off the record, as is standard practice, and I will be obliged to respect that. I am not sure how one conducts a journalistic interview with an NDA, but perhaps you should send me a draft of what you intend so that I can understand if it provides a workable framework for a useful exchange.'

Nine months after our first contact, Wierzycka finally consented to a meeting – but 'without prejudice and strictly off the record'.

*

Magda Wierzycka, according to sources close to her, had received a call in 2017, while she was negotiating her support for the sources with Brian Currin, from someone in the Reserve Bank who said they believed there was some important material related to the Guptas that was about to emerge and they were concerned to know about it because it might have an impact on the financial markets.

The journalists were talking too much and too many people knew about the email leak, Wierzycka thought. She took legal and security advice and was told that if this was the case, the Guptas would know about it within a few days. The best way forward was to disseminate the raw information as widely as possible, through a platform like WikiLeaks.

Wierzycka's attitude towards Currin and *amaBhungane* had soured. She thought they were concerned only with monetising the data for their personal profit or achieving journalistic fame. 'They treated me like an ATM,' she told those close to her.

SO, FOR THE RECORD

'This is starting to smell like a commercial transaction instead of helping the country,' she messaged Currin. Clearly, she thought she was the only one who had the interests of the country at heart and was prepared to put this before personal concerns.

According to sources close to her, shortly after breaking with them, she took her family off to London, where she tried to upload the data to WikiLeaks. But the WikiLeaks platform was unstable and she was unable to do it. She even went to the Ecuadorian embassy, where WikiLeaks founder Julian Assange had taken refuge in 2012 to avoid arrest on allegations of sexual assault, seeking a way to pass the material to him. She failed, but kept a photo of herself, with a copy of the data, outside the building.

Her next step was to make 200 copies and distribute these to 'people of influence'. Once she did that, it was only a matter of days before the information made it to the newspapers.

In this way, acting unilaterally, Wierzycka up-ended the approach originally agreed on. She made all the data available to scores of people, and it included some quite salacious personal emails which would undermine the argument that they were dealing only with information in the public interest. She cut out the journalists, so there was no one to make sense of the material and ensure that it had maximum impact.

Also, the sources were still in South Africa, so they were at risk. Sure, Wierzycka had waited until the deadline by when they'd agreed the sources would leave, but by withdrawing her financial support she had delayed their departure.

As Brkic and the *amaBhungane* team saw it, she had endangered the whole story and the lives of the sources and others. She had taken their material, broken their trust, made her own decision about how to handle it, and destroyed their partnership.

Most astoundingly, she had been disingenuous about it. When confronted by the journalists, she'd been adamant in written messages that she had not kept a copy of the material nor had she leaked it to the newspapers. She sent a note to Brkic to say they were wrong if they

174

thought it was her. This was, however, semantics: what she'd done was give the material to many people, knowing it would get to the media; and she had destroyed her copy only after distributing the 200 copies.

Wierzycka believed she knew better than anyone how the matter should be handled. In her view, she'd paid for the material and therefore could do with it as she pleased. She had little patience for those she thought were slow or unwilling to take her lead. She was used to a world in which money could buy her control over information and people and organisations.

She told people afterwards that she had no regrets for following this path, would do it again, and would ask for no credit or recognition for it.

Aftermath

#GuptaLeaks was 'probably the greatest investigative journalism coup in South African history', journalist and commentator William Saunderson-Meyer wrote on *Independent Online* in July 2017. 'From the very outset, this seemed in its detail and cadence to be authentic, damaging material. When it grew into a journalistic torrent, a deluge drawing on some 100 000–200 000 emails, it became clear that they contained revelations that potentially could reshape political and commercial dynasties, both locally and abroad.'

'#GuptaLeaks became the biggest work of investigative journalism by South African hacks since *Vrye Weekblad's* Vlakplaas exposés [into apartheid killing squads],' wrote Adriaan Basson and Pieter du Toit in their book. 'The emails reveal the extent of state capture and destroy any notion that this was a dreamt-up concept by the so-called Western media, Zuma's opponents and "white monopoly capital".'

In March 2018 I convened the judges for the Taco Kuiper Awards for Investigative Reporting, the country's biggest journalism award, where we said:

> For the last few years, it seemed that we were facing an impervious culture of impunity as many state institutions of accountability faltered and corruption appeared to be undermining our democracy and destroying our economy. But investigative journalists beavered away, piecing together the elements of what grew into a remarkable story.

For some time it was a back-and-forth of allegation and counter-allegation, charge and denial, but
in the last few months things turned around and all
this work came to fruition. We now appear to have
started – and I say only started – the process of forcing
accountability and transparency on those who were
responsible – and today we can celebrate that journalists were central to this apparent turnaround …
I know of only a few times in the history of a nation
when journalists have played such a clear and crucial
role in bringing a country back from the brink.

This was one of a string of awards won for the story, culminating
in *amaBhungane*, the *Daily Maverick*, News24, OpenUp and Finance
Uncovered sharing the 2019 Global Shining Light Award from the
Global Investigative Journalism Network.

*

#GuptaLeaks not only shook up the country, it also shook up the
media industry.

The stories provided the breakthrough for *amaBhungane*, with outlets vying for its copy, and foundations and wealthy individuals stepping
in to support the team. They even had success in crowdsource funding,
unheard of in South Africa. Small contributions from the public jumped
from about R800 000 the year before #GuptaLeaks to R2,3 million the
year after, then R2,5 million.

The *amaB* model took off across the subcontinent. Investigative-
journalism centres – mostly supported by the George Soros-funded
Open Society Foundation – sprang up in Lesotho, Botswana, Mozambique, Malawi and Zimbabwe, leading to a boom in accountability
reporting.

The *Daily Maverick* also got new financial backing and was able to
expand, having found a new mission and direction.

*

The ones who carried the heaviest load were the whistleblowers. Stan and John were able to take their families out of the country and go in search of new and safer pastures.

It took me many months, working through intermediaries, to meet Stan and his wife. They appreciated the support they'd had but they spoke unhappily about having to rent out their house in a hurry, close their business and find homes for their dogs.

Stan's wife spoke with pain of the disruption it had brought to their lives. Leaving the dogs had been particularly difficult, they said, and now, two years later, they had no business or home. Stan himself had the mild paranoia that was probably inevitable after two years of uncertainty and instability.

The relationship with a source is always tough in journalism, and it played out in this case in a way that typified the difficulties. In public, the focus was on the protection of the sources, and the lengths to which journalists had to go to preserve the sources' anonymity. But behind the scenes it was a complicated and shifting relationship that required careful handling.

While journalists and their sources may be locked together in a forced partnership, their interests don't always coincide, and the journalist can be torn between the desire to get a good story out as strongly as possible, and the interests of the source, both legitimate and not. It was even tougher when the story was one of enormous importance, and the source was naturally more inwardly focused, protecting themselves.

Brkic and Brümmer stayed in close touch with Stan and ran everything past him. It was fundamental to their work and reputation that they protect the identity of their sources. And Stan had the highest praise for Brümmer and Brkic. He had contempt, however, for Wierzycka, who he felt had been self-serving and had let them down; and anger with Brian Currin, who he felt had 'betrayed them'. He was angry at how Currin had handled the hard drives, saying he'd compromised the chain of evidence that Stan had been so careful about, and compromised him at a meeting with the US Federal Bureau of Investigation (FBI) in Nairobi, Kenya.

Currin, as an intermediary, had had a tough time managing what he saw as his partnership with Stan and John. With his lawyer's training, he was also thinking about securing the evidence that would be needed in future. The FBI had been pushing him for some time for the original hard disk of emails, which they said they needed for their own investigation into the Guptas.

Currin didn't want to give it to them, because the project had to remain based in South Africa and prevent the Guptas from labelling it – as they did with so much of the criticism of them – as an international, 'neo-colonial' plot; but at the same time he didn't want to block an FBI investigation which could assist in holding the Guptas to account. He offered the FBI agents a copy of the clone copy, but they needed the full evidence trail from the original material.

Stan and Currin met the FBI in Malawi to try to hammer out a solution. They agreed that Currin would hand the material to the Zondo Commission of Inquiry into state capture. Judge Raymond Zondo would then have experts access the information on the damaged disk and certify the evidence trail for both his commission and the FBI.

They set up another meeting, in Nairobi, because that was where the FBI said it had the equipment to make a copy. And it was after Nairobi that Stan lost faith in Currin: he felt, he said, that his identity had not been properly protected.

Sitting together at Nairobi airport on their way out, Stan was quite distraught, Currin told me. 'I think because he, understandably, felt an extreme case of anti-climax because he now had nothing. The story was now completely out of his hands. The original was with Zondo and he still could not trust Zondo's commission completely. He had no bargaining power left, it was no longer his project, and I think it deflated him. He was dejected.'

Currin, however, was 'delighted' that the whole thing was 'done and dusted'. 'I'd done my job, what I had set out to do,' he said. But he regretted not showing more understanding for Stan's position. 'I didn't show the empathy I should have, on reflection, and after that the nature and tone of our communication changed radically.'

Stan wrote to Currin in 2018 to ask for the original of his and John's signed affidavits, also key elements in the evidence chain that linked the hard drive to the Guptas. Currin declined: the affidavits didn't belong to Stan or John, he explained, and he needed to keep the originals.

Currin told me he was saddened that his relationship with Stan had soured, though he could understand the reasons for it. 'As much as I admire what he did and appreciate the impact it had on his and his wife's lives, I found him a difficult person to work with.' This left Currin with some tough dilemmas: 'At some stage, I had to choose between trying to please him on the one hand, and achieving the objectives of what I regarded as our joint project [on the other]. I chose the latter, and have no regrets that I did.'

This, sadly, is not an unusual outcome for whistleblowers: their lives torn apart, they enjoy a brief period of pride and satisfaction, and then are left to stand alone and rebuild their lives when the story moves on. They watch others being honoured for their work, and they stay in the background.

South Africa has legislation to protect whistleblowers, but it doesn't prevent the deep disruption of the life of an individual who speaks out against wrongdoing, nor can it stop the sense of letdown and abandonment that is common among whistleblowers.

PART III
'DUPES OF DECEIVERS'

The admission

'We got it wrong, and for that we apologise' was the *Sunday Times* headline on 14 October 2018.

Editor Bongani Siqoko wrote that there had been two major stories by their senior journalists in 2011, before his appointment, that had been 'manipulated by those with ulterior motives' and had contained errors.

The first was the 'renditions' story, the allegations that senior policemen Anwa Dramat and Shadrack Sibiya had been involved in illegally handing over criminals to Zimbabwe, some of whom had been tortured and killed. This story had brought down the two respected officers.

The second was the story of the Hawks' Cato Manor 'death squad'. This story had ended the 40-year career of another respected officer, Johan Booysen.

Siqoko undertook to return the awards won for these stories, and gave space in the paper for those who'd been accused to put their cases at length, something that had been denied them for years. Two key journalists – and two of the country's best-known and most respected journalistic sleuths – Mzilikazi Wa Afrika and Stephan Hofstatter, were let go from the paper, as was Ray Hartley, who'd been editor at the time of the Cato Manor story and who'd spoken out in defence of the reporting.

A few months earlier, Siqoko had retracted the SARS 'rogue unit' stories that had run over two years. This series of stories had driven a number of senior officials out of SARS and left the organisation gutted.

Siqoko had used what was becoming his regular series of euphemisms: 'We got some things wrong,' he said, and 'we have found serious gaps … in our news-gathering and production'. He then gave a long list of a succession of compounding errors that had taken place in more than thirty stories over many months. The newspaper had reached a settlement with the subjects of those stories, and journalist Piet Rampedi had resigned in protest.

These three reports had led to a band of the country's top policemen, prosecutors and tax officials losing their jobs and facing criminal charges. This had allowed President Jacob Zuma to replace these individuals with his cronies, to seize control of these institutions, to stop them from investigating and prosecuting his friends, his allies, his family and himself, and to turn them on his political rivals. They had hollowed out key institutions of state and destroyed the capacity of the police and the tax collector to do their jobs.

These stories had been instrumental in the capture of the state by a corrupt elite around President Zuma.

*

One bad story would have been a serious problem. Three meant that one of the country's top investigative-journalism teams, and some of its best-known reporters, were in disgrace.

The *Sunday Times* and its investigative team had had the best motives, Siqoko said: the search for truth to serve the public good. But they'd been played. 'While we were interrogating, investigating and reporting these stories, there was clearly a parallel political project aimed at undermining our democratic values and destroying state institutions, and removing individuals who were seen as obstacles to this project. We admit that our stories may have been used for this purpose.'

Siqoko didn't say how his newspaper and journalists had been played or who had done it. He brushed over the fact that the paper had stuck with its stories for many months, even years. Not even a devastating 2015 Press Council ruling had led his predecessors to reconsider.

In the SARS case, the council panel had ruled that the *Sunday Times* reporting was 'inaccurate, misleading and unfair'. The paper hadn't verified its information, hadn't given subjects reasonable time to respond and hadn't obtained its information legally, honestly or fairly. The *Sunday Times* had committed 'tier 3' breaches of the Press Code, the most serious kind, and they were ordered to retract and apologise on the front page. Such an unequivocal, even angry, ruling was rare.

Many questioned whether the newspaper and the journalists had been innocent. Pete Richer, one of the SARS staffers targeted in the reports, confronted the journalists at a September 2018 book launch, noting that 'scurrilous and unethical journalists' had set up a fiction to get rid of 'ethical, hardworking, conscientious public servants'.

One of the country's best-known journalists, Max du Preez, wrote that this was 'the worst chapter in the history of South African media since 1994':

> We're not talking about a small mistake or slip-up under pressure. A small group of *Sunday Times* journalists wrote a series of utterly false reports ... These stories were then used by those who had planted them

on the journalists to get rid of dozens of some of the best senior civil servants we ever had … Our democracy, the rule of law and clean government were all seriously undermined … SARS and the Hawks are still struggling to recover from the damage.

Investigative journalist Jacques Pauw said this was 'not just sloppy reporting or journalists that got it wrong. This was manufactured journalism that was meant to disinform and to ultimately damage our law-enforcement agencies.'

Another commentator, Chris Vick, said the *Sunday Times*'s integrity was 'on trial'. These were 'not merely small factual errors requiring correction … [they were] orchestrated smear campaigns – manipulation of news, through the manipulation of journalists, resulting in a complete misinterpretation of the facts … so that state capture could progress.'

If the country's biggest newspaper was on trial, South African journalism was in the dock with them. This was an opportunity that would be grabbed by those who wanted to discredit the country's news media, those who would say we couldn't believe or trust any of our journalists, who would dismiss us all as purveyors of 'fake news', who wanted greater control over the media. It was a victory for those who would benefit from obfuscating the distinction between truth and falsity, those who wished to operate from behind a grey cloud of confusion.

What had led to the *Sunday Times* going down such a dark and destructive path? How had some of the country's best investigative reporters come to this? Was it well-meaning reporting that had gone wrong, or was there a malignancy in the newsroom? Were they victims of manipulation, or were they – or some of their reporters – part of the project to undermine and damage these institutions? Was this a *Sunday Times* problem, or did it point to a deeper problem in our news media?

Early warning bells

An early sign that all wasn't well in the country's largest paper began with a series of front-page stories back in 2007 and 2008, all of which had to be retracted, some after scathing Press Council rulings.

'How fat cats looted Land Bank billions' on 11 November 2007 revealed details of a forensic audit into problems at the Land Bank, but without telling readers that the journalist had never seen the audit report, nor that it was still in draft, unsigned form. Given this second-hand sourcing, it wasn't a surprise that there were errors in the reporting.

The '*Sunday Times* treatment', though, meant that it was all stated as fact, without the qualifiers that would alert readers to the risks of such a hearsay story. Nor did the writers tell the reader anything at all about the source of the hearsay, to enable any judgement on its reliability. And they couldn't get hold of the key subject of the story, Land Bank CEO Alan Mukoki, before going to print. They tried to fix this the following week, but managed to misquote Mukoki.

The biggest surprise was that when the *Sunday Times* did see the audit report later, they didn't admit to or acknowledge that they had misreported it. The newspaper's attitude was that it had got most of the story right, and – despite a strong policy to make corrections voluntarily and quickly – it fell prey to the common temptation of avoiding admitting embarrassing mistakes.

Mukoki's complaint to the press ombudsman in February 2013 drew a stinging rebuke for the newspaper: it hadn't exercised sufficient care and should have reported the audit content as claims and

187

allegations rather than fact; and it should have acknowledged its mistakes and carried Mukoki's side of the story more fully. 'This [the way the paper handled the story] makes for sensationalist journalism,' the ombudsman concluded, ordering the *Sunday Times* to take the humiliating step of publishing his ruling, laying bare the paper's blunders.

The ombudsman is part of the country's Press Council structures, a self-regulatory system set up and funded by newspaper owners to enable quick resolution of disputes over their coverage. It's often derided for being too close to the industry and lenient on journalists, so such a sharply worded judgement was unusual – and should have alerted the newsroom to problems in its operation.

The Sunday Times's front page of 3 August 2008 was devoted to revelations about the controversial arms deal, the result, it said, of a six-month investigation by the newspaper. 'Mbeki took R30-m and gave some to Zuma' was the splash headline, and above it the strap expanded, 'Secret report fingers both men in arms-deal bribes'.

These were sensational claims, implicating the sitting president and the next in line, then the president of the ruling party. You would expect extra care over such claims. The two were described as 'partners in crime'. An editorial called for Mbeki's dismissal and criminal prosecution.

What was the source of such a major claim? The report quoted one paragraph from a report compiled by an unnamed UK specialist risk consultancy and also an unnamed South African official 'who had access to such information'. It was third-hand information, an anonymous source quoting another anonymous source, but stated as fact. The newspaper promised more 'sensational allegations' the following week, but these never materialised. Nor was the story ever confirmed or retracted.

Another story, around the same time, was so ludicrously over the top, and so universally mocked, that even the all-powerful *Sunday Times* had to take steps to shore up its credibility. 'Transnet sold our sea to foreigners' the front page screamed on 24 August 2008, with a diagram showing large parts of the sea around Cape Town's prestigious

V&A Waterfront development apparently ceded to foreign investors by Transnet, the parastatal transport company. It included 22 kilometres of coastline and 90 square kilometres of sea, running all the way out to Robben Island. If the legislation currently before Parliament was passed, the paper stated, the sale would be illegal and Transnet could face a R20-billion claim.

The story ran on the same day as the retraction of the Land Bank story, as if to signal to readers that they should treat the newspaper's reports with scepticism.

Two weeks later the *Sunday Times* published a front-page retraction of the Transnet story, saying coyly that the headline, the diagram and the statement about the extent of the sea area sold 'went too far'.

*

I was one of four people commissioned by editor Mondli Makhanya in mid-2008 to review 'systems and processes at the *Sunday Times* to gain an understanding of how recent stories which fell short of standards of journalistic excellence were printed'. Two other former editors, Paula Fray and Franz Kruger, media lawyer Dario Milo and I interviewed more than eighty members of staff and studied internal documentation, policies and international best practice to try and recommend what needed to be done to fix the newspaper's credibility problem.

The report of this *Sunday Times* review panel in December 2008 outlined a series of practices, bad habits, policies, attitudes and newsroom cultures that bedevilled not just the *Sunday Times* but all newspapers, to varying extents, as they grappled with economic and political pressures. The paper's successes had led to complacency, we said, and over time its policies, practices and structures had become inadequate to deal with the challenges they were facing. The newsroom was top heavy, with lots of editors and managers and too few reporters. There was a need to redirect resources to reporting.

Rewriting by seniors was a major problem, with many reporters expressing unhappiness at the '*Sunday Times* treatment' that turned a story into a splash. This style, we said, 'had sometimes come to be used in a way that is out of touch with the paper's audiences and with the mainstream of journalism. This sometimes also leads to inaccuracies ...' We gave a list of instances where shoddy rewriting had introduced errors: 'six horses' had become 'six white horses'; 'unmarried' had become 'divorced'; a schoolgirl had become 'a shy schoolgirl'. Even quotes were occasionally changed. Indeed, when we reviewed the newspaper's published corrections, many of them were apologies for misquoting.

One senior said they dreaded it when their story was chosen for a front-page splash, because that meant it went through multiple layers of editors to get the full 'treatment' and you never knew where that would end. Sometimes, when a reporter objected, the response was to take their name off the story rather than pay heed to their warnings.

Policies on sourcing, fact-checking, corrections and apologies had to be reviewed, tightened up and properly implemented, we said. The single biggest factor causing the missteps, we noted, was arrogance – a word that came up often in our investigation.

We reported a 'high degree of unhappiness' among staff and poor morale. And we highlighted 'an unusually high level of family and personal relationships between staff'. Our language was delicate: 'Some are related, others are married, or involved with or divorced from each other.'

And then there was the secrecy of the investigations unit. Tucked away in one of the few offices in an otherwise open-plan space, and the only one that had a keypad lock, the unit's behaviour caused 'considerable unhappiness'. They considered themselves different and special, a newsroom elite. Their stories seldom appeared on the diary, the weekly story plan that formed the core of the planning of each edition. Sometimes, we were told, their work was only submitted on the day of publication, making it difficult for the stories to be put through the normal scrutiny. In a place that reeked of arrogance, the unit was ground zero of a curdled culture in the newsroom.

Clearly, the problems ran deep – but it would be wrong to single out the *Sunday Times*. Most of these problems were evident to some extent in all our newspapers, which were facing the same combination of financial, political and new-technology challenges. Many of them were inevitable, given the changes taking place in media and the society around them. Even *The New York Times* suffered the 'Jayson Blair scandal' in 2013, in which a well-known writer was exposed as a fraud who'd made up many parts of his reports.

The *Sunday Times* had had the courage to confront its issues, and we recommended at length and in detail far-reaching fixes.

Now, would the newspaper have the strength to implement them?

*

Six months later, midway through 2009, I wrote a *Business Day* column saying that few of our recommendations had been implemented at the *Sunday Times*. Publisher Mike Robertson called the staff together and denounced me, saying that I wouldn't work for them again.

One of our recommendations had been that the newspaper publish at least the executive summary of our report, so that its readers could see the extent to which it was going to rebuild. It didn't, though the report eventually and inevitably got out anyway.

When someone who understands tradecraft saw the report much later, he said to me, 'If you were a spook working out how to play the *Sunday Times*, you would start with this report. It outlines all the problems in the place, all the weak links. You wrote the manual.'

The men who knew too much

George Darmanovic held court at the Doppio Zero restaurant in Greenside, Johannesburg, most weekdays around 2010. He carefully orchestrated who was there, who lunched with him, who popped in, whom he saw and whom he was seen with. People came and went, some for a quick chat, some for a meal.

Darmanovic was always the centre of attention: he had to be; he earned his living from it.

Sometimes senior policemen joined him so that he could show who were his friends and allies. Sometimes he asked potential 'clients' to be there, so that they could see what influence and clout he had. Sometimes he asked SSA agents to pass by, so that he could offer their services to those who were with him.

Well-known politicians would also join from time to time. Blade Nzimande, a minister in Jacob Zuma's government and a leading figure in the South African Communist Party, was at the table at least once.

A well-known Johannesburg attorney, one whose clients included known underworld figures who had money to spend on buying influence in state structures, or were in trouble and needed help, was a regular, and Darmanovic was the go-to guy. A senior person from SARS was often there, as were top officers from the Hawks. Glenn Agliotti, one of Johannesburg's best-known gangsters, would drop by. Sometimes Darmanovic would invite Jacques Pauw or other investigative reporters.

If you had trouble with the police or with the taxman or with the courts, Darmanovic was the man who could help sort it out. It would cost you money, but he could help you.

Like all half-good intelligence operators, Darmanovic was also a conman and a showman: for hire, but in the end always working for himself. The policeman might only have been interested in tucking into his steak, but to Darmanovic he was a prop. He had someone else at another table, and he was saying, 'See who's there, he's the best guy in Crime Intelligence, he's our man, he can look after you ...'

Darmanovic didn't take notes, but he would remember that person's details and what they needed. That night, Darmanovic would be on a burner phone saying, 'This is what it's going to cost you; you need to get the money together, preferably cash.' The next morning, Darmanovic would send someone round to that person's house to collect a down payment on whatever favour he was asking or influence he was buying. Darmanovic might pass some of that money on to a helpful official, or he might keep it himself; usually he would split it. He was running the show and setting the rules.

'Darmanovic was in control, and he bamboozled all of us,' one of his men said.

Born in South Africa of a Yugoslav father and Lebanese mother, George Darmanovic had grown up in Mayfair, Johannesburg, and later moved to Emmarentia. He had a steady daily routine. Weekends were family time, but weekdays followed a regular pattern. From first thing in the morning, as early as 5am, he would be messaging his contacts. 'How you, my brother, just saying good morning, whadda-whadda ... Everyone got that message, and everyone thought they were the only one. He made everyone seem special,' one of his friends told me.

Between 6 and 7am his team of men would come to his house and he would dispense their tasks: collect money from so-and-so, deliver money, collect a document from a policeman, take an envelope of money, pull the paper.

To 'pull the paper' meant to get the documentation on someone. He would send one of his men to a police station with, say, R1 000 and that person would give a policeman R200 to pull a file, and pocket the rest. This person would return later in the day and deliver the envelope, maybe with the printout of someone's record or of cases opened against that person. Now Darmanovic would have information on someone, and Darmanovic traded in information.

From 7am was his exercise time. Some of his men would walk with him, around the Melville Koppies nature reserve, or the nearby Parkview suburb, and back to his house. Then it was down to his basement gym for two hours of push-ups, sit-ups and hitting the boxing bag.

'He could hit that bag harder than anyone. He would boast about the well-known fighters he had knocked out, and his followers would all nod happily. It was all about buying into his cult,' a source told me.

Darmanovic was strong and kept himself fit. He was known as 'The Butcher' and probably liked the fear the nickname instilled in people. But it came from being a blockman in his father's butchery when he was younger.

Around 10am they would move to Doppio Zero. 'From the work the day before, he would have his men report back. They would get their instructions for the day and off they would go. Nobody knew the full extent of what he was doing because he only let certain people know certain things, and only certain people would collect the cash and deposit it into accounts.'

Then the meetings would start, and a range of people – clients and contacts – would come and go. Some were there just to get lunch and be seen there, probably hoping to pick up some information of their own; others were trying to find a way out of some trouble; some had been summoned by Darmanovic to do a deal. Sometimes there was a journalist looking for a lead.

Darmanovic gave information, and he gathered it. Pauw describes one meeting where Darmanovic walked him to his car and took from the boot large dossiers on two of President Jacob Zuma's keenest enemies. Also in his boot was some heavy weaponry.

Doppio Zero was just one of his hangouts. When he had to meet someone from Crime Intelligence, he used a restaurant near their headquarters in Erasmuskloof on the edge of Pretoria. When he had contacts to meet in Pretoria, notably from the presidency or foreign diplomats, he could be seen at a restaurant called Café 41 in Groenkloof. These would more likely be one-on-one meetings.

Darmanovic was on contract to the SSA. The cash he carried all the time and handed out lavishly he called 'Inzo's money'. This was a reference to a man known as Inzo Mohamed, a senior member of the NIA and later the SSA who was close to Darmanovic, and whose real name was Inayet Ismail. The money was from the secret agency funds used and abused to enable people like Darmanovic to operate.

And the ultimate source of his power? He claimed to have access to President Jacob Zuma. He'd rallied his troops to help Zuma get the presidency, channelling money into his campaign from those who wanted to curry favour with the next president, and now he had access.

Or at least he said he did.

Darmanovic had gained this access to Zuma during his election campaign through Paul Stemmet, a well-known former special-ops man turned policeman turned private-security and intelligence operator. As one person who worked with him said, 'Stemmet went to Zuma to tell him that [then president] Mbeki had taken out a hit on him, because he [Mbeki] knew Zuma was his biggest threat and if he could neutralise Zuma, [the ANC election in] Polokwane would be a walk through the park. That information was taken to Zuma and Darmanovic tagged along. And Darmanovic being George, he turned it all about himself, and he became the go-to man for the president on these things.'

The person went on, 'Darmanovic's agenda was that if Zuma was brought into power, he would owe a debt of gratitude to certain individuals, and they would be lining up for their pound of flesh. Darmanovic and those around him milked the relationship with Zuma. Darmanovic could sit there, get the necessary people on the phone, show whom he was connected with, bamboozle everybody.

'This took a dark turn because there were a lot of people around thinking they were giving money to Zuma but it wasn't necessarily going to him. It could be going to someone's back pocket, one of those people connected to George.'

Darmanovic was the point at which the SSA, the gangsters of Johannesburg and the journalists who wrote about them intersected. It was a three-ring circus, and he was the ringmaster.

*

One of the people at that table at Doppio Zero was, occasionally, Chad Thomas. 'This is the best disseminator of raw intelligence in the industry,' was how Darmanovic would introduce Thomas, particularly if he wanted to flatter him. He meant that if you wanted someone with contacts among journalists, someone who knew how to work the media, Thomas was your man.

Thomas prided himself on his intimate knowledge of the media. He could chat about the personal lives and habits of the best-known investigative reporters. He talked of them as friends and acquaintances. He knew the inner workings of places like the *Sunday Times*: who was in and who was out, who was up and who was down; what their deadlines were, and how to play them. I was constantly surprised at how familiar he was with newsrooms and journalists' gossip.

Thomas is a large, powerful man with an imposing presence. His path from Hillbrow street kid to intelligence operative was an unusual one, showing how the intersection between state security and gangsterism in the back streets of Johannesburg goes back a while.

He lived with his mother on the 42nd floor of the circular tower block that dominates the Hillbrow skyline, Ponte City. 'It was phenomenal,' he told me in an extensive set of interviews in his Parkview home and Emmarentia office in 2018, 'coming from conservative Pietermaritzburg to Ponte. We had a tenpin-bowling alley downstairs, and a little Italian restaurant and a supermarket in the building.'

Soon he was hanging out in the coffee houses, bars, pool halls, clubs and dives of Hillbrow in the 1980s, mixing with gangsters, prostitutes, drug-dealers and cops in the rich non-racial atmosphere of this buzzing cosmopolitan area. 'From being a very good boy, I became quite a naughty boy, not in the sense that I harmed people, but in the sense that I moved with the wrong crowd, I got involved with some less-than-kosher blokes, and my mom didn't like it.'

Thomas got to know both the cops and the gangsters, who operated side by side. 'I met everyone from hookers to drug dealers, you name it. If you got to know the guys, the Greeks, the Jews, the Lebs, the Porras, the Yugoslavs, the coloured guys, the black guys, the Indian guys, the cops got to know you, and everyone knew everyone. There were different places you would go every day, but our base was the Allied pool hall in the basement of Highpoint,' he said, naming the landmark Hillbrow skyscraper.

The 'real dangerous guys' in Hillbrow were those of the Civil Cooperation Bureau (CCB), a notorious military-intelligence operation on the dark side of the apartheid regime, mostly ex-policemen, some of them with serious crime convictions. They hung out at the Lodge, also known as Breakers, in Abel Street, Hillbrow. Thomas won't go into who would be there, but it was known that Darmanovic was in close touch with the most notorious of them: Eugene Riley, Staal Burger and Calla Botha. Darmanovic was also linked to Ferdi Barnard, who went to prison for the assassination of anti-apartheid activist David Webster.

But Thomas was to tread a long and winding path on the edges of Hillbrow's murky police-gangster world before he came back to work with Darmanovic.

*

Thomas says that when he was 'a little bit naughty' – when he ran into trouble with the police while still at school in 1990 – they recruited him to work under cover. The Hillbrow crime-prevention unit asked him to help with drug busts 'because I was young and willing to do just about anything'.

After he left school, he was – in what was a proud moment for him – sworn in as a police reservist in 1992. In this role, he took part in some 'serious busts … We were making a serious dent in the buttons [mandrax] industry. We would find a small dealer or user, follow him, and land up some nights in Newclare or Westbury, sometimes in Bertrams.'

This was where Thomas found his skill in intelligence. 'The hookers were our informers. We would look after them and they would look after us with intelligence. I was gathering information from informers, not realising that this was the crux of intelligence work.'

Thomas's mother had wanted him to become a journalist, and perhaps that planted a seed. So when he had his first encounter with the media, helping a *Scope* magazine journalist do a feature on drug addicts in Hillbrow, it was a memorable moment for him. He still treasures the letter of thanks he got from *Scope* editor David Mullaney.

As an undercover agent for the Hillbrow police, Thomas initially worked with the crime-prevention unit that was responsible for drug busts and other undercover work. He partnered up with fellow reservists Lenny Govender and Fareed Hoosen. The trio had some success, especially with drug busts; but, being reservists, they were frustrated that they never had access to the resources that the permanent-force members had.

Eventually the three transferred to John Vorster Square police station. During this time, Thomas had cause to investigate a person who'd joined their team claiming to be an undercover military-intelligence agent. Thomas's digging revealed that the person wasn't who he claimed to be. He built a dossier on the man and took it to the military police, who charged the man with impersonation of a military official.

In this process, Thomas met the head of the then Witwatersrand Command Provost Unit (Military Police), Lieutenant-Colonel Clive van Ryneveld. Van Ryneveld offered Thomas a permanent post in the military as an investigator and liaison with army counter-intelligence.

Van Ryneveld became a father figure to Thomas, who did well in his new position. 'I received the achiever of the month award for April 1994, which was the month that the first democratic elections were held, and the Officer Commanding Witwatersrand Command merit award in August 1994, the month of my 21st birthday. I felt like I'd found my home.'

This was soon to change when Van Ryneveld resigned from the defence force. 'My intelligence gathering in the military police was much the same as in the police – unorthodox but successful. This meant that I wasn't particularly popular among my peers, who referred to me quite openly as "*die kolonel se witbroodjie*" [the colonel's favourite].' Thomas bought his discharge, although he remained an active citizen-force member, and was appointed to an intelligence unit in Germiston. Later he transferred to a signal group as a member of the reserve forces and stayed active until the mid-2000s.

But it was an unstable period, when Thomas led something of a double life. While outwardly, he seemed on top of his game, Thomas was suffering from his own personal demons. 'I was on a downward spiral. My abuse of alcohol and drugs got worse. I landed up doing things I regret to this day: getting into unnecessary physical fights with strangers and using my connected status to neutralise the situation, and other incidents that frankly sicken me when I think back to them.

'Make no mistake, I am no angel, no white knight, but for a time I was fooled into thinking that I was fighting on the right side for the right reasons. There are many things that happened that I deeply regret, mostly the harm I caused my family, relationships that are irreparable, and people that were unknowingly caught up in the collateral damage.'

He was young, living on the edge, and developing a reputation for intelligence work and a fascination for the media – it was quite a combination. He also had a presence and charm that seemed to open doors for him. Big-handed and warm-hearted, Thomas was (and is) a great talker, open and welcoming, the kind of person who gave and won confidence with ease.

He – like many ex-military and police members of the time – joined the private-security industry in 1995, and then became security manager at Bedford Centre shopping mall in Bedfordview, at the time a meeting place for some of the city's seedier characters. In the two years he was there, 'I met many of the underworld figures that Bedfordview later became known for, and have maintained relationships with them over these 25 years,' he told me.

After some time in security and investigation roles in the banking sector, Thomas set up his own operation, Integrated Risk Solutions, which became IRS Forensic Investigations, in 2001. It was what was known in the polite language of security as a 'risk management and financial crimes investigation specialist' and it represented the privatisation of the police function by ex-policemen. Thomas was hired by individuals or companies who had a crime problem but didn't believe they could rely on the police. He and his team would investigate the case, gather the evidence, take the statement and draw up the docket to hand over to the police. He'd use his contacts to shepherd it through the courts. 'We are a team of professionals that understand the workings of the criminal justice system and are able to use this expertise to ensure, where possible, successful prosecution.'

For a period, he supplemented his income by working with Darmanovic. He was quick to say he never worked *for* Darmanovic, but received sporadic payment from Darmanovic, purportedly from the SSA. One of Darmanovic's men would regularly drop off cash at Thomas's house. The amounts varied, but were 'generally small amounts'.

Every now and then Darmanovic would talk to him about renewing his contract and getting him a raise. But there was no contract. And no formal raise. In fact, the amount of cash varied significantly.

Thomas was adamant that he didn't believe himself to be an SSA agent. He was just doing work for Darmanovic, and it was work that 'could benefit the state'. 'We knew that George had SSA connections, but we didn't quite know whom he was working for … George stated that the people at the SSA appreciated the work I was doing … although

I met other confirmed members of the SSA who always complimented me on my work, I was never certain whether I was ever in fact on the books of the SSA.'

This dissembling was typical of the grey areas of operation around the SSA. Thomas was what SSA would call an 'asset' – not a staff member, not a contractor (which is what Darmanovic was), but the next rung down. 'This is not unusual as all intelligence agencies have assets that work via intermediaries so they can ensure plausible deniability should something go wrong,' Thomas said.

*

Chad Thomas's specialisation was working the media. 'I inserted myself in the media world some years ago. ... I inserted myself as best I could ... I deliberately set out to ... I don't want to use the word "capture" ... to cultivate relationships with the journalists.'

Thomas was unusual in this world of secrecy and anonymity: he was comfortable with a media profile, and was quick to respond and speak out. The walls of his office were decorated with media by and about him stretching over three decades, and it was a source of great pride. There were media events he'd hosted with top law enforcement people and introduced them to the media. There were media comments of his on a wide range of security-related topics. And there were pictures of him with all sorts of officials, particularly senior policemen.

Thomas was a good talker who put himself at the centre of much of the activity, but his was a world of half-truths, embellishments and manipulated information. It was about information as a weapon for political ends, a soft and malleable weapon, like putty that could be shaped for one purpose and then reshaped for a different purpose. He enjoyed the image of being someone who was handy with this putty. He could have been exaggerating his role, and, listening, I had to try to work out what was true and what was embellished.

None of it was patently false, because that wasn't how it worked.

Information wasn't invented, it was manipulated. It might consist mostly of facts about a person or an event, but perhaps with something else slipped in, something that may be half-true or unproven or intended to lead a journalist along a certain path. Good intelligence was mostly true, with some exaggerations or insertions.

Thomas talked fondly of the 'dozens of local and foreign journalists' he'd got to know and work with, but is reluctant to discuss specifics of whom, he worked with on what. He knew and understood journalists because they worked with the same currency: information. He could use it to curry their favour and they could use him as an entree into the world of spooks.

'They would phone me first, and by them phoning me for confirmation on something, I would learn about it immediately. But I would give them stuff that they could verify with their sources. So that was me creating that network, and it was the network that was used and abused later on.'

It was for this media network and this knowledge that Darmanovic wanted and needed Thomas: when Darmanovic wanted to pass something on to the media, he would often go through Thomas. They would discuss whom to give it to and when to give it. Should they give it to the Sunday papers on a Friday or a Saturday? If they gave it to competing newspapers, those papers would be under pressure to beat their rivals. They had to have enough time to do the story, but not enough to dig too deep. So late Friday or even Saturday morning was good.

They would work out who the journalist was likely to phone for confirmation. Sometimes they would set someone up for this task, and brief them to confirm the story.

Sometimes they would find another way to get it to the journalist, in the expectation that they would phone a pre-determined source to confirm. They would set up a circular system, so that the journalist might not realise that the second source they were using to confirm it had got it from the same place as their first source.

'There were times when there was stuff I didn't want to touch, but

I didn't want to disappoint. I would pass on info that I didn't necessarily believe or buy into in the hope that it would then be verified or discounted.' So he would pass on information that may have been false on the assumption that it would be checked out by the investigative journalists.

'I would literally pass an envelope and they could do what they liked with it. Other times there were things that I packaged into a dossier.'

But he was insistent that he wasn't part of the team that was targeting and discrediting SARS. 'I can categorically state that,' he said.

Thomas tells of receiving a dossier from someone in the elite police unit, the Scorpions. It contained allegations from a Cape Town gangster about senior policeman Anwa Dramat, alleging his involvement in perlemoen smuggling. The information had been investigated before, and dismissed. But this agent believed there was something in it, and didn't want the dossier to disappear when the Scorpions were being shut down. Dramat was about to become head of the Hawks, the organisation that replaced the Scorpions.

Thomas gave it to a journalist and he also gave a copy to Darmanovic, and that found its way to other journalists. Some investigated and rejected it, others reported parts of it. But it was to become part of a bigger dossier on Dramat.

Changing times

A critical moment in the evolution of the *Sunday Times* investigations unit came in 2011, with a call from its keenest rivals at Media24. This emerging giant of South African publishing, which owned *City Press*, all the Afrikaans titles and the country's biggest online news service, offered jobs to the three members of the crack unit – Rob Rose, Stephan Hofstatter and Mzilikazi Wa Afrika – with salaries almost double what they were earning.

It was an aggressive and provocative move that signalled the major shifts taking place in South African news media, with Media24's ascendancy in the face of decline in the rest of the field.

Media24's parent company, Naspers, had begun in 1915 as an intrinsic part of the Afrikaner nationalist project, and its history was closely tied to that of the ruling party of apartheid, the National Party. Cabinet ministers had sat on its board and its papers' political editors had attended closed party-executive meetings, giving their support to the reformist wing of the party.

In the 1980s they'd been rewarded for their support with control of a monopoly in pay-TV, with M-Net and later DStv, which gave them the platform to move forcefully into Africa and beyond as South Africa opened up post-1990. Under the visionary leadership of Koos Bekker, the company changed remarkably quickly from a conservative Afrikaans group into a modern, open, technologically aggressive multinational. It positioned itself at the forefront of digital change, staying ahead of the curve.

After the online bubble burst in the early 2000s, the group shifted focus to the developing world and, with a mixture of serendipity and foresight, hit gold in China when a small investment in some smart young entrepreneurs gave the company a big early stake in Tencent.

They grew massively with what quickly became a Chinese giant, and by 2019 they were active in 120 countries and valued at US$63 billion – just short of a trillion rands.

The group's vision lay in being first in all new technology; its good fortune was that pay-TV gave it the finances to do it; and its real skill was in negotiating its relationships with whichever government was in power wherever it operated.

Its journalism evolved similarly from its ideological roots into some of the most independent post-1994 reporting in the country. The group used its pay-TV cash adventurously and aggressively, which meant that its South African arm, Media24, quickly established an overwhelming dominance in local media. From the mid-1980s it expanded from its Afrikaans media base to go after English-language and black readers.

In 2003 it launched the tabloid the *Daily Sun*, which was a roaring success, quickly becoming more than three times the size of its nearest daily rival and overtaking the *Sunday Times* as the country's biggest newspaper for a few years. Media24 had also bought the *Golden City Post* and *Drum* magazine from Jim Bailey, heir to a mining fortune who'd spent much of it on black journalism since the 1950s; and it changed the *Post* into *City Press*, aimed at the black Sunday market and the nearest rival to the *Sunday Times*.

By the early 2000s, Media24 was the biggest South African publisher of newspapers, books and magazines, and dominant on the internet and in pay-TV. The market value of the group was at least twenty times that of any other media group, though the South African portion of it was by this time just a small segment of the global operation. It was nonetheless still by a number of factors bigger than its local rivals, having the advantage of the backing of the massive international group.

So when it swooped in on the *Sunday Times*'s core and crack investigation team, it was an act of intentional and aggressive disruption. Media24 was second in the lucrative Sunday-newspaper market, and Bekker didn't like being second.

The company initially tried to recruit one person in the *Sunday Times* team, but that person said it was the whole team or nothing. The offer extended to all three: Wa Afrika, Rose and Hofstatter agreed to stick together and make the move. They'd been clashing with the *Sunday Times* deputy editor, Marvin Meintjies, who was assigned to look over their shoulders, and they were promised at Media24 the freedom and resources that all recruiters offer in these situations.

The shrewd *Sunday Times* publisher, Mike Robertson, stepped in quickly and over the head of the editor, Ray Hartley. He called Wa Afrika alone into his office for a marathon conversation about what he could do to keep them. He offered to match the salary offers they'd received (which meant they'd be earning more than the most senior editorial managers) and to free them from Meintjies's oversight: they would answer only and directly to Hartley.

With persistence, patience and wile, Robertson won over Mzilikazi, and the rest of the team stuck with their pledge to stay together.

Media24 couldn't have anticipated that its failed recruitment attempt would do much more harm to the *Sunday Times* than a successful one would have.

*

These three reporters had been a newsroom elite, but the Robertson deal made them untouchables, a special task squad without the normal constraints and oversight of news conferences, news diaries, news editors, subeditors and others who would filter their plans and materials.

Already, the 2008 report, three years before, had indicated that the attitude, conduct and relationship of the investigations unit with the rest of the newsroom was a serious problem. Now they were given a status and immunity that would elevate them even further. They weren't part of the hurly-burly of the open-plan newsroom; in their closed and locked office, they were set apart from the rest.

To be invited into that room was a rare concession by the team that others may be able to assist them in their work. It was always temporary and tactical, though, for only a few had the keypad code that permitted access.

The investigations unit seldom submitted its story ideas to the news conferences during which the paper was planned because the team didn't trust that open meeting. It became standard practice that the weekly diary, which listed each reporter's input for the week, recorded only 'To be informed' next to their names. The work they were doing was too sensitive and too important to share, and only the editor-in-chief could know what they were planning for that week. They sent their finished work straight to the editor-in-chief, often at the last minute, and many of the other seniors didn't know what it was about until they saw printouts of the front-page drafts.

It was a recipe for disaster.

*

The *Sunday Times*'s sense of its own power and influence came from a period when its dominance was unchallenged, and nobody could really take it on. But its world had started to change in the 1990s, and that change had accelerated in the 2000s, and this would catch up with the paper.

In the 1990s, with the rise of the internet, the traditional media had started to lose readers, advertisers and clout; but it was the emergence of social media in the following decade that shattered the news market, changing reader and advertising patterns and undermining the hegemony of institutions like the *Sunday Times*. In a decade, *Sunday Times* sales dropped from the steady 500 000 weekly average it had enjoyed for decades to under 300 000. It was in line with the national trend –

the average of 3,2 million weekly/weekend newspapers sold in 2006 had dropped to 2 million by 2018 – and the pattern in most countries.

The internet gave readers and advertisers more choice, and the balance of power shifted from the newspaper to the advertisers, who now had a surfeit of opportunities to reach their markets, and the readers, who now had a global range of reading options and social media to challenge the dominance of legacy outlets like the *Sunday Times*. Sources, too, were less dependent on traditional media to get their information out. They could now set their terms, or threaten to publish on the internet.

As the new millennium wore on, the country's economic situation began to deteriorate – GDP growth in South Africa went from a lively 6% in 2007 to 1% in a little over a decade – and advertising dipped dramatically. And then the rise of the search and social giants – Google, Facebook, YouTube, Instagram and others – started to sweep up most of the remaining advertising. It was a triple whammy.

There were two approaches to this being taken by newspapers around the world. The 'low road' entailed cutting costs to maintain profitability. This was a short-term strategy because if you reduced your newsroom size – and this was the only real way to find substantial savings – it showed quite quickly in the quality and range of your journalism, and this would just encourage your readers to start seeking out their news for free somewhere on the internet. You may reap profits for a while, but you'd enter a death spiral: lose audience, cut costs, lose more audience, cut more costs …

The 'high road' was to increase spending, or at least maintain editorial spend, to ensure that you produced a good enough product that people would continue to come to you for news, and even pay for it, because what you offered was unique and valuable to them. At the same time, you would have to spend money on shifting this audience over to your digital outlet and developing online skills and resources. This route was risky and expensive and took nerves and deep pockets, since nobody around the world was yet recouping the cost of digitising a newsroom. You couldn't beat the search and social-media giants on advertising, so you had to rely much more on convincing readers to pay for your news – a hard thing to do when so much was available for free.

Alan Rusbridger, editor of the UK's *The Guardian* during much of this period, captured the stress and pressures of this time of unrelenting and radical disruption in his memoir:

> The moment you felt you had cracked the web along came Web 2.0. Once you'd grappled with desktop, there was mobile. No sooner did you feel at home with search than you were told it was all about social. The minute you'd learned the basics of audio podcasting the commercial team (not to mention Facebook) were mouthing the latest mantra: pivot to video. You'd get up to speed on platforms, only be told it was all about personalisation. You might think you understood data, only to learn it was now all about structured data. You'd crack your platform strategy only for [Facebook's] Mark Zuckerberg to change his mind.

This route of expensive experimentation and extreme flexibility favoured those who could benefit from a switch to a more global market, like *The New York Times, The Economist, The Wall Street Journal* and the *Financial Times*. They could gather online subscriptions from a much wider worldwide pool, and it helped if you were going for a wealthier market more able to pay for subscriptions.

The Guardian had a large trust behind it and was able to use this backing to turn from being a relatively small left-leaning London paper into a leading global brand – and then start getting people to pay for it.

Business and financial papers led the way, because they had a market able and prepared to pay for reliable information. The *Sunday Times*'s sister publications, *Business Day* and the *Financial Mail*, though, were slow to move in this direction, enjoying what they thought was safe market dominance.

In South Africa, not only were there limited possibilities to get to a wider world audience, but we had few owners with the capability, vision and motivation to take the high road. Since internet penetration was slow and expensive, most opted to sit back as their peers in other countries spent the money on research and development, while they watched from relative safety.

The sole exception was Media24, which was backed by the giant Naspers group and could afford to be aggressive in its spending on digital experimentation and innovation. It was no coincidence that it was growing its dominance in the South African media world.

The Sunday Times *in the new era*

The media company that owned the *Sunday Times* underwent several name changes as consecutive owners juggled with this political and financial hot potato: originally Johnnic Communications, in 2007 it became Avusa, in 2012 it was renamed the Times Media Group, in 2017 it became Tiso Blackstar, and most recently, in 2019, it was bought by Arena Holdings.

During the Times Media/Tiso Blackstar era, the group was in the hands of an investment-fund mogul, Andrew Bonamour. Bonamour came with a fund-manager's three- to five-year framework to get his returns and bail out, which stretched for longer as it became clear that he'd bought at a market high point and couldn't easily extract himself from a business in a downward spiral. Most importantly, though, this meant the man at the helm had a short-term vision, and would do little of the long-term planning and investment that was required in a sector going through deep changes.

The group's newsrooms – like all of those in the country – saw a steady reduction in staff numbers over this period. The *State of the Newsroom 2018* report estimated that the number of journalists in South African newsrooms dropped by fifty percent in the preceding decade, but anecdotal evidence suggests it was higher than this. Again, this was a global trend: in the US, newspaper employment dropped 45% in that decade. Those few institutions that had the vision, courage and deep pockets to maintain their staffs – like *The New York Times* and *The Guardian* – were the exceptions, and reaped the benefits.

The *Sunday Times* also had to go through the same transition as all other newspapers – and all South African institutions – of shedding its apartheid baggage and adapting to a new political, social and demographic order. Addressing editors in the first months of his presidency in 1994, Nelson Mandela was elegantly diplomatic when he highlighted the ownership of South Africa's media – 'concentrated in a few hands, reflecting the patterns of racial exclusion characteristic of the old era' – and the 'composition of management, editorial executives and senior journalists, which mirrors the same pattern'. He didn't even delve into issues of content, because it was apparent that this racial exclusivity in the ranks also meant that the paper, its politics and its news choices were distinctly white, reflecting the suburban lifestyle and attitudes of its editors.

These challenges on three fronts – the technological, the financial and the political – were formidable, but the *Sunday Times's* historic dominance shielded it from many of these realities. When the 2000s came, the paper didn't have the strength and clout it had had for the previous century, but most of those inside the newsroom still strutted the stage as if it did. They still said, 'It's not news until we say it is,' even as social media was changing the definition of news and young people were consuming it in an entirely different way. This smugness was to lay the ground for the troubled times to come.

Yes, they understood that the internet was changing how journalists worked, and they made use of the new tools it provided for their communication and research. Journalists became much more mobile and research became much easier.

Yes, they knew that reading habits were changing and they had to move to provide the news when and wherever their readers wanted it. They couldn't rely on readers to come to buy the print version every Sunday; now it had to be available on whatever electronic platform readers wanted to use, and wherever they wanted to be when they used it.

Yes, they could see that the competition for readers' time and attention was greater than ever, as readers could access a whole new range of information and entertainment on their mobile devices.

Yes, they were aware that they needed to include video and audio, ending the long distinction between print and broadcast journalists.

Yes, they understood that news was moving much faster and that people weren't going to wait around until Sunday to know if a major story broke.

Young readers didn't need the *Sunday Times* to tell them what was happening or what they should be doing in their lives, because they could get it from many more online sources – and these sources were faster and cooler than the Sunday newspaper. People could find opinions, events, trends and opportunities, identified not by the fuddy-duddies of the Sunday papers but by their peers around the world and around the corner.

These people didn't want to be lectured to any more. Now they expected to take part in a conversation. They wanted to interact, and produce media, not just receive it.

But a big machine like the *Sunday Times*, confident in its ways and arrogant in its dominance of readers and advertisers, didn't adjust easily. Publishers and editors went to international conferences, and saw what was shifting and changing, but they also saw that few of the world's newspapers were making money on the internet, or knew how to do it. They tagged websites onto their print operations, like digital append-ages, or they set up digital news operations quite separate from their conventional newsrooms.

They experimented cautiously with the new rules of engagement and interactivity. They knew they couldn't stand still, but the shift was difficult and expensive. They would have to move from a weekly pro-duction routine to a 24/7 quick-response operation. They would have to go from print to multimedia, requiring new equipment, new skills and new production processes.

The *Sunday Times* took a gradual approach, moving only when it had to and hoping to let others around the world make mistakes it could learn from.

The paper banked on its traditional way of doing business: build the readership, whether in print or online, and sell it to advertisers. If those readers were middle class and had disposable income, advertisers would pay a premium to get to them. Traditionally, advertisers had few other ways to get a national audience, so the balance of power had for many years lain with the *Sunday Times*: the advertiser needed the newspaper more than the newspaper needed the advertiser.

That had worked this way – like all newspapers – for over two centuries: advertising effectively subsidised the cost of news gathering to make it cheap for readers. It took a while to realise that this wasn't working any more. They got the readers online, but the advertisers had many more ways to get to those readers, and wouldn't pay nearly as much. And anyway much of the traditional advertising just didn't work in the same way on the internet.

The world defined by the days in which the *Sunday Times*'s presence in every middle-class home, and its power to tell us what was important, was fragmenting. Each person in the house could find websites that gave them exactly what they wanted, and they didn't need to plough through all the material aimed at others around them.

The notion of a shared sense of national news was being torn apart. Every niche, every demographic, every group, whether defined by age, race, class or geography, could get just the news that most affected and interested them. And the internet enabled the marketers, politicians and others who wanted to communicate with people to do it directly, without going through traditional media like the *Sunday Times*. They could set up their own websites and send their own email and electronic newsletters.

As news started to break on social media, and spread instantly, papers like the *Sunday Times* found themselves having to follow rather than lead. The internet started to break down the role of media like the *Sunday Times* as gatekeepers and agenda-setters. Powerful editors who had been able to decide what news and opinions could be shared with the nation found they could be circumvented: the internet allowed everyone to speak directly to everyone else if they wished.

The news agenda was much more contested, fluid and uncontrollable. Previously those whom reporters wrote about, criticised and exposed could write a letter – and it may or may not run in the paper. They could take legal action or go to the Press Council, but this was costly and time-consuming, and people often felt these forums were weighted against them, particularly since the *Sunday Times* had the resources to fight back. Now, unhappy readers could take to social media, challenge the newspaper and inflict damage on it and its journalists. The editor's powers were slipping away, imperceptibly but quickly.

*

Perhaps the first sign that all wasn't well was that the paper went through a succession of editors within a few years. After Ken Owen, Brian Pottinger took the helm for only three years before being kicked upstairs into management. Mike Robertson was the first person of colour to play a leading role in the paper, briefly as editor and then for longer as publisher. He was followed by Mathatha Tsedu, the first black African in the position, whose attempts to shift the paper radically led his to being pushed aside within eighteen months. Mondli Makhanya, the first of a new generation of younger black editors, occupied the seat for six years, followed by Ray Hartley's brief stint. Then Phylicia Oppelt took the reins – the first woman in the paper's 107-year history to do so.

The most prestigious job in South African journalism had become the most precarious, making the careers of a new generation of journalists, but breaking them as quickly. The editorship was still the most powerful post, but it had also become a near-impossible one.

By design

Consider the front pages of great global newspapers like *The New York Times*, *The Guardian* and *Le Monde*. They have a flexible format that displays a range of the most important news of the day. On most days, they have a lead story across three or four of the front-page columns, intended to first attract the reader's eye but not dominate the page. The rest of the page is usually designed to showcase the range of stories on offer, so that if the main one doesn't draw in the reader, another will.

There's a hierarchy of stories, and the status of each story is signalled by typography, placement and subheads. Some newspapers have placement conventions, such as a light story across the bottom of the page, or – in the case of the *Los Angeles Times* – the 'column one' spot, the left-hand column that every day kicks off a showcase piece of long-form writing coveted by writers because it gives them more scope than usual.

A few times a year, newspapers will throw this out and splash a big story with a massive headline across the front page. They do this only when a plane crashes into the World Trade Center, for example, or a president is brought down – something of large enough significance to scream it out and capture everyone's attention. They use typography and design to tell readers that this isn't a normal news day.

The *Sunday Times's* design is less flexible: it's the same basic front-page layout every week, a template with a screaming headline dominating the page, however big or small the story may be. The design demands a regular cracker of a story to fill that splash space.

This design reflects an attitude and a policy. For some years editors placed overwhelming importance on having a big splash to dominate the front page every week. From the first conference on a Tuesday morning, through to the last on a Saturday, the primary concern was what would fill this space on the front page and command enough attention to get everyone talking, and buying the newspaper. Mike Robertson as editor heightened this priority, and the editors who followed told me that nothing gave them more anxiety than the demand for an agenda-setting front-page breaking-news splash.

Generating such a splash every week would always be difficult, but it was possible in the days when the *Sunday Times* had a large and strong newsroom and stories weren't breaking first on the internet. But consistent cutbacks from the mid-2000s had halved the size of the newsroom, and the remaining staff were now shared among all the group titles and media in a common newsroom; and as modern, multi-media and high-tech as it was, this newsroom had once served only a weekly print newspaper, and now had to serve multiple outlets and platforms around the clock. It was a display of the diminished resources and standing of the biggest newspaper of all.

In addition, the rise of the internet and social media meant that exclusivity on breaking news lasted no more than a few minutes before the story went viral and was picked up by all outlets.

The paper's static design meant that at least two weeks out of three, or perhaps even more often, reporters struggled to fill it with a story that was fresh and unique enough to command attention, and they would have to take a story normally destined for the inside of the paper, and sex it up to validate that front-page headline: they had to give it the *Sunday Times* treatment to justify the massive headline, not the other way around.

'We were placed under enormous pressure to produce a large number of scoops and splashes,' Stephan Hofstatter said, with pride for how they'd met this demand. But it also meant that there was pressure to rush stories, to avoid waiting until they were complete, and to take ever-increasing risks.

*

There is little evidence, incidentally, that a front-page splash boosts circulation in the long term. People buy a paper like the *Sunday Times* for a host of reasons, but mostly out of habit, a sense that it's part of their weekend life, and a routine that connects them to an imagined community that shares a sense of what news is that day.

For the *Sunday Times*, it was for a long time the overall mix that mattered: the comics for the kids, the sport for the fans in the house, business and personal finance for the breadwinners, the political news that would be discussed at dinner, the celebrity gossip for the workplace, recipes for the cooks, and so on. It was a family package.

But as budgets tightened, the paper did too, and it became less of a total package and more dependent on a powerful front page.

That front-page splash might push sales up a few percentage points in a good week, but it was the long-term standing and position of the paper that brought people to it week after week. And that depended on credibility – a quality that had to be built up and nurtured over time, but which can be lost with one bad story.

Heavy is the head that wears the crown

Phylicia Oppelt drove into the basement of the *Sunday Times* building and parked. She sat still, staring ahead, frozen by a deep sense of dread.

She couldn't get out of the car. She knew that when she did and went up in the lift and into the newsroom, she would face an onslaught. Waiting for her would be the usual barrage of complaints, queries, requests, demands from the powerful who either wanted the *Sunday Times*'s attention or resented it. She knew it was a good sign if all the political leaders from all sides gave her hell, but the relentless pressure was taking its toll. As were the newsroom and boardroom battles.

She was struggling to bring out a newspaper with a staff she felt to be inadequate and ill equipped. She was under massive pressure from the publisher to deliver sales and revenue, to cut costs, to produce a great newspaper every week. She couldn't do it all. How could she motivate staff when they were overstretched? How could she deliver sales figures when the budgets were too tight for her to do what she needed to do? If she pleased her bosses, then her staff were unhappy. If she pleased her staff, then the people they were writing about were unhappy. How could she coax great work out of her young and inexperienced team under these pressures?

There weren't many among her staff whom she felt she could trust to do a good job. When they gave her a news diary that was thin and dull, how could she not show her frustration? This – the most power-ful job in South African journalism – was the one she'd always want-ed, and she'd fought hard to get it, so why was it that today, after a few months as editor, she couldn't get out of her car and go to her desk?

She was highly visible as the most senior black woman journalist in the country, and the pressure was huge. She felt so vulnerable, yet had to keep the demeanour of an iron-strong woman. She had to keep command, like a general trying to summon for a counter-attack a bedraggled army that had lost a series of battles.

This wasn't the first time she'd sat in her car in this garage, having to gather the strength to go out and face the day. It was happening more and more often. Every week it was becoming harder to go into the building.

She remembered one Saturday morning when she'd left the newsroom for a few minutes of quiet time. Her phone had rung and she saw on the screen that it was the publisher, Mike Robertson. A Saturday call from him meant a problem.

Robertson told her the group CEO and main shareholder, the ultimate boss, Andrew Bonamour, wanted to pulp the *Business Times* section that had been printed the previous night. Section editor Rob Rose had gone after the head of the PIC, the controversial controller of the massive government pension funds, running a picture of his Lamborghini in the PIC garage. How did he afford this? Was it at the expense of the workers whose money he handled?

Rose was being provocative in running the story – but that was Rose.

Oppelt had never liked the story idea much. It was a cheap shot that would feed the accusation that papers like the *Sunday Times* treated conspicuous black wealth in a way it never treated white wealth, that the journalists couldn't help themselves questioning black success. It boiled down to the charge that the paper had black editors, reporters, even owners, but its newsroom culture was still white.

The hard-headed Rose had gone ahead with the picture. It raised legitimate questions about a lifestyle that might not match the man's position. Rose knew that stories were emerging around this person, and he was probing and pushing, in the hope that something would come out. It had nothing to do with race, he argued, and those who said it did were using race to protect someone who shouldn't be protected.

What he didn't know was that Bonamour had been negotiating a PIC investment or loan for the company, and now the fund's head was angry and wanted Rose fired. The future of the company hung on a picture of a flashy sportscar. Bonamour was insisting they trash the whole print run, and reprint the section without the picture.

Allowing a corporate deal to prevent the publication of a story would mean a deep compromise in journalistic principles. It would also cost a great deal and delay the whole newspaper, leading to a loss in sales. How was she to hit sales targets if the paper came out late? How was she to make her budgets with such an unexpected cost? How was she to handle Rose, an enormously talented journalist, a key member of her staff, but a wilful troublemaker who gave her constant headaches? How was she to maintain credibility among her staff if she was seen to give in to such pressure?

In the end, Robertson had held off Bonamour until it was too late to reprint the section. He'd protected Oppelt. But the pressure was enormous. And Bonamour was angry.

Oppelt recalled a previous incident when Rose had been part of the global consortium of journalists who investigated the ground-breaking Panama Papers leak, the biggest corporate leak ever, which revealed the secret accounts and shell companies that the global elite were using to hide wealth and avoid taxes. Among the South Africans whose names had come up in the papers were the owners of Thompsons Tours, major *Sunday Times* advertisers to the tune of about R25 million a year. Oppelt had backed Rose on that story – she thought the evidence was sound and no one was questioning its accuracy. It was great to be part of such an important international exposé and to collaborate with journalists around the world to break such a major story together.

The Thompsons Tours owners, though, were livid and threatened to pull their advertising if the story wasn't retracted. The *Sunday Times* bosses wanted to find a compromise to placate them. Apologise, Robertson and Bonamour told Oppelt, but she didn't want to. There was nothing to apologise for, and it was important to stand by her reporters when they got it right.

But the threat of a major loss of advertising was too much to bear, and her managers wouldn't let it go, so she crafted a 'Matter of Fact' to go into the paper the following week. It had the tone of an apology, but never quite said sorry. The wording went through a number of delicately negotiated iterations until the managers were happy it would placate the Thompsons Tours owners, and she could live with it.

But when it appeared that Sunday, the Thompsons Tours owners weren't satisfied and they pulled their advertising.

Robertson told her she would have to fire Rose. She stood firm, saying Robertson would need to fire her first.

Roberson had let it go, but had made Oppelt undertake significant editorial cuts to make up for the lost advertising. So in the end it was she and her staff who took the pain.

And now it was Rose again. She was trapped between these two men: Rose and Robertson. Rose was a valuable journalist, one of the best, but unmanageable, like so many of the best. Robertson was the corporate powerhouse. He'd been the best editor she'd ever worked under, and it was great to have a publisher who understood the editor's job, loved good writing, and knew the paper and the editor's burden better than anyone.

Bonamour was the CEO but he was new to the media business and cared only about the bottom line. He relied on Robertson and his knowledge of the business, so Robertson was powerful. Oppelt trusted Robertson and believed he was doing what was best for the newspaper, but he was always looking over her shoulder. He hadn't wanted to move out of the editorship when he had, believing he was the most successful editor, so he was all over the editors who'd come after him and who reported to him, especially Oppelt, who was his protégée. But he'd backed her for the job, and protected her from Bonamour, who didn't like her – or at least that's what Robertson told her. He'd shown her emails from Bonamour saying she had to go.

Some called her 'Mike's girl'. But from her point of view, the relationship was strained. He'd once called her on a Sunday to say that she'd produced the best edition in the paper's history. She'd treasured that moment. But more often he told her what he didn't like or just stayed silent. He was paternal towards her, and when she fought back, he withheld approval, treating her like a naughty girl.

She was also not popular among many of her staff, and knew it. A willingness to be unpopular is a good trait for an editor, who has to make quick, hard decisions on matters that will almost always hurt someone, whether it's the reporter, the subject of the story, or people not even mentioned in the story. Sometimes it hurts those who deserve it, sometimes those who're just caught up in it, who become collateral damage. Often it's someone the writer hadn't even thought about when doing the story.

Every decision an editor has to make has some potential to do good, and massive potential to do harm, and the best she can do is hope that in the long run the good outweighs the harm. An editor can only guess how much good a story can do, and how much damage, and hope to make the right guess. Do no harm, the ethicists say, but the truth is you can only try to anticipate harm and mitigate it. To risk no harm would be to do no journalism; to do no harm, a fantasy.

The weakest editors were those who tried to please, those who wanted to hang out with the rich and powerful, and were tempted to protect them to keep this status. The best were those who knew the job meant they had to live with enemies and more fake friends than real ones. Good editing often came down to a careful choice of enemies and a sceptical handling of fair-weather friends.

When she'd got this job, she'd insisted that before she began, Robertson clean out a bunch of staffers she didn't trust or want to work with. So when she'd arrived there was already blood on the floor, some of it from senior journalists who'd been there for some time, and everyone knew it was she who'd had Robertson wield the knife. The newsroom was jumpy, even hostile. They knew her to be tough, and she

223

kept up that facade. The atmosphere in the newsroom was outwardly welcoming, but below the surface ran a stream of hostility.

She'd built up her defences over the years: she came across as tough, invulnerable, in command of herself and all around her. That was what was needed to survive, never mind to get ahead, as an uppity black woman. But it was also her weakness, because it meant she shared with no-one her worries, her concerns, her vulnerabilities, her sense that the world was closing in on her. She even eschewed female solidarity, partly because she was alone at the top, partly because she could show no vulnerability.

*

We could never read her, a number of her colleagues said to me about Oppelt. You never knew what she was going to say or what she was thinking. She had us guessing all the time. What would she like or dislike? What did she want or not want? When would she laugh or blow up? When would she love you and when would she scream? We never knew what to expect. It wasn't easy to disagree with her, they said. She could be prickly.

Everyone knew Robertson had her back, so they couldn't mess with her. It also meant she wouldn't last long without Robertson's support. She was in his grasp, and his grasp was tight.

'What Mike wanted, Mike got,' was the reality, she told me during our interview in 2018. She could be unpopular with everyone, but she would lose her job if she wasn't popular with Robertson.

Robertson initiated many of the cuts and restructurings that the paper went through while Oppelt was in the hot seat, like the controversial decision to cut back the number of staff photographers. It was her budget, but he often took the initiative that should have been hers. He had results to deliver to Bonamour, what he thought necessary for the prosperity of the paper. And he had his own substantial bonuses and share options to look after. But he wasn't crude, and he deferred to her editorial status, especially in front of others.

Every Friday there was a general management meeting that looked at the previous week's sales and revenue numbers. The trend was downwards, so the commercial pressure was relentless, week after week, Friday after Friday, as she was preparing to make that week's critical decisions. Robertson only had to ask her what she was going to do about it, and approve or disapprove of her answers. Or nudge her in a certain direction. Over time, she'd come to realise that she didn't have the power she'd expected to have when she got the job of steering this behemoth of a newspaper.

It hadn't turned out the way she'd expected. Her dream job was feeling like a nightmare.

She used to say that what she was doing was the best fun. 'I was being paid to be doing what I loved. I was in the best place in the world.' She had fought long and hard to get to this pinnacle, and when she got there she had moved sharply to assert her leadership. She hadn't been afraid to assert herself. She hadn't minded that she wasn't popular: she'd known she was the person for this job and this was the job for her.

Within a few months, she wasn't loving the job any more. The stress was wearing her down. She was getting messages on a Sunday morning from Bonamour saying the paper was crap, advertisers were complaining, the guy from his local supermarket said the paper was so depressing. He would forward messages from people who worked on the paper, complaining. Bonamour said she should try this, or do that, issuing thinly veiled instructions, and it was irritating because he knew so little about editing.

She'd tried to tell him that she didn't have the calibre of people she needed to do the job. When she'd joined the paper back in 1994, a junior like her wasn't allowed to write for the main news section until they had years of experience. It used to be that you learnt the trade on a small newspaper, and you came to the *Sunday Times* when you had proven yourself. And when you got in the door, you started on the soft stories, and the less important sections, and had to graduate to serious news. You earned a byline over some time, and celebrated when you got it. And when you made the front page, you bought drinks for everyone.

Now the newsroom was half-empty, and those reporters who were there were mostly juniors. Pile up their years of collective experience and it would be less than one of the towering and intimidating seniors who were dominating the room when she'd started in journalism. There were some good people, but they had little of the experience needed to deal with the extraordinary pressures of this newsroom. And then, for some others, she didn't understand how they'd come to be there.

This meant that she relied hugely on the investigations unit for big stories, as there were few others in the newsroom who could break a story. Every Tuesday she would ask for the news diaries for the week and would send them back with questions. Didn't you read that in the papers already? That's not a news story. Did you think of this angle?

She felt that she was doing the news editing herself. Once she even sent a copy of the marked-up diary to Robertson and Bonamour to show them what she was dealing with.

As an editor-in-chief, you have to trust your reporters and copy editors. By the time the material comes to your desk, you have to believe that the checking and verification have been done, that it has passed all the screenings. She couldn't do it herself with every story, but she didn't have people she could rely on to do it. She lived in constant fear of things going horribly wrong.

They'd already had two clangers – stories with amateurish errors that were deeply embarrassing and for which they'd had to publish retractions and apologies, what they called 'grovels'. They'd reported that cricket hero Graeme Smith had advised his wife of his plan to divorce her in an SMS, that he'd lied to her and that he'd a 'secret divorce plan'. It wasn't true. Smith took the paper to the Press Council, which ordered them to retract and apologise.

They were still hurting from that when, a week later, they reported that a cousin of comedian Trevor Noah had been murdered. The young reporter described the funeral. Turned out he'd been to the wrong one.

The Noahs had never heard of the deceased. Noah tweeted, 'Thanks to some crafty journalism, my family and I have spent the whole day trying to find out if one of us has died. Awkward'. Noah had more Twitter followers than the *Sunday Times* had paper sales, so that hurt.

She lived in terror of more errors like this. It burnt you, having to retract a story that everyone was talking about. Your pride was dented and newsroom morale suffered. You were the butt of social-media jokes. 'You have to scrape yourself off the floor and go back the next week to start again,' she said. And live in terror that it could happen again at any time.

*

This is what she was thinking about as she sat in her car in the garage. She sat there for about fifteen minutes before she could open the door, walk across the concrete, and get into the lift.

A tale of four reports

In the six months between June 2014 and February 2015, four reports into SARS were commissioned, all of them by respectable legal and accountancy professionals. These reports – or versions of them – were cited by the *Sunday Times* to back their stories.

First, SARS commissioned attorney Moeti Kanyane to establish the facts around the Walter-Van Loggerenberg relationship. Kanyane's report raised concerns about Van Loggerenberg's potential conflicts of interest, but cast serious doubt on Walter: 'We are unable to conclude that the evidentiary material presented by Ms Walter in support of the allegations is credible … they should not be a basis upon which to grant a decision.'

The *Sunday Times* was leaked two different copies of this report, one signed, one unsigned, within 24 hours of its completion. The unsigned one was missing a paragraph that said that Kanyane hadn't spoken to Johann van Loggerenberg for more than a few minutes, but that it didn't matter as he'd made no adverse finding against the tax man. Knowing that Kanyane hadn't heard Van Loggerenberg's evidence nor put allegations to him would have rung an alarm bell if the *Sunday Times* reporters had known it.

When the reporters phoned Van Loggerenberg just hours before going to print to say they had the report, he didn't believe them, as he was still preparing his own submission for the report. They didn't report this, though it seems more than a little pertinent that a key player hadn't yet made his submission when the report was leaked. Nor did they report Kanyane's doubts about Walter's credibility, or that Walter had declined to give an affidavit in support of her wild claims.

As the controversy continued, in September 2014 SARS appointed independent senior counsel Muzi Sikhakhane, with two other advocates, to inquire further. Sikhakhane's brief was to look into the issues raised by Kanyane about the Walter-Van Loggerenberg relationship. While he was doing that, Tom Moyane arrived as the new SARS commissioner and the 'rogue unit' reports began to appear in the media.

Sikhakhane's conduct became bizarre, to say the least: he unilaterally expanded his mandate to look into the 'rogue unit'. He never, though, told key SARS people that he was doing this, so they weren't able to present evidence or answer allegations in this regard.

In December of that year Sikhakhane's report was leaked to the *Sunday Times*. He found that Van Loggerenberg's HRIU had been established unlawfully and that there was 'prima facie evidence that the unit may have abused its power and resources by engaging in activities that reside in the other agencies of government and which it had no lawful authority to perform'. This may have included 'rogue behaviour that had the potential to damage the reputation of SARS' and created 'the real possibility of undermining the work of those agencies tasked with the investigation of organised crime and the collection of intelligence'. This included printing fake ID cards, using false names, bugging, tracing vehicles, and conducting surveillance of individuals. Van Loggerenberg had 'no appreciation of the domain of ethics and standards by which senior management must conduct themselves', and his 'failure to see conflicts of interest in his conduct demonstrates that he should remain in positions in which he must be an operator rather than a senior manager'. His interaction with the media was improper, said Sikhakhane, and had the potential to bring SARS into disrepute. He had shown 'poor judgement' in his handling of his relationship with Walter.

Sikhakhane concluded that SARS should charge Van Loggerenberg with leaking information to Walter and to the media, bringing SARS into disrepute, and a breach of the SARS code of conduct. (It didn't add to Sikhakhane's credibility that he quoted the wrong section of the law in doing so.) The unit, he said, should be disbanded and a full judicial inquiry held into its activities.

SARS's acting commissioner, Ivan Pillay, who'd briefed Sikhakhane, wrote a 26-page detailed response, shredding the report. Sikhakhane hadn't met his brief on the key issue, and had unilaterally extended his mandate, causing 'procedural and substantive problems'. Pillay identified numerous errors of fact and interpretation in the report. He pointed out that there were simple explanations for some of the accusations – such as the fake identification cards and bugging equipment – but since these allegations had never been put to those responsible, they hadn't had the opportunity to present these explanations. The report reached conclusions with little reference to the evidence or its validity.

The issue of whether the unit was legal was fundamental, but Sikhakhane had never spelt out how he'd come to the conclusion that it was not. SARS had taken legal advice when they set it up, had the necessary permission from the then Finance Minister, Trevor Manuel, and had enacted a host of policies, rules and regulations to prevent the unit breaking the law – so it wasn't as if the tax authority had done it without consideration for the law. Manuel and SARS Commissioner Pravin Gordhan were both consistently adamant that it was above board, and they had legal opinions to confirm this.

SARS officials were obligated to do covert investigation into tax evasion; as Pillay pointed out, it was ludicrous to suggest that SARS should not have a covert unit collecting intelligence in pursuit of its tax-collection mandate. The legislation says that only the SSA may do covert investigations into issues of national security, so the key question was whether SARS was going beyond its tax-collection mandate and encroaching on issues of national security. Nowhere did Sikhakhane cite a case where SARS had encroached on the terrain of national security. In fact, he didn't deal with these debates, offering only that there 'may have been' rogue activity and there was the 'possibility' of certain improper actions.

In August 2019 I wrote to Muzi Sikhakhane to try and clarify these issues. His response was truly extraordinary: he didn't just decline to discuss it with me, or restate his position, but launched a sweeping attack on all journalists who'd covered the story, and me personally, laced with a bewildering bitterness:

> First, I am not at liberty to give interviews or details regarding a matter in which I was briefed. Second, an interview with me would serve no purpose as you and many journalists have long commented on my report and, in fact, have a particular position on the issue and narrative you wish to perpetuate.
>
> I regard your request as both late and *mala fide,* and an attempt to legitimise your pre-existing media views on the issue. You and others are at liberty to believe and perpetuate narratives you find convenient for race, class or other purposes. With the greatest of respect, I do not believe any of you are pursuing truth in this matter. You have commented on this matter in the past five years since my report was published and it would serve no purpose to interview me now. For consistency, I suggest you put in your book the views you have already expressed in this regard.

I had never previously commented or written about his report. Sikhakhane was showing a propensity to jump to conclusions based on something other than hard evidence.

*

There were two more reports. The Kroon Report was commissioned in February 2015 by the Minister of Finance to tell him what to do about the Sikhakhane report, essentially in a bid to put a cap on an issue that was plaguing the Ministry and which they wanted to bury. Judge Frank Kroon hired as one of his team Rudolf Mastenbroek, who'd become an advocate after being pushed out of SARS. Mastenbroek nursed a deep resentment towards Pillay and Van Loggerenberg, and had been linked to key *Sunday Times* people, notably his ex-wife, editor Phylicia Oppelt. It's hard to think of a person more conflicted than this to work on what was supposed to be an independent report.

This alone would undermine the standing of Kroon's report, but it wasn't the reason the judge later retracted it. He didn't hear evidence, nor test what Sikhakhane had so wildly concluded – he took Sikhakhane's reports as factual and assumed them to be truthful. By 2019 Kroon had come to realise that he couldn't rely on Sikhakhane's reports, and apologised for his findings.

When the new SARS Commissioner, Tom Moyane, was appointed, he didn't take up Sikhakane's recommendation for a judicial inquiry, but asked consultancy firm KPMG Forensic South Africa to review the evidence and give him guidance on what to do. Since KPMG later retracted its report's conclusions and recommendations and apologised for it, fired nine of its top executives, returned the R23 million they'd been paid for the work, and undertook to donate R40 million to good causes by way of self-inflicted penance, it isn't worth delving into the details of what the consultancy concluded, though the 139-page report – an amateurish, badly drafted, error-ridden, often incomprehensible, self-contradictory mish-mash that didn't pass the most cursory assessment – largely mirrored its predecessors.

KPMG claimed that a team of about thirty individuals had spent months on the documentary review (there were no interviews and no investigation), reviewing 850 000 emails and 1,36 million documents – figures so unlikely, and so clearly designed to justify the outrageous R23-million fee, that they're hard to believe. Let's do the numbers: if all thirty people had read the emails for eight hours a day, spending just one minute on each email, it would have taken the team 58 working days just to do this; and one minute on each of the other documents would have taken them 94 working days. And that's just the speed-reading, not allowing for any analysis.

Nowhere in the report could KPMG confirm the *Sunday Time*'s core allegation that Zuma had been bugged, or that the unit had broken into homes, had millions in secret funding or operated a brothel.

If that weren't enough, the statement issued in January 2016 by SARS's Ivan Pillay, Pete Richer, Adrian Lackay and Yolisa Pikie might have alerted journalists to the fact that what was contained in KPMG's report should be taken with a grain of salt:

> The public must know that none us have ever been engaged by KPMG during the process leading up to the alleged report. We were not afforded any opportunity to make representations on the allegations against us. Conducting investigations and making findings without giving affected parties a right of reply to allegations against them is procedurally flawed and untenable in law. Thus we must caution anyone who may want to attach any value to a report that is the result of a legally questionable document and process. Until such time as we have been afforded a right to reply to its content, it is of no consequence.

There was also a mysterious clause in the report, saying it couldn't be used 'for the resolution or disposition of any disputes or controversies thereto and may not be disclosed, quoted or referenced, in whole or in part'. In other words, it couldn't be used for the purposes for which it was commissioned!

So when the *Sunday Times* trumpeted on 4 October 2015 that the 'KPMG report confirms our story' and called for a probe into Pravin Gordhan, they were not on solid ground. The story was accompanied by a garish graphic headed 'Exposed: SARS's rogue unit', with a picture of a shady 1950s-looking spy with his hat pulled low over his eyes.

The paper devoted its most prominent news spaces, pages one

and three, and an editorial to the report, using it as vindication. It revealed, they said, 'that SARS blew more than R106m in taxpayers' money running "a covert and rogue intelligence unit" that spied on South Africans, and then repeatedly lied about its existence to the public'. The unit operated outside the normal controls, protocols and oversight structures of SARS, agents of the unit were known as 'ghost employees', they unlawfully intercepted taxpayers' communications, and unlawfully monitored conversations at the NPA offices.

The article purported to show an organogram of the rogue unit, but mysteriously included Belinda Walter, Judge Kroon and – at the bottom of the pile – former SARS Commissioner Oupa Magashula and the current one, Tom Moyane. At the top was the target, former commissioner and Minister of Finance at the time, Pravin Gordhan.

This was a low point in the *Sunday Times's* reporting, lacking even the most basic attempt to make sense, let alone match reality. It was reckless and crude, undercutting the credibility of SARS and inevitably having the long-term effect of weakening tax compliance and undermining the economy.

The newspaper had gone in search of back-up for its story and found it, and had overlooked how dubious some of the evidence was – a textbook case of confirmation bias. A hint of how it came to this was evident in the careful, passive-voice phrasing of the source: the KPMG report had been 'seen by *Sunday Times* reporters', which likely meant that one reporter had been shown the report, or parts of it, but they did not have it in hand and had not read it in full. They also never told the reader that it was only a draft report, not a final one.

It turned out to be worse than this. In December 2015, the newspaper told the press ombudsman that only eight copies of the report had been produced, each watermarked with the name of the recipient. Piet Rampedi had been shown one, but couldn't make a copy of it, as the watermark would have identified his source. So the source 'produced an executive summary which he or she gave to Rampedi', and 'the journalist checked the summary against the report to confirm its accuracy'.

He also took a photo of the document. 'We submit that … the summary is accurate,' the newspaper said. Accurate it may have been, but the newspaper was staking its credibility on a report it didn't have in hand, and therefore couldn't critically assess.

An executive summary, which should list the main features and key points of a complete report, is easy to distort simply by being selective about what's included. For example, they could have plucked out this quote from Sikhakhane: 'The covert unit operated outside of the traditional SARS environment, printed fake SARS cards, bugged, traced vehicles, conducted surveillance of individuals and disguised themselves as drivers to certain political figures.'

Or this one, saying the opposite: 'It is generally accepted that the unit never progressed to conduct anything more than the limited intelligence it did when it started. This limited intelligence work entailed desk-top research and physical surveillance and tracking (following), with the use of borrowed vehicle tracking devices in two or three cases in its entire lifespan.'

These two quotes appeared to contradict each other, and raised questions about the quality of the KPMG report.

And whose name was on Rampedi's copy? Who was the origin of the abbreviated version he received? It was Tom Moyane himself. That was confirmed for me by someone who saw Rampedi's photo of it, with the watermark. It indicated that Zuma's appointee as the new SARS Commissioner, who was systematically attacking the 'rogue unit' and using the *Sunday Times* reporting to dismantle SARS's investigative capability, was working hand in glove with members of the *Sunday Times* investigations unit.

In the same edition of the *Sunday Times*, the investigations unit slipped into what appeared to be a recasting of the 'brothel' story. They quoted Fanie Bothma, the former SARS employee accused of running the brothel, saying there had been no such thing: there had only been a party at an informant's house with a couple of prostitutes brought in. The story was presented as an update, not a retraction or apology, though the paper was acknowledging that its previous report had not been accurate. And it didn't mention Johann van Loggerenberg, although the original brothel report had linked it to him.

Bolstered by the KPMG report, that week's editorial lashed out at the newspaper's critics with a smugness that was extreme even for the *Sunday Times*. SARS officials and media outlets that were critical of the newspaper were dismissed in the editorial as 'a convenient club of malcontents aggrieved by real or imagined slights or hurts … [who] insisted that an alternative narrative existed to the one we published'. These malcontents 'cast aspersions on the integrity of this newspaper and its reporters. We were accused of being cynically manipulated as part of a plot that sought to bring down good men and women who had sacrificed their lives for the South African struggle'. The *Sunday Times's* reporting had now been unequivocally corroborated, according to the editorial.

This went to the core of the *Sunday Times's* attitude. There was something deeply un-journalistic about dismissing the notion that there could be more than one narrative.

Perhaps the most egregious of the *Sunday Times's* claims was that the unit was secretive and SARS had denied its existence – in spite of the fact that Pillay and Van Loggerenberg had at various times going back to 2010 briefed the media, including the *Sunday Times,* on the unit and its work. Such briefings were what you would want from a responsible government agency that had to be open but also cautious about sensitive operations. But the very editors and journalists they had briefed at the *Sunday Times* persistently repeated the charge that SARS had been secretive about it.

The paper also continued to pay no more than lip service to the right of reply. Van Loggerenberg was given less than five hours to respond to a series of seven questions that dealt with issues going back to 2001, and wasn't shown the KPMG report he was being asked to comment on. He answered all the questions, but his answers to only three were used.

Gordhan was given three hours and also not shown the report.

It was notable that the net had widened to take in Gordhan, whose picture now featured prominently. Gordhan was at the time at war with Tom Moyane since he'd tried to block Moyane's radical restructuring of SARS. And he was at war with President Jacob Zuma, as he and the Treasury were attempting to block many of Zuma's wilder attempts to take control of state and parastatal institutions.

The pattern had been established: when someone got in the way of Zuma and his allies, such as Moyane, mud was thrown at them, no matter how spurious, and the *Sunday Times* was happy to report it.

The first mention of Gordhan in this way was in a letter from Moyane's lawyers to KPMG, published by journalist Marianne Thamm in the *Daily Maverick*, making recommendations for KPMG's findings. KPMG reproduced these recommendations precisely in its report – including the push to target Gordhan.

*

The earlier *Sunday Times* stories had cleared the way for President Zuma to appoint Tom Moyane – who had no experience in tax – as SARS Commissioner in September 2014, in the midst of the 'rogue unit' row, and provided him with the excuses he needed to tackle the institution.

Within two weeks of his arrival, the 'brothel' story had appeared in the *Sunday Times*, and Moyane used it the very next day as a reason to unilaterally disband his entire executive committee, though there was no evidence that any of them were implicated or even knew about it (or, of course, that the brothel actually existed).

The *later* stories wreaked havoc at SARS. Johann van Loggerenberg was suspended and the work of the HRIU was derailed. The tax authority's spate of successes in chasing down high-profile tax criminals ground to a halt as key people fought for their jobs and reputations.

The big tax dodgers, politicians and gangsters alike, must have been celebrating.

Moyane moved swiftly to drive out other senior staff. On 5 December 2014, Ivan Pillay and Peter Richer were suspended. This was reversed by the Labour Court, but they were suspended again in January 2015, and later resigned.

Adrian Lackay was blocked from speaking on SARS's behalf, and Moyane took over this role himself.

Fifty-five senior officials left in the nineteen months after Moyane's appointment.

When Van Loggerenberg resigned in early 2015, one of Moyane's conditions – oddly – of accepting his resignation was that the tax investigator withdraw all the cases he had before the Press Council against the *Sunday Times*. And within 24 hours, Van Loggerenberg's resignation letter was in the hands of Piet Rampedi at the newspaper. Moyane and Rampedi were working hand-in-hand, it seemed.

Within a month after his arrival, Moyane had appointed consultant Bain & Co to review the SARS operating model. After a perfunctory diagnostic analysis, and little or no consultation with the operational management, they proposed a radical new operating model and it was immediately implemented. Moyane appointed an entirely new executive, drawing in all but two members from outside the organisation and without any tax-collection experience.

According to Judge Robert Nugent, who in 2018 and 2019 led an inquiry into SARS, Bain had met with Moyane and President Zuma to develop the restructuring plan nine months before Moyane's appointment. It had been the *Sunday Times*'s stories that had enabled them to put it in motion so quickly and so radically. Moyane's disbanding of his executive committee on the basis of a newspaper report shortly after arriving at SARS was 'extraordinary in any rational terms', Nugent said.

Moyane wasted no time in destroying most of the institutional knowledge in SARS and ensuring that few of those who had so successfully built the organisation in the previous two decades remained: he displaced 200 managers from their jobs, 'many of whom ended up in positions that had no content or even job description'. 'Reckless mismanagement', Nugent labelled it, as Moyane 'dismantled the elements of governance one by one'.

SARS had been on a decade-long trajectory of modernisation 'that had earned it accolades domestically and abroad', and Moyane had summarily stopped it, Nugent said. 'What SARS was, and what it has become, is sufficient proof ... He [Moyane] turned a world-class organisation upside down, leaving SARS as it is today: wracked with intrigue, suspicion and distrust and fear of senior management; information technology that is in decay ... space for the illicit trade to flourish; loss of long-serving skills; experienced personnel [finding themselves] in supernumerary positions doing little if anything at all; and revenue collection compromised.'

Nugent's conclusion was brutal: 'The day Mr Moyane took office was a calamity for SARS ... a massive failure of governance and integrity.'

And who benefited from this? Nugent was clear: it was 'delinquent taxpayers' who were rejoicing. 'Measures to counter criminality have been compromised and those who trade illicitly in commodities like tobacco operate with little constraint.'

On the question of the legality of the SARS investigative unit, Nugent was unequivocal: 'I find no reason why the establishment and existence of the unit was indeed unlawful.' And he pointed out that this view had been supported by a senior-counsel opinion given to Moyane himself in 2015. Moyane hid this opinion, and it only surfaced after his suspension years later.

The fallout begins

It was the SARS stories that revealed the cracks within the *Sunday Times* and its sister paper, *Business Day*.

Malcolm Rees had quietly resigned early on, in late 2014, when the stories took a turn that he couldn't live with.

Cape Town-based reporter Pearlie Joubert was less discreet: a formidable investigator and fierce individualist with a tough, hard-headed, in-your-face manner, best known for her relentless pursuit of her targets and a wicked, profanity-laced sense of humour and raucous laugh, keeping silent or toeing a line wasn't her forte. 'Hard to manage' was how her superiors described her – a sobriquet usually taken as a compliment by a journalist.

Joubert's work occasionally overlapped with that of the investigations unit, and editor Phylicia Oppelt tried to get them to work together. 'Phylicia once asked me to fly up and work with them on the Glynnis Breytenbach story,' she told me. Breytenbach, a prominent prosecutor who'd tackled corrupt senior policeman Richard Mdluli, was in the crosshairs of the Zuma team. 'I walked into that office, said there was some shit-hot story about Breytenbach that I was asked to work with them on, [and] Mzi [Wa Afrika] stood up, walked out the room and slammed the door.

'I said, "What the fuck just happened here?" Stephan [Hofstatter] said he didn't know, but he briefed me on the story. I said I would check out the Hermanus story and go and speak to Wim [Trengove, an advocate who represented Breytenbach and whom Joubert knew well].'

The 'Hermanus story' was that Breytenbach had supposedly improperly helped a friend whose son had been arrested for drunken driving in the holiday town of Hermanus in the Western Cape. That was Joubert's style: get straight down to it, confront the story head-on.

The *Sunday Times* and others had received a 'Breytenbach dossier' drawn up for the SSA by Chad Thomas. It contained three allegations against her: that she'd let a large construction company off the hook when they were caught colluding in the tenders to build stadiums for the 2010 World Cup; the 'Hermanus incident'; and, most dramatic of all, that she was a Mossad agent, working for the Israelis. None of these gained any traction. For example, the evidence for the Mossad connection was a lunch Breytenbach had attended in London with businessman and philanthropist Natie Kirsh. With them was an Israeli, a retired agent for the country's internal security, not for Mossad.

Joubert told me in a 2018 interview in Cape Town, 'I checked out the Hermanus story and it was so insignificant. All she'd done was give the boy's parents the phone number of the local prosecutor. That's it.'

At the time, in mid 2014, Joubert was on to another SARS tobacco story. She'd been investigating a Cape Town underworld character, Mark Lifman, and had received a tip-off from a police officer that during a drug bust they'd found Lifman's car and cigarettes from a company owned by another dubious character, Yusuf Kajee. Kajee was in business with Edward Zuma, the president's son, and SARS was investigating the two of them. 'It was real underworld stuff, so juicy, such dubious characters, and all brushing up against the president and his family, which made it so much more interesting.'

Again, Oppelt asked Joubert to fly up to Joburg and work with the investigations unit, which was also on the trail of the SARS tobacco story. Joubert described being allowed into the locked unit room to meet with the team. 'I didn't really want to work in that room. It was a bit of a boys' club, to be frank.' Describing the macho atmosphere in a radio interview in 2018, she said that as a woman 'you often gag on the testosterone in those investigations units in newsrooms'.

And Joubert faced hostility from Wa Afrika. 'It was clear to me that Mzilikazi didn't want me in the team. I don't know if it was a territorial thing, or if it was about race or gender, but it was clear to me that I was intruding. They were so *vas* [tight] with each other.'

One Saturday evening late in 2014, Rob Rose called her and said, 'Bokkie, we're running the SARS story tomorrow.'

Joubert: 'I said you are out of your fucking mind, you are getting it from a spy.'

You're just jealous, Rose told her.

Joubert phoned Oppelt. 'I said, you're publishing the biggest Stratcom story.' Stratcom was the strategic-communications arms of the apartheid police, notorious for planting fake stories in the media; to evoke them was to evoke the worst of the apartheid propaganda legacy. 'There's something very wrong here,' Joubert went on, recounting her phone conversation with Oppelt. 'The purpose of all this is to get rid of Pravin Gordhan. They couldn't do it directly, so they are going via SARS. We are making a mistake here. I want in on the story.'

Instead, said Joubert, she was quickly isolated and kept away from the story. She was left out of the investigations unit's Monday-morning Skype meetings and wasn't invited to the annual seniors' strategy meeting. And Oppelt told her staff to stop sending the weekly diary to Joubert.

'I had a drink with Phylicia one night and I told her that this story was all about big tobacco, and the president's people, and getting rid of Pravin Gordhan. I said we were being used as a wrecking ball against SARS.

'She said that she had evidence that SARS was working illegally, but wouldn't tell me where she'd got it. She said she couldn't have me working against my colleagues.

'I said I wanted to work with them. It wasn't acrimonious. I would join the team.

'The next day was what I called the ambush meeting. Phylicia was there and so was the whole unit, packed into that office. Mzi was running the agenda. He was sitting at the head of the oval table. He said he was very disturbed because he did not trust me. He said I had been criticising them in public. He said I had killed their Breytenbach story.

'Then Piet [Rampedi] said: "You are speaking to Van Loggerenberg behind our backs. We want you to explain your relationship with him." I said, of course I was speaking to him. I was speaking to a lot of people at SARS. That was my job.'

Rampedi's concern about Joubert speaking to Johann van Loggerenberg was telling: the reporter had always had a problem dealing with the tax man. When they had to approach him for comment, Rampedi would let Hofstatter do it. Once, at a press ombudsman hearing at the height of the rogue-unit stories, Van Loggerenberg had seen Rampedi and taken the chance to try and speak to him. Rampedi had turned his back on him and walked away – an extraordinary thing for a journalist to do to someone he's writing about.

Perhaps the story that Van Loggerenberg had been an apartheid police spy had poisoned Rampedi against him. Perhaps Rampedi just never cared to hear anything that contradicted his story. Perhaps Joubert was simply trampling on his toes.

But Joubert wouldn't back off. She tore into the investigations unit's SARS stories. 'You want to run stories about them bugging the president's office, but your sources are all unnamed. I said, where is this brothel? Have you found it? Have you found anyone who worked there? Have you got one of the girls?'

Well, nobody questioned the investigations unit like that. Oppelt intervened and said she wouldn't have Joubert working against the team. Joubert said she didn't understand what they were doing. 'They were on a roll then. There was no stopping them,' she said.

'Then the Anwa Dramat thing happened. I heard, just before Christmas [2014], that he had lost his job. I went to his office on the Saturday morning with my kids. He left us in the office and there was a dismissal letter on his desk. I took it, ran to a printing place across the road, and copied it.'

She filed what was a major breaking story, and news editor Archie

Henderson called her and told her that the investigations unit was also working on the story. 'I said to Archie there was no way that we could have a joint byline. I wanted nothing to do with them. I said you could put my story on the sports pages, and theirs on the news pages, but you couldn't put them together. Oppelt was away and her deputy overruled me. They ran the story as the front-page lead with our joint bylines.

'It was the most bizarre story they ever ran. The intro said Dramat was fired because he had made powerful enemies who wanted certain investigations closed down. Then the rest of the story said he was guilty of renditions.

'I decided then that I had to leave. I had no option. I couldn't breathe any more.

'A few weeks later I received a whole bunch of emails and faxes from a whistleblower at SARS, who said they'd heard they could trust me, and said what was happening in the organisation – all typed in capital letters and with *kak* spelling. So what must I say to this person? That I can't show it to my colleagues because the *Sunday Times* took a different view?'

She submitted her resignation in January 2015. Oppelt asked to discuss it with her but never followed up.

Joubert was in purgatory for many months, jobless until she gave up on journalism and went to work in the non-profit sector.

The *Sunday Times* did a cursory investigation into her allegation that there was a conflict of interest over the role of Oppelt's ex-husband, Mastenbroek, with the company lawyer doing no more than asking Oppelt a few questions and leaving it at that. No report was ever published.

In December 2015 Oppelt launched a malicious public counter-attack on Joubert, suggesting Joubert was unethical, had clashed with her colleagues, and had an improper relationship with Johann van Loggerenberg.

*

Songezo Zibi, the respected editor of *Business Day*, a sister-title of the *Sunday Times*, fell out with his Tiso Blackstar bosses because he didn't fall in line behind the *Sunday Times*. He told the story much later, on 29 September 2018, in a Twitter thread.

A few weeks into the *Sunday Times* story, he tweeted, they had a call at *Business Day* to say 'a senior SARS executive was prepared to speak to us on a deep background basis. Deputy editor Sharon Chetty and I went to meet with him days later.

'The meeting was a detailed background on the various investigating units SARS had historically had, what they investigate, how they work and what had happened recently. I left the meeting confused, and also disappointed there were no exciting leaks.'

Zibi decided that *Business Day* would take the time to do its own investigation, trawling through all the documents and interviewing sources, witnesses and experts. 'I realised we could get caught up in a game of smoke and mirrors and get ourselves into a credibility trap if we ran stories without background-checking the sources themselves.' Zibi vowed, he wrote, to 'not chase a scoop at all costs ... [to] patiently build our story no matter what'.

And, he said, 'we would ask stupid questions'. An example he gave was that the *Sunday Times* had used the SARS unit's purchase of night-vision goggles to show that they were involved in illegal surveillance. 'I asked how they were supposed to see perlemoen poachers they were [legitimately] following at night [without night-vision goggles]? ... Dololo [No] answer.'

Zibi went on, 'I also had conversations with my colleagues at the *Sunday Times* on the story. Where was the brothel in Durban? Why didn't they have a picture of the brothel? How does someone run a cash business in Durban while sitting in Pretoria with a day job? Actually, no answers.'

Since the two newsrooms were on the same floor, with doors opposite each other, things would get tense as it became clear to Zibi that his paper was on a different path from that of its sister paper.

'We did not struggle all that much to find information they [the *Sunday Times*] could not find, for some reason. One simply had to read the same documents they were reading in some instances. It made no sense.'

Zibi said that although he was the editor, not the writer, he personally met more than twenty sources, and read the documents and screen grabs. He didn't believe the Sikhakhane reports, lost his temper when he saw that KMPG had done its report without interviewing the 'culprits', and dismissed Kroon as 'a disgrace that should not be called a judge'.

'Over time it became clear to me that SARS was seen as being politically uncontrollable and this had to stop. People needed to be purged and ... [a] smokescreen ... used to dismantle SARS.'

Business Day published an unusual two-page spread on 2 March 2015. Its coverage was measured, thoughtful and understated, weighing up the complex issues at stake, careful – perhaps too careful – not be seen to attack its *Sunday Times* colleagues. Political writer Natasha Marriam went only so far as to say there were two competing narratives on SARS, and that these were tearing apart 'the most efficient and cleanest institute of state'.

Legal reporter Franny Rabkin dissected what covert work SARS could do within the law, and the evidence of what it did do. She concluded that by relying on the dubious Sikhakhane report, SARS 'may be out on a rather narrow ledge'. She could have said the same of her colleagues across the corridor.

The writers stayed away from the 'brothel' and 'bugging' storylines, but the undertone of doubt was enough to anger the *Sunday Times's* editor and its Times Media boss, Andrew Bonamour.

Zibi said his staff started to get threatening phonecalls after this, and he was followed. When his reporters covered the Press Council hearings into the *Sunday Times* story in December 2015, his boss was furious that they were reporting it straight, and the *Sunday Times* was coming off badly.

In January 2016 Songezo Zibi resigned, suddenly and unexpectedly.

*

In February 2015 *Carte Blanche* presenter Bongani Bingwa interviewed Mike Peega and Belinda Walter. They dressed it up as 'a story that rivals the famous Hollywood spy thrillers' and embellished it with dramatic lighting and lavish James Bond-like recreations.

Carte Blanche is a respected television programme on the satellite station M-Net which has for three decades tackled a range of investigative stories. It has built a reputation for solid reporting – but in this case, *Carte Blanche* produced one of its worst stories ever, far more crude and uncritical than anything the *Sunday Times* did.

They let Peega and Walter make the most outrageous claims without asking for any substantiation and gave these claims credence, calling them 'revelations'. Another of their presenters, Devi Sankaree Govender, tweeted: 'Belinda Walter is one very brave woman who spoke to us without hiding her ID. I take my hat off to her.'

In fact, *Carte Blanche* had been warned. The producer of the piece, Bernadette Maguire, had sounded out investigative reporter Julian Rademeyer, who had written about Peega in his book about the rhino-poaching industry, *Killing for Profit*. 'I suggested that *Carte Blanche* should do their own investigation. I told her my doubts about Peega's reliability as a witness ... She later put me on the phone with the insert's presenter, Bongani Bingwa, and I repeated my concerns to him.' But executive producer George Mazarakis wanted a 'quick hit' on a story they could not ignore because it was appearing week after week in the *Sunday Times*. What they produced, Rademeyer told me, was 'a shocking travesty'.

Van Loggerenberg took *Carte Blanche* to the Broadcasting Complaints Commission in May of that year. Mazarakis waited until just before the hearing to offer Van Loggerenberg a deal: they would withdraw the piece and give him a 45-second right of reply.

Van Loggerenberg accepted and had a brief appearance on the show shortly afterwards. The piece was removed from *Carte Blanche*'s website and all reference to it disappeared. They never apologised or explained. Sankaree put her hat back on and pulled it over her eyes.

Bingwa, though, came back to the matter in 2017, having become a presenter on Radio 702. On the same day as his colleague Eusebius McKaiser tore Hofstatter apart on air, he felt a need to explain himself. 'It sometimes becomes clearer much later what was being done by whom, against whom and for what reason,' he said.

His words stand as an indictment of his and the programme's journalistic standards: 'At the time, a number of those people [Van Loggerenberg and his colleagues] would not speak, and you can only reflect what you are told. You can't reflect on what no one has actually said ... Once a story has broken, we can easily repeat it without always checking for ourselves, that does happen ... that was the story we were told.'

And then he trivialised it, by asking listeners to phone in with stories of when they had been duped. 'Is your mother really actually your sister? Was your husband married to someone else? Give us a call ...'

'Inaccurate, misleading and unfair'

The *Sunday Times* stood firm on their stories, despite growing pressure on every front.

They ignored public pressure, reader pressure, and pressure from their own newsroom colleagues. 'We stand by our stories,' was their mantra, echoing through the news fraternity with increasing hollowness.

In 2016 Mzilikazi Wa Afrika came to speak to my students at the University of the Witwatersrand, and I asked him if he stood by the 'brothel' story. 'Every word,' he said. But three years later you haven't produced the evidence, I said. 'It will come, you'll see,' was his response.

The fact that almost all the other media appeared to accept SARS's version of the story and denounced the *Sunday Times*'s version as 'a spurious and ... untested narrative', as Marianne Thamm of the *Daily Maverick* put it, didn't lead them to a rethink, or even to consider running the counter-narrative. In fact, it seemed to spur them on to dig deeper into the hole they were in.

In March 2015 a critical point for most media came when SARS's Adrian Lackay gave evidence to a parliamentary committee with a gravity and sincerity that struck a chord: he'd come to realise that Moyane had made him issue statements that 'contained false and incorrect information'. Key facts were 'being ignored deliberately, adapted to advance a particular narrative and used as a basis to effectively muzzle, frustrate, victimise and suspend key officials in SARS'.

Certain SARS officials, and media such as the *Sunday Times,* had put forward a narrative that was 'false and contrived'. Allegations such as those of the brothel and spying on the president 'had their origins in a little truth and much fiction'. Anyone who attempted to counter this narrative was 'muzzled, bullied, threatened, suspended and their tenure at SARS made unbearable', Lackay said.

The *Sunday Times* ignored this, reporting not a word of it.

The newspaper faced a string of complaints to the Press Council. SARS employees Ivan Pillay and Johann van Loggerenberg, and Johan Booysen, the fall-guy of the newspaper's Cato Manor 'death squad' pieces, had been slow to turn to the industry-standards body, probably because they were all fighting for their jobs, and their hands were tied by their employment and then severance contracts – but when they were free to do so, they scored crucial moral victories. Over a two-month period in late 2015 and early 2016, press ombudsman Johan Retief repeatedly savaged the *Sunday Times*, becoming progressively more strident in rulings against the paper.

The hapless *Sunday Times* legal editor Susan Smuts was having to prostrate herself before the ombudsman on a regular basis, defending material that was increasingly indefensible, sometimes with the authors not even coming to hearings. Each complaint charged that the *Sunday Times* had not asked the subjects of their stories for their comment or had given them insufficient time to respond, or that they'd been selective in what they'd used of the answers. Sometimes the subjects of the stories weren't told accurately or fully what was being written about them before being expected to respond; or they were asked for comment on reports they hadn't seen, and had to guess what they were responding to.

Taken together, these complaints became not just a critique of the paper's practices, but a comprehensive denunciation of its professionalism.

In December 2015 Retief found that the *Sunday Times* report of 4 October of that year, 'Call to probe Pravin over SARS spy saga', a front-page splash that had pointed a finger at Gordhan's role in authorising the SARS 'rogue unit', had been inaccurate, misleading and unfair; that the paper's editorial comments had not been based on fact and therefore were not fair comment; and that reporters had failed to allow Gordhan to respond appropriately. The *Sunday Times* was ordered to retract that report and editorial comment, and apologise to Gordhan on the front page, above the fold – the most prominent position in the newspaper.

At the same time, the ombudsman considered a complaint from Ivan Pillay. Again, Retief found the *Sunday Times's* reporting to be inaccurate, misleading and unfair, and the editorial comment not based on fact. He let the paper off the hook for giving Pillay only a few hours to respond, because the tax man had, in fact, managed to respond in that time. But, the ombudsman said, the *Sunday Times* had erred in not showing Pillay the KPMG report summary he was asked to comment on.

Of course the reporters hadn't shown Pillay the report: it would have revealed that they were relying on a third-party summary.

Piet Rampedi was the subject of specific criticism for saying he'd seen the report. There were only two options to describe Rampedi's reporting, the ombudsman said: 'Either he was misled by his source, or he deliberately misled the public, his newspaper as well as this office.'

Again, the paper was told to retract and apologise on page one, above the fold.

Just a month later, in January 2016, Retief found that the paper's treatment of Johann van Loggerenberg was – you guessed it – inaccurate, misleading and unfair, and its editorial comment not based on fact. Because Van Loggerenberg had rushed to reply to the paper's questions in the limited time they'd given him, the ombudsman didn't uphold his complaint about how little time he'd been given, but the newspaper was reprimanded for not allowing him to see the document they were asking him to comment on.

For the third time the *Sunday Times* was told to retract and apologise on page one, above the fold. This key position, designed to cause maximum discomfort to the journalist responsible for the story, was becoming a regular focus of humiliation and embarrassment.

'Damning findings,' Marianne Thamm wrote in the *Daily Maverick*, 'tarnished the reputation of the country's biggest-selling newspaper which, it appears, was drawn into an elaborate cloak-and-dagger campaign to discredit SARS.'

The paper did win one, secondary case: in January 2016 Johan Retief dismissed Pearlie Joubert's complaint that the paper hadn't treated her fairly in its reporting of her departure.

*

In early 2015 Mike Robertson's share options matured, enabling him to afford to leave gracefully after 29 years at the company. But clouds had been gathering around him for some time, and he was smart enough to pre-empt them.

Two key things in the company that Robertson had been responsible for were coming back to haunt the operation. The first was his consistent backing of Phylicia Oppelt, which had enabled her to avoid confronting the problematic stories for years. Robertson had always been ruthless in dealing with problems, but he'd seemed unable to do it in this case. In the face of the paper's fast-eroding credibility, Robertson was too close to Oppelt to do what had to be done.

The second was *The Times* daily edition, which he had pioneered. This spunky new daily, launched in 2012, was at first given away for free to *Sunday Times* subscribers – perhaps the most costly subscription promotion ever. The costs, many of which Robertson had hidden in the *Sunday Times* figures, became unsustainable, and an attempt to turn *The Times* into a paid newspaper never got off the ground. Robertson's baby was carving holes in the balance sheet.

Robertson's departure would leave Oppelt immediately vulnerable. On 28 April 2015, before Robertson had even left the building, CEO Andrew Bonamour reassured the editor that her position was safe, emailing her at 3.30am while on a trip to Ghana: 'I am getting a lot of calls saying that Mike resigned as I asked him to fire you and he refused and resigned instead. This is totally untrue. I wanted you to know this. I think you are doing a great job and you will continue to be ST editor with no interference from me. I will support you 100%.'

Oppelt must have had to think for a while why her boss was sitting up in the middle of the night in a foreign city and feeling the need to give her immediate unsolicited reassurance that her job was safe. She didn't reply until late the next morning, when she sent a terse one-liner: 'Thanks, Andrew. I would be interested to know where this comes from.'

'Me too,' Bonamour responded, and then decided to spell out all he knew. 'You must hear these rumours,' he said.

1. I fired Mike because he refused to fire you over Tollmans [the owners of Thompsons Tours, who had pulled out R25-million-worth of advertising].
2. I fired Mike as Tiso guys [major shareholders] were unhappy at strat session due to the fact that it was purely focused on print.
3. I fired Mike due to The Times and his protection of it.
4. I intend to asset strip TMG [Times Media group].

Then he pointed a finger at Oppelt's own restless staff: '[It's] all nonsense and definitely coming from internal,' he wrote.

His email was a neat summary of what kept media owners up at night: advertisers unhappy with editorial treatment; how to balance print and digital; managers who were throwing money at unhappy print ventures and were too powerful to stop; and the prospect of asset stripping.

The speculation came from journalist Alec Hogg, who had reported that day on his BizNews website that he'd had a phone conversation with Bonamour, who'd dismissed the rumours that Robertson had been pushed out either for his 'print first' strategy, or for his backing of Oppelt.

Bonamour must have been worried about Hogg's reporting and

decided to pre-empt it. In his response to Hogg, he publicly committed to Oppelt: 'Let's talk in six months' time. She [Oppelt] will still be there.'

A few days later, on 6 May, Oppelt wrote to Bonamour to express concern about what had been said at a meeting with her top team: 'Had meeting with senior managers today about rumours and concerns about bias and being played. Good points raised until it was said that Mike was fired because he refused to fire me. Said with great authority.'

It seemed her colleagues were worried about the increasing allegations that the *Sunday Times* was being played and showing bias. They knew that Robertson had been her backer.

Again, Bonamour gave her reassurances: 'If Mike was fired cause he wouldn't fire you he would have a great claim against TMG. Besides, now with him out the way I could arguably do that. Let's see. You have my guarantee.' A close reading, though, with a touch of paranoia, might make this sound like a thinly disguised threat: 'I can now fire you,' he could be saying.

Oppelt didn't let it go: 'You could persuade the board that I'm a liability and they should fire me. You could do that.'

'I could but I didn't,' Bonamour came back quickly. 'I would come to you first (which I did on this issue). Please ask Mike [who by this stage had left] directly to put your mind at rest.'

In August that year, Oppelt asked Bonamour how he was feeling about the paper. Again, he reassured her: 'I must say over the last few weeks I think it's been great. You gone back with your gut [sic] instead of worrying about single copy sales.' This latter point might have been a dig at Robertson's weekly meetings, which had focused on the previous week's sales.

By September there was a nervous tone in an Oppelt's note to Bonamour: 'Just wanted to say that I understand the challenges and I was not dismissing those when I sent the first email. I appreciate the investment in our journalists and our work. I was not trying to be obstructive or difficult.'

In his response to that email, Bonamour told Oppelt of his disagreements with her *Business Day* counterpart, Songezo Zibi, who'd recently run his SARS stories that did not accept the *Sunday Times*'s view. Bonamour hinted at action against Zibi and made a bold promise to Oppelt: 'This afternoon I had a very annoying conversation with Songezo. You doing a great job [sic]. I will fix the other areas. I want to have the best products so that we can pay ... everyone a lot of money. I am going to put you on our new long-term incentive [scheme] at Tiso Blackstar level.'

Putting her into this incentive scheme was a clear signal that he saw her position as long term – either he was dissembling, or he was out of touch with what was going on in his newspapers. At no stage did he raise the furious controversy over the SARS stories, or the press ombudsman's devastating rulings.

In the midst of this, in October 2015, Johann van Loggerenberg wrote a 29-page letter, with dozens of pages of annexures, to the Tiso Blackstar board, setting out his grievances. He said his many attempts 'at seeking recourse in a civilised manner with the *Sunday Times* [had] failed' and he asked them to investigate matters at the newspaper and the activities of Oppelt and the investigative team. This weighty tome could not easily be ignored or dismissed.

A month later, on 24 November 2015 – exactly six months after Robertson had left and Bonamour had told a journalist that Oppelt would still be there in six months' time – Phylicia Oppelt was fired.

The clean-up

In Bongani Siqoko's second week as the new *Sunday Times* editor, he had to face the ghosts of the SARS story.

Siqoko had arrived on 11 January 2016 as an outsider, one of the very few *Sunday Times* editors who hadn't come through the ranks of its political team. He came from a small, local but respected newspaper, the *Daily Dispatch*, based in East London. Suddenly, he was in one of the most powerful journalism seats in the country, and the seat was hot.

Andy Gill, who'd succeeded Mike Robertson as group managing director, gave Siqoko a firm mandate: 'Clean up this place.'

Taking over the *Sunday Times* at any time would've been a formidable challenge, and now the paper was facing one of its most difficult periods since its launch 111 years before. It wasn't doing well, the economic climate and advertising decline were hitting it hard, it had just had a series of devastating Press Council rulings against it, and its reporters were being widely criticised and increasingly denigrated by the community of journalists.

Siqoko had his hands full. 'The atmosphere here was hostile, there were threats of suing, so I wanted to deal with it once and for all, I wanted to start with a clean slate,' he told me in 2018.

He knew that something was wrong with the SARS story, and he would have to deal with it and the embarrassing Press Council findings, but he'd barely settled in when Piet Rampedi came with the latest leak from tax boss Tom Moyane's office. Moyane, locked in a power battle with Pravin Gordhan over his restructuring of SARS, had commissioned a legal opinion to prevent the Finance Minister from interfering in SARS, and a copy had gone straight to Rampedi.

Siqoko had to run it, as the fight between the two men was big news, but he told me he'd tried not to revive the controversy over the 'rogue unit' story, and instructed Rampedi to steer clear of it.

'Tax boss moves to block Pravin', was the screaming headline on 24 January. Rampedi did manage to get in, low down in the story, his favourable view of the tax commissioner: 'Moyane was appointed in 2014 to clean up the mess at SARS amid ongoing probes into the rogue unit.'

It was slipped in as fact, but was, of course, a highly contested view. By this stage many people and other publications were reporting that Moyane had been brought in to stop the unit's investigations into those close to the president and his restructuring had been a politically motivated purge, not a clean-up. But the *Sunday Times* stood with Moyane, reflecting his perspective. They'd dropped the quote marks around the term 'rogue unit', as if its existence and role were uncontested.

The story mentioned Van Loggerenberg only as one of those officials 'close to Gordhan ... [who had resigned] after the rogue unit was uncovered' and one of those who had issued a statement the previous day denouncing the KPMG report. Van Loggerenberg emailed immediately to complain that he hadn't been contacted about the story – not that he was surprised, he said, as he'd tried many times to meet the previous *Sunday Times* editor.

Siqoko agreed to meet. In his reply email, he asked what Van Loggerenberg wanted, 'and the answer was the retraction of the entire story. I said I was willing to listen, but doubt I'm going to retract anything. I will investigate.'

When Rampedi heard his editor was talking to Van Loggerenberg, he resigned. 'He wasn't even interested in what we talked about,' Siqoko said.

In Rampedi's 2 000-word letter of resignation, he said he was leaving the newspaper with immediate effect because of the 'unethical' decision to enter into an 'underhanded deal' with the SARS officials he, Rampedi, had been investigating. The deal was cut, he charged, 'without my consent and behind my back' and it was 'a self-serving and unethical attempt to sacrifice me for commercial and political expediency'.

He was being isolated in his work, he said. Sources were responding 'derogatorily to me when I contact them for comment' and 'some of my own colleagues are now pleading discomfort to share a byline with me … claiming their sources had threatened to abandon them for continuing working closely with me'. It was 'untenable' to be part of the newsroom any longer.

Rampedi was very concerned that media should tell all versions of a story, and not stick with one narrative, he claimed. 'I am of the view that the *Sunday Times* or any media for that matter must avoid being used as a platform for one narrative … all versions must be told.'

This was an unexpected complaint about a newspaper that had doggedly stuck with a single narrative, and ignored all competing versions, and more so from a reporter who'd refused to speak to some of the people he was reporting on. But then he made clear what narrative he didn't want: 'I think the narrative being pursued is a racist one seeking to discredit all those who are African in the dispute …'

And he said it again: 'The *Sunday Times* has joined the well-orchestrated media chorus that has abandoned its journalistic ethics in pursuing the narrative that only those who are African are capable of acting illegally, irregularly or in a corrupt manner and those who are Indians and whites aren't, and must be protected at all costs.'

And again: 'I think the *Sunday Times* must desist from entertaining a narrative that in the SARS saga only those who are African did wrong, regardless of the facts to the contrary.'

Since the narrative the paper had carried was one that tore down mostly whites and Indians, this was a strange concern. But then, Rampedi's letter didn't engage with the issues of the stories or their veracity at all. There was no acknowledgment of any errors made, and the Press Council rulings were dismissed out of hand. What emerged was his motivation for the whole story: a racial Africanism that viewed Zuma, Moyane and their allies as those who brought transformation and promised radical economic change, and who were prepared to confront whites and Indians who were seen to block it. He was oblivious to the damage Moyane had wrought on the country's tax institution and its capacity to fight serious crime, or the fact that men like Ivan Pillay and Pete Richer had substantial progressive and struggle credentials.

*

Siqoko had a series of meetings with Van Loggerenberg. He took group media managing director Moshoeshoe Monare and political editor S'thembiso Msomi with him, and Van Loggerenberg brought his former colleagues Ivan Pillay and Adrian Lackay. Lackay was, as always, friendly and relaxed; Pillay said hardly anything.

The meetings were 'very long and very difficult', Siqoko said. 'You know Van Loggerenberg: something he should say in three paragraphs, he sends you twenty pages.'

Van Loggerenberg relayed his long string of grievances, accumulated over the years. He'd tried to meet the reporting team, but they'd said no. He'd tried to meet the editor, but she'd demurred. He'd tried to engage with Rampedi, but he wouldn't talk. He and others tried to show documents to journalists to tell their side of the story, but the *Sunday Times* wasn't interested. Almost every week the reporters would come to them late on a Friday with a whole string of allegations, and not give them time to respond properly. It wasn't fair treatment.

Siqoko was very different from his predecessor. A gentle, approachable person, remarkably frank and trusting, he sat in his modest office at the edge of what was now a sprawling single newsroom, bringing together all the staff from all the group publications. This giant room was overlooked by the offices and boardrooms of the bosses, who sat on a mezzanine with glass windows, gazing down from the quiet of their solitary offices on the buzz below.

Siqoko asked Susan Smuts to give him copies of everything they'd written about the SARS 'rogue unit', the Cato Manor 'death squad' and the Zimbabwe 'renditions', and he looked at these in a meeting with Hofstatter and Wa Afrika. Rampedi had already left.

Given that this was years after the first story had appeared, you'd think that the reporters would've had more than enough time to gather their evidence and get their story straight. But they couldn't back up some of their claims, and wouldn't answer some questions. 'These guys would not admit to anything,' Siqoko said.

The story that convinced Siqoko that he had a problem was the one about the brothel.

> I said I want to be able to defend you, so tell me where this brothel was. In Durban, they said. I said where in Durban, one said Durban North and the other said it was behind a certain hill, so they argued. They didn't know where it was. They said the brothel was mentioned in a document. But even that document does not say it. It says the guys had arrived at this house that belonged to the unit and there had been a party, and there were women, and it felt like a brothel. So I asked, how did they pay the women? Did we even go to this place?
>
> They did not agree when I said we should apologise. They felt their stories were solid, and they had done a thorough investigation.
>
> There were also issues of fairness and balance. The culture here was to only start making calls to people they were writing about [on] Friday. They were scared of leaks, and there were some of these. My argument was that we are not fair to the people we are writing about. Sometimes you have to do this, but sometimes they were working on a story for a while, so there are issues of fairness.

When he questioned the reporters about the Cato Manor story, he couldn't believe how poor their sourcing and proof was. 'I asked them where they got the photos and they couldn't really tell me. They said they got [them] from someone in Crime Intelligence, but they didn't know his full name. They didn't have his phone number, because he always called them. I asked them what he looked like, and they didn't know. They said he always had his face covered. They even argued over who had met him, Rob or Mzi.'

When Siqoko asked about eyewitnesses, they told him they were given two names, but they had only spoken to them through Mary de Haas and didn't have their phone numbers.

Another set of witnesses were a soccer coach and a 14-year-old player who happened to have seen a shoot-out. The coach was Wa Afrika's cousin. Did the editor at the time know that one of Wa Afrika's key sources was his cousin? No, was the answer.

'You can see the pattern,' Siqoko said. 'I even asked for their note-books and was only given a few photostats, so I don't know if they were genuine.'

Siqoko hammered out an agreement with the SARS three, in return for their dropping legal and Press Council actions against the paper. 'I said [to Van Loggerenberg] we can't retract everything. The establish-ment of the [SARS HRIU] was controversial. They said they could have explained it to us, but we refused to hear their side of the story. So we said we were ready to do a deal. We won't retract everything, but we can apologise for what we got wrong.'

The compromise reached was an apology with some front-page presence, and then two pages inside, including pieces by Van Loggeren-berg and Pillay. It appeared in the *Sunday Times* ten weeks after Van Loggerenberg's email to Siqoko, on 3 April 2016. They tried to bury it on page one, putting a mystifying blurb in small type at the bottom of the page: 'SARS: Right of Reply Page 18'. Those who turned to that deep inside page found a piece by Van Loggerenberg, '"Rogue" unit never broke the law and was very effective', and another by Pillay, 'The "rogue unit" narrative was a great disservice to public interest, and made up of lies and distortions'.

In the same issue, Siqoko's editorial, blandly headlined 'Our response', took a while to get to the point. It started with lavish praise for the newspaper's history and the investigations unit's long and 'exemplary' record, and the importance of covering the 'rogue unit' allegations. 'Today,' the new editor finally said, about seventy lines into the story, 'we admit to you that we got some things wrong'. Although he said that the newspaper had stated 'some allegations as fact, and gave incomplete information in some cases', he didn't say what these allegations or cases were. In the 'Zuma bugging' story, they should have said it was allegation not fact; and in the 'brothel' story, again, it should have been reported as an allegation.

Siqoko also conceded that there had been 'more errors repeated in other reports'.

The issue of the SARS story had given the paper 'an opportunity to take a closer look at our news-gathering and production processes. We have found some serious gaps,' he said. Efforts were being made to fix these: the news desk was being restructured, quality assurance was being strengthened, and experienced editor Andrew Trench was being made investigations editor to oversee this kind of work.

Siqoko had made some brave moves. He'd turned around the attitude towards the story and finally given space to those the *Sunday Times* had criticised. He'd stood up to the investigations unit and withstood Rampedi's tantrum.

But Trench soon moved on to another role, and a great weight was placed on Susan Smuts to keep an eye on potentially problematic stories – even though she was the one who'd vetted and defended many of the reports that had caused all the trouble.

There certainly was no big clean-out, beyond the dismantling of the investigations unit. There were no dismissals of the culprits, and not even disciplinary action. The promises of reform were vague.

While Siqoko admitted to certain errors and poor practices, he didn't acknowledge that it had been a long and sustained campaign that had done huge damage to an important institution.

It was an important climb-down, but it was incomplete.

*

Bongani Siqoko put aside the 'death squad' and 'renditions' stories for some months, and tried to move on. But the subjects of those stories were stewing.

It was Hofstatter's insouciance that brought them back into the news. He'd kept a low profile for some months, but in September 2018 he held a launch of a book he'd written on the collapse of Eskom, *Licence to Loot*, and his detractors, enraged at his speedy re-emergence as a journalist, took the opportunity to confront him. They came to the launch, at a small boutique bookshop, and stood in the audience with posters that read 'Hofstatter, when did you switch from pro-corruption to anti-corruption?', 'Hofstatter is a Tom Moyane stooge' and 'Hofstatter: State capture crony, profits from helping capture the state, then dishonestly profits from state capture resistance'.

At question time, Pete Richer jumped up: 'I lost my job because of Stephan Hofstatter,' he said, his anger and hurt boiling just beneath the surface. Then he gave a neat encapsulation of how state capture had happened: 'Let me tell you how the story came about. In order to get hold of primary institutions of the state for state capture, you need to get rid of ethical, hardworking, conscientious public servants. In order to do that, you set up scurrilous and unethical journalists, like this one,' he said, pointing at Hofstatter, 'who write stories that create the basis for those public servants to get pushed out.'

He went on:

> And we have many examples of this, all coming from a clique in the *Sunday Times*: Johan Booysen, General Anwa Dramat, General Sibiya, Ivan Pillay, Johann van Loggerenberg, myself and others.
>
> How it works is you create a fiction, a scurrilous story, and on the basis of that the public servant gets suspended, and in most cases pushed out. Your

> reputation is ruined, so there is no chance you can find another niche, you are unemployed, your family is compromised, and then a stooge get puts in place [in that institution].

Anticipating Hofstatter's defence, Richer said,

> Journalists, like everyone else, can make mistakes, we understand that. But multiple mistakes look like a pattern, which went on for years, 35 stories, and led to us getting ousted.
>
> In those three years, not once did the writers of those stories contact me. The stories are so bad that the date on which I was accused of doing some of these things at SARS, I was not even employed there. They turn out to be complete drivel.
>
> There were no basic journalistic ethics about contacting people, no attempt to verify facts. As a result, the anti-smuggling unit is no more, and SARS's ability to go after smugglers has completely broken down. It has been decimated, along with the Hawks, with IPID, the police, one institution after another, through the same completely unethical journalism.

Hofstatter listened with a wry half-smile, and then, caught before an audience, went further than he ever had to admit personal culpability.

> You are absolutely right. There is no way of saying it. We made mistakes with those stories.
>
> I have to say that those stories were produced by quite a large team of journalists, but I was a member of them.
>
> I certainly never saw myself as a journalist wanting to cause harm, or wanting to create stories that would do ill. I have spent many years working on

264

other stories and my purpose was always in my mind to expose wrongdoing and stand up for the down-trodden.

... There were serious errors, and I apologise for those. You are right that the stories were used to attack those institutions and [it] was certainly never my intention for that to happen.

I am very sorry, and very sorry for what it did to your life. I can't take it back, I can't change the fact that I was a member of the team that produced those stories or those stories were used to attack those institutions. All I can do is apologise. And say that it was not intentional and to learn something from it.

And what had he learnt? asked another audience member.

Hofstatter responded:

The biggest mistake was not to insist on them giving us enough time to drill down into the story. In that pressure-cooker situation at that time, the pressure was to produce a scoop and it was a big mistake not to step back and say, is this the right scoop, or will it damage people it was not intended to damage?

When things are massively contested, when history is itself being contested, you have to put things in their proper context, and that was a huge mistake as well.

Also, I have learnt to be transparent with readers about gaps in my knowledge. There were huge gaps in my knowledge, but now I know to be transparent about that.

The disruption of the book launch was widely reported and a video circulated on social media. It highlighted that Hofstatter continued to be employed as a journalist and had not been held accountable.

The next day, radio host Eusebius McKaiser replayed an interview

265

he had a year earlier with journalist Jacques Pauw, who had been sharply critical of the *Sunday Times* journalists in his book, *The President's Keepers*. During that interview, Hofstatter and Wa Afrika had decided to turn up at the studio uninvited to have their say. *Sunday Times* editor Bongani Siqoko phoned Wa Afrika when he was on the way there and told him he would be fired if he spoke out about the story. Wa Afrika turned back, but Hofstatter, who no longer worked at the *Sunday Times*, arrived. What do we do, McKaiser said to Pauw. Invite him in, Pauw said, let's hear what he has to say.

Hofstatter now faced two tough questioners. Asked if the 'rogue unit' story was bogus, he said it wasn't. He cited the Kroon and KPMG reports, standing by them when even their authors had denounced them. When Kroon had said wrongful acts had been committed, 'I can't consider that completely bogus. In the KPMG report, even though the conclusions were withdrawn, the findings in the body of the report found possibly some criminal acts. That's pretty rogue,' he said, grasping at straws.

And did he believe there was a SARS brothel? 'No. But there was an internal memo from an official who said that he was at what he called a brothel. We reported that.'

He would have liked to have done things differently, he conceded: 'More context, more rigour.' But he still thought they had done a decent reporting job. Hofstatter seemed to constantly admit there were problems with the story, then backpedal when asked to take responsibility for them.

When this was replayed in 2018, it was devastating, for both Hofstatter and the *Sunday Times*. The issue was once again thrown wide open.

Played again

In that same month, September 2018, the *Sunday Times* fell into the very trap it said it had learnt to avoid: it ran a page-three story based on leaked documents that said that IPID was working improperly with controversial forensic investigator Paul O'Sullivan.

Reporter Poloko Tau didn't say the story was another element in an ongoing feud in an intra-police war, or that his source was the highly dubious former Acting Commissioner of Police Khomotso Phahlane; and, once again, the newspaper gave only the most token right of reply to both O'Sullivan and his business associate Sarah-Jane Trent.

O'Sullivan was a formidable enemy, a man who liked a good fight. His approach was to escalate the disagreement, boldly and aggressively, into a full-on, bare-knuckle conflict. 'Fake news!' he trumpeted in *Business Report* on 10 October, citing the article as 'evidence that the *Sunday Times* was an integral part of state capture'. He wrote an email to the *Sunday Times* saying he would 'take them down': he would lead an advertising and reader boycott if they didn't retract the story, as well as their Cato Manor 'death squad' and Zimbabwe 'rendition' stories, and apologise to all the people they'd hurt. He sent this email all over the place, including to other media.

O'Sullivan boasted many successes over twenty years of a private fight against corruption, including the jailing of former Commissioner of Police Jackie Selebi. Fearless and flamboyant, he always fired first with threatening emails and colourful text messages, making extravagant use of upper-case hollering, and taunted his targets in public.

'Come on, Mr Tau,' he wrote, 'let's get the last tango in Johannesburg going. Who knows, maybe you will go down in history as having unwittingly helped me consign your morally corrupt publication to the gutter where they truly belong.'

To Phahlane, he was straightforward: 'I told this to Selebi 15 years ago, and I'm telling you now. PREPARE YOURSELF FOR PRISON. I will send you there.'

Like all bullies, the *Sunday Times*, already vulnerable, crumbled when someone stood up to them. Within hours, media managing director Moshoeshoe Monare was on the phone, trying to set up a negotiation between the editor and O'Sullivan, to get him to back off from organising a boycott.

O'Sullivan's response was to up the ante: when they came to see him, he'd covered his boardroom table with what appeared to be boycott-campaign material. He said he'd hired staff to start the following week to phone all the *Sunday Times*'s advertisers.

Two weeks later the *Sunday Times* ran an odd page-three note from the editor, 'A transformed *Sunday Times* that you can trust'. It must have mystified readers. 'Over the past few weeks there have been calls for the *Sunday Times* to publicly account, apologise and testify before judicial commissions about its role and involvement in state capture … The most vocal has been from a group of people who want you, our loyal reader, to doubt whether this newspaper can be trusted.'

Can the paper be trusted? he asked, before answering with 'a resounding yes'. 'You can trust the *Sunday Times*. You can trust me, its editor, and you can trust the team …'

There followed a grandiose set of journalistic clichés about the paper's integrity and mission, and a vague description of steps taken to improve its verification and editorial controls. But still there were no dismissals, and no naming of the sources who had misled them.

O'Sullivan just revved it up some more. Stephan Hofstatter had assisted state capture and was now trying to make money from it through his book. The *Sunday Times* was the enemy of the people. He demanded an unequivocal retraction of all three 'fake news stories', that the newspaper return the awards won for these stories, that it publish a front-page apology, and that it give an undertaking not to write stories fed to its reporters by criminals. If this did not happen, O'Sullivan warned, he would start canvassing all advertisers to abandon the paper. 'I will gladly pay for an articled clerk to sit at [our] offices ... and drive [your] shareholder value into the ground,' he wrote in an email to the *Sunday Times*.

*

Only now, finally, did Bongani Siqoko sit down with the investigations unit and question them fully about the Cato Manor and so-called rendition stories. And when he did, the stories fell apart. It quickly became clear that they had made mistakes, that their sources had been dubious and their verification shaky, that documents had been doctored, and that they had stuck doggedly to their single narrative.

It's worth remembering that many journalists make mistakes because we're over-eager to get a great story. I'm not a journalistic puritan, and have been prepared under the right circumstances to push the ethical boundaries for stories which are of overwhelming public interest. One example, from the early 1990s, was when I was editor at *The Weekly Mail*, which prided itself on tackling stories no one else would cover. The township violence and train shootings of that period were horrific, taking a huge toll, and there were constantly reports of a secret white hand in promoting the violence, probably from the far-right-wingers who didn't want the constitutional negotiations of the time to succeed. A young and courageous journalist called Philippa Garson was one of a team of reporters who worked bravely to expose such activities. Although they persistently published bits and pieces of evidence and first-hand accounts, they were treated with scepticism. We needed the smoking gun.

One day, in 1991, Garson came to tell me about a source who worked in a seedy Hillbrow hotel who'd told her of a group of former policemen – some of them previously convicted for murder – and known right-wingers meeting weekly in secret in the hotel. It looked like they had a hand in the violence. We debated long and hard how to approach this. Garson was convinced the only way was to hire someone to plant a bug in the room, and hear what they were talking about. Her contact could get us access.

There were obvious ethical and practical risks in doing this but there was no other way to get the evidence, and there was no question that there was overwhelming public interest to justify stretching the boundaries of the rules. Those were not normal times.

The private detective who did it for us got caught. He and I were charged and convicted, and received a fine and a suspended sentence, but most of all we were embarrassed. We'd got so close to what could have been the biggest story of the time, but messed it up.

Another case involved Eddie Koch, a brilliant investigative journalist and a pioneer environmental reporter on *The Weekly Mail*. One day he arrived with copies of a cargo manifest that showed that the SAA *Helderberg*, a plane that had mysteriously crashed into the Indian Ocean, killing more than a hundred people, had been carrying dangerous cargo that would explain how it had caught fire and crashed. It was sensational and the documents appeared to be genuine.

We ran the story, but had to hastily retract, as it turned out that the manifest was from a ship, the SS *Helderberg*, and had been doctored. So nobody is immune to making mistakes and anyone can be played. What was important, though, was that we admitted it, apologised and climbed down quickly. It hurt, but we got over it.

Journalists don't have to prove a case, whether beyond reasonable doubt or on a balance of probabilities, and they don't have to say where they got the information. As Ivan Pillay put it in his submission to the Sikhakhane inquiry, 'The media are not bound by the same standards that would apply to our courts or the prosecutorial processes or in the investigating agencies.' They only have to take reasonable steps to verify their story, provide some credible evidence to back it up, and have a public-interest reason to publish. They can present it as an allegation, even one they themselves don't believe. This often shifts the burden of proof to the target of the information, rather than the source.

This allows the media to play its role in ensuring that allegations in the public interest get aired relatively easily and quickly. Where the courts can be slow, expensive and even hostile, and while Parliament puts everything through a political filter, the media can do it quickly and often powerfully and effectively. (That said, journalists don't always have tools such as powers of search and seizure, or access to bank or telephone records, to verify the information given to them.)

This makes the media a powerful weapon of accountability, if handled responsibly. If it's done irresponsibly – in other words, without verifying the credibility of the evidence, critically analysing where it comes from and what it signifies, putting it into context, and offering a genuine and substantive right of reply – then journalists can be used by those who leak the information to them for personal, political or financial advantage. This danger is heightened when a newspaper is under pressure, particularly financial pressure, and journalists are tempted to allow the hunger for a big front-page story to cloud their judgement – and all the more so when they're running to keep up with an unfiltered, unchecked social media, where these stories and allegations can flow freely.

A journalist's instinct is to get information out, not sit on it. Journalists hate knowing something that they can't pass on to their audience. A journalist or editor establishes for themselves what level of proof they require in order to publish, and that level isn't consistent: it's based on an editor's judgement under pressure, with the advice of peers, legal advisers and other experts. It's not based on precedent, or a set of rules and procedures, or subject to appeal, as happens in the courts.

This allows journalists to shine light into dark holes, to get into the open all the secrets that those with power and authority want to hide. This freedom is essential to transparency, without which democracy cannot function. But this isn't always done with care and responsibility.

'Often,' Pillay wrote in his 2014 submission to Sikhakhane, 'the only defence they [the media] raise is public interest, where they fail to distinguish between "public interest" and "what is interesting to the public".' There was, for example, certainly interest in a story of love, tax and spies, but what parts of it served the public interest? What parts of it needed to be in the public eye?

*

In October 2018 Bongani Siqoko negotiated a settlement with Johan Booysen and Ivan Pillay: for a full apology for and retraction of both the 'death squad' and the 'rendition' stories, and space to put their cases, they would drop their legal actions and the matter would be put to rest.

The grand climb-down came the following week, 14 October 2018: 'We got it wrong and for that we apologise,' Siqoko admitted on behalf of his newspaper. He did exactly what O'Sullivan had asked for, to the letter, including promises to return the awards won for these stories. Hofstatter and Wa Afrika were let go, with payouts and non-disclosure agreements to prevent them from talking.

O'Sullivan's response? 'You are not quite out of the woods yet.' He wanted a personal apology and insisted they should name the sources that had misled them.

A series of long and unusual encounters

In January 2019 – long after the *Sunday Times*'s big apology – Johann van Loggerenberg sat around a meeting-room table with Stephan Hofstatter, Rob Rose and Malcolm Rees in the Morningside office of the private-investigation outfit that the one-time tax man now did work for. He had a bunch of files with him, and a notebook with pages and pages of prepared questions. The three journalists had their computers open, and were mining their records to answer him. The atmosphere was friendly but with an underlying nervous tension.

Van Loggerenberg had asked the reporters to meet with him to try and work together to unravel what had happened. Piet Rampedi and Mzilikazi Wa Afrika had no interest in dealing with Van Loggerenberg, but the other three had agreed.

Van Loggerenberg had constantly expressed a sense of disbelief about the events of the time. He told me that he'd thought of the reporters as friends, who could approach and ask him anything, and that they'd done so until the point where it really mattered. When Walter had asked him for a journalist she could trust with her life, he'd recommended Rose. Why had they turned on him?

He recalled how he used to wait at the end of each week for their calls and their latest accusations. 'To this day, on Friday 4pm or Saturday mornings, I get this feeling of dread,' he told me.

I sat in on some of those long and unusual encounters between the former tax investigator and the writers, and watched as Van Loggerenberg took the journalists systematically through every word they had written, parsing every sentence, and asking why they had written it and where they had sourced it from. It was their own, mini, private Truth and Reconciliation Commission. Around the table were four men whose lives had been ripped apart, their careers upended, by what three of them had written about the fourth. Van Loggerenberg wanted them to see and admit to what they'd done wrong.

The meetings were off the record, so I can't reveal the content. But what was said was consistent with what we know of the reporters' attitudes and responses from other pronouncements and discussions.

Van Loggerenberg, as always, cited paragraph and verse, pointing out factual errors, and things he'd told them and they'd ignored. He wanted to understand their motives, their responsibilities and their ethics – not to point fingers, but to try and steer them towards an understanding of their responsibilities and get them to acknowledge their errors and omissions.

In other forums, the reporters had said repeatedly they had not been personally responsible for parts of the story written by others, or that they were ethically prohibited from identifying the sources, or that they couldn't remember where various bits of information came from – a litany of evasions and obfuscations, made possible by the fact that two of the journalists most responsible for the work had stood adamantly by their stories.

Rose had consistently been the most willing to acknowledge that things had gone wrong and was most keen to move on. He was the survivor: when the other two were let go, his position was hanging by a thread.

Rose argued to me that he'd come in late to at least some of the stories and mainly helped with the writing. But to let one white man off the hook wouldn't have been received well. In late 2018, at the time of the apology and retraction, Tiso Blackstar had asked him to take six months' leave, to let the storm blow over. He'd resisted, and the publishers had had a dilemma on their hands, until former editor Ray Hartley – who by then had been kicked upstairs and was more expendable – wrote a letter criticising the decision to withdraw the story.

Hartley had been editor at the time of the Cato Manor reporting, and his detailed response to the paper's retraction noted that his '30-year reputation as an ethical, fair and accurate journalist and editor' had been severely damaged. 'I am greeted in the street with looks of pity and, sometimes, anger,' he wrote.

He asked the new editor, Bongani Siqoko, to run the letter. Siqoko declined the request, and Hartley circulated the letter among his friends. News24 got hold of it and published it. In it, he conceded that the words 'death squad' in the original subheading had gone too far; there should have been an 'alleged'. Where Siqoko had said in his retraction that only twelve of the killings had been suspicious, not eighteen, as they had originally reported, Hartley said this made no difference in his mind. 'One killing would have been too many.'

He challenged the view that the articles had made Johan Booysen directly responsible. 'The articles did no such thing. They said the police accused of the killings fell under "the ultimate command" of Booysen.'

Hartley said he didn't believe Booysen had ordered the killings and accepted Booysen's innocence. Why, then, did the newspaper never give substantial space to Booysen's version of what was happening? Why did they ignore his cries that he was being framed for political reasons?

'These journalists [Hofstatter, Rose and Wa Afrika] put their lives at risk tackling this story. They waded knee-deep through the blood of KwaZulu-Natal's killing fields, and that deserves to be honoured, not dismissed. Did they make errors? Yes, they did. Were any of these errors fatal to the conclusion that irregular killings occurred? No, they were not.'

Then he gave the *Sunday Times* treatment to those who'd questioned the stories: 'Many allegations by hucksters, charlatans, disgraced journalists and, tragically, some doyens of the media profession have been made against the reporters on the Cato Manor story. Not one shred of credible evidence has been produced to back this up.'

Never mind the rich language of 'wading knee-deep through blood', what was critical here was that a former editor of one of the most influential newspapers in the country was saying that it didn't matter much that his reporters had made errors, and that some of these errors hadn't been corrected. It wasn't terribly important that they'd got some key facts wrong, even if that had discredited the story.

So Ray Hartley went.

Hofstatter had lost his job in October 2018 and was now doing freelance research work, mostly for an international market. He stood by his position that they had made mistakes and misjudgements, but that the core of the stories was valid, and he continued to emphasise that his personal life had been a mess and that this had affected his work.

The publishers felt that with two white men and one black man having been cleared out, they could get away with letting Rose off the hook. So Rose survived, and was made editor of the *Financial Mail*.

Malcolm Rees, whose life had also been turned upside down, had always had the strongest sense of grievance: the initial story he'd been pushed into doing had some validity, but it had been manipulated and the story had run away from him. He'd resigned early on because he hadn't been able to stomach what was happening at the *Sunday Times*, but this hadn't been acknowledged. The accusation that he'd been bribed had since been resurrected by *Noseweek*, and it popped up on Google every time he tried to get a job.

The three journalists attended the series of meetings with Van Loggerenberg because they were desperate to put these events behind them, and had a grudging respect for Van Loggerenberg. But Van Loggerenberg wouldn't let them get away without accounting for themselves, working at them with grim determination. He challenged them on their individual and collective responsibility. The reporters had always struggled to take individual responsibility for what had happened, and had constantly pointed to the group and newsroom dynamic to explain it. They had had little trouble taking the credit when stories under their bylines did well, but were quick to disavow them when they did not.

The two black members of the team had stood by their stories unapologetically and the three white men had always been cautious about blaming their absent partners. Loyalties were complicated and confused, as was the interplay of personal and group responsibilities, and issues of race didn't make it easier. Some of the key material had come through Wa Afrika and Rampedi, and only they, Hofstatter had often argued, could name those sources. And to name these sources would mean betraying their colleagues and they wouldn't do that – even though they now differed on the stories they'd done together and had parted ways.

The journalistic rule that protects sources was intended to promote truth, to enable and encourage whistleblowers to speak out and be assured of their anonymity, but here it was being used to protect fake whistleblowers, those who deceived rather than revealed the truth. It was an inversion of the ethical rule.

Also, their hands were somewhat tied. Rose had been promoted and couldn't risk these issues coming up again, and Hofstatter's departure agreement prevented him from speaking openly without endangering his settlement. At most, they would admit to being responsible for a fact here, a paragraph there, a quote somewhere in the story – but never for the whole and sustained reporting, or its stark presentation.

There's a journalism aphorism that says it's possible for a story to get every fact right, and still be horribly wrong. Here, the journalists, or at least some of them, were saying – and still say – that they got many facts wrong, but the story was still right. That's like an architect saying a building was beautiful, pity it fell down because the foundations were weak.

After many months of meetings, Rees agreed to write a letter apologising to Van Loggerenberg and his family for the harm caused by the accusation that he'd been an apartheid spy. The statement had been inserted into his story, he said, shortly before going to print. He hadn't believed the accusation then, and he didn't believe it now. In his letter on 8 September 2019 he wrote, 'I have been falsely branded an unethical journalist who accepted bribes from criminals and who took instructions from nefarious individuals to publish manufactured news articles ... As such, I am intimately familiar with the personal, relationship, career and financial harm that such attacks cause, and I deeply empathise with you [Van Loggerenberg].'

Van Loggerenberg accepted the apology and shared it on social media.

He continued the meetings with the other two for a while, with the aim of getting something similar from them. He later expressed satisfaction that he'd made progress with Rose, though it was kept under the radar, probably because Rose couldn't risk his job. But he cut off discussions with Hofstatter, because Hofstatter couldn't face up to what he'd done. 'He cares not for truth or the journalism profession. He cares for himself,' Van Loggerenberg said.

Wa Afrika and Rampedi were nowhere to be seen.

*

For this book, Mzilikazi Wa Afrika had agreed to meet me, and then ignored my attempts to set it up. And when we retracted his Taco Kuiper Award, he wrote me an abusive email.

When I approached Piet Rampedi, he said he'd said all he wanted to say, and I had already made my views clear, so he saw no point in talking to me. He later named me at number 19 in his 31-person Twitter list of the 'media cabal' that had driven the agenda against him and his stories.

Wa Afrika and Rampedi reappeared after some time in Iqbal Survé's Sekunjalo Independent Media group, and reopened the campaign around the 'rogue unit' and against Pravin Gordhan. What was becoming clear was that rogue journalists, subject to little or no editorial scrutiny, could find a platform to disseminate their own personal invective. It was one thing to do it on social media, but it was also true of parts of the traditional media. It polluted our political debate and degraded our journalism.

The story got some additional oxygen when the new Public Protector, Busisiwe Mkhwebane, appointed under President Zuma, resuscitated the issue in 2019, but her standing was by then so low that it proved little more than a distraction.

By this stage Sekunjalo had little credibility and had itself gone rogue, abandoning all the industry self-regulation and oversight organisations, and serving mostly as a promotional tool for Survé's other businesses.

The players

When, in 2018, the award panel I chaired withdrew the Taco Kuiper runner-up award that Rob Rose, Mzilikazi Wa Afrika and Stephan Hofstatter had won in 2012 for their Cato Manor 'death squad' story, Rose graciously returned his trophy. Wa Afrika and Hofstatter refused to return theirs, and sent me a lawyer's letter saying that I had not spoken to any of them nor sought to interview them to hear their side of the story, and asking to meet me with two other members of the judging panel. It was an extraordinary display of how out of touch they were with reality.

I'd met and talked at length to Hofstatter, though not fruitfully, as he'd said he wasn't ready to talk about the details of the story. And I'd written to Wa Afrika to ask for an interview and he had agreed, and then ignored repeated attempts to set up a meeting. But these interviews were about this book, rather than about the award, they argued.

I declined to set up a meeting for them with the judges. Wa Afrika emailed:

> It is clear that you have an agenda or working for your masters, we have requested to meet with you and at least more than one of your panel members, instead of arranging that meeting as requested, so we can set the record straight and clear our names that you have been, without any shame, dragging through the mud, the only response we get from you is when are we

returning the trophies, I am not returning any trophy until my side of the story is heard ... you have been dishonest and misled the public ... even a murderer is given a fair trial unless you want us to believe that panel is a kangaroo court ... stop wasting our time we have very important things to do rather to entertain you.

The Global Shining Light Award organisers quietly removed the 2013 *Sunday Times* award from its website.

Hofstatter and Wa Afrika wrote a long letter to my fellow board members on the Global Investigative Journalism Network, saying their story might have had some errors but it was sound journalism, and accusing me and others of dishonesty. They asked the Global Network to intervene and mediate this situation. The Global Network ignored the letter. As one of the board members said to me, 'They know you are writing a book, and they have fired a shot across your bows.'

Hofstatter would still not meet with me, but agreed to answer questions through his lawyer. I asked him if there were elements of the Cato Manor 'death squad' story, for example, that he regretted or would do differently with the benefit of hindsight. 'None,' he said. 'We uncovered and exposed solid evidence of serious human-rights violations. It was manifestly in the public interest to do so.' He conceded there were some factual errors in the story, but these were not fatal, he said, and had been corrected in the newspaper.

He also resorted to abuse, saying I had become 'one of the most effective vehicles for Booysen's smears'. 'You uncritically swallowed his Kool-Aid ... you caved in to public pressure ... a grave injustice has been done to dozens of people killed under suspicious circumstances ... I urge you to resist the pressures to become part of the cover-up,' he wrote to me.

Although he'd been let go from the *Sunday Times*, he said that his departure agreement with the company wasn't based on any wrongdoing on his part, and that he'd still like an independent investigation.

Nine years after the story appeared, Hofstatter could still not come to terms with the fact that he and his fellow reporters had been played.

*

Some years after her fall from grace, I met with Phylicia Oppelt in a café in Norwood, Johannesburg.

A small woman, she's as fierce as she's diminutive. When I first knew her, when she was a young intern in the early 1990s, her demeanour showed all the toughness and determination required to be a successful black woman in a white male domain. She didn't speak a lot, but when she did, she had a sharp tongue. She did little to hide a burning ambition that had her carefully plotting her professional ascent from the early days.

Now she was a different person, carrying on her face and in her carriage the pain of the *Sunday Times* years, and her rapid fall from the highest of journalistic offices. Gone was the steely look of the woman who'd risen quickly through the ranks to the high-profile job of her dreams. She was now scrambling to build a new life in a relatively dull, low-profile, mid-level job, out of journalism. She was nervous while talking to me, her eyes darting around, showing a vulnerability I hadn't seen in her before.

But once she started expressing her anger and frustration, the words and emotions came tumbling out. After she'd been let go from the *Sunday Times*, she couldn't easily get a job in Johannesburg, or in media anywhere, for that matter, and had had to take a position at the University of the Western Cape, with a two-hour flight each way on weekends to see her daughters in Johannesburg.

'When I was fired, my bum was cold because of all those noses being withdrawn so quickly. None of those who had laughed at my jokes [for] all those years ever bothered to speak to me after I was fired. Suddenly, I was a nobody. I would bump into old colleagues and they would pretend not to see me.'

She gave me a statement she had written but not published. It was dripping with bitterness. She had just been doing her job as editor, she wrote, but now 'I am accused of having acted in concert with shadowy figures to overthrow our republic, destroy the reputation of the revenue service, damage the reputation of the *Sunday Times* in particular and South African journalism in general'.

She had repeatedly been asked to atone for her misdeeds as editor, she wrote, but her settlement agreement with Tiso Blackstar had silenced her. The longer she remained silent, the more commentators such as me – 'the righteous whites', she labelled us – had stuck with 'a singular narrative' that held her responsible for the destruction of SARS and the demeaning of the *Sunday Times*.

Her criticism of a singular narrative was breathtaking: here was the queen of the relentlessly single narrative complaining that she was herself a victim.

She wasn't surprised that her successor as editor, Bongani Siqoko, who had apologised and retracted on behalf of the newspaper, 'was apparently buckling under the relentless pressure placed on the *Sunday Times*', she said. 'I have sat in that chair that Siqoko occupies and I have felt the unbearable pressure when commercial and editorial interests collide,' she wrote.

How was she expected to have known 'the confluence of history and ulterior motives' that lay behind the SARS story, she asked. There were no warning signs. The documents her team had gathered were almost all part of the statements submitted to the Sikhakhane panel, which was led, she said, by an advocate of significant reputation. His report was eloquent and damning about the activities of the SARS rogue unit: '... a tiny ugly black spot that lay deep in the belly of this august institution ... the unit that was established without the requisite legislative framework, and operated in isolation and outside the official premises of SARS'. She asked: Were we to dismiss this evidence?

Every single story in the SARS series went through the normal editorial processes at the *Sunday Times*, she said. 'Not one went straight onto the pages, deemed to be classified or untouchable ... each one was scrutinised, queried and accepted ... the senior executive team – all of those who still occupy senior positions within Tiso Blackstar – all had sight of the stories, sat in our editorial conferences and left satisfied.'

Lead writer Piet Rampedi would be invited to the editorial conferences to explain aspects of the story or the sourcing. 'Not once did he shy away from answering and not once did the editors deem the story too risky to be published.'

On Saturdays, as pages were finalised and approved, they would be printed out and pinned to the newsroom wall. 'Every single page of the main section of the *Sunday Times* – including every page that contained a SARS story – was there for everyone to read.' Perhaps these senior editors, she said, 'were so cowed by me that they could not bring themselves to openly raise their doubts and concerns'.

On only two occasions had Tiso Blackstar management asked about the stories, and both times arose out of 'outside interference'. The first was when former Finance Minister Trevor Manuel had phoned her boss, Mike Robertson, to offer to act as an intermediary between Oppelt and SARS. Robertson told Manuel to approach Oppelt directly. He did not.

The second was an attempted intervention by the well-known head of reputation management company Brunswick SA, Itumeleng Mahabane, who asked for a meeting between SARS's Ivan Pillay and Tiso Blackstar management, without Oppelt. The meeting never happened.

Her bosses had never raised the SARS story when they fired her. Only a few months before, they'd been so happy with her performance that they'd promised to bring her into the group's long-term senior-executive share incentive scheme. Then they turned around and said the paper needed a new strategy and redesign, and that she wasn't the person to do it. Not a word about SARS.

But the pressure had been mounting, she said. Johann van Loggerenberg sent a string of lawyers' letters. Pravin Gordhan had called one Saturday morning 'and offered a lecture on how I was destroying good men'. Much had been made of her ex-husband's role as a former SARS official, but a *Sunday Times* inquiry had cleared her on that front.

She deployed the sharp tongue for which she was known, and part of the reason her colleagues were often 'cowed'. The reason rival journalist Jacques Pauw had been so venomous in his criticism towards her, she said, was because she'd refused to run a food column he'd offered when he opened a restaurant. 'In response, he and [former editor and columnist] Max du Preez took to social media to lament my abuse of power. I guess it smarted being sacked by an uppity black woman,' she concluded.

And then, near the end of her nine-page unpublished statement, finally, after all these years, she admitted a single error: 'A statement given to Sikhakhane mentioned that the unit was running a brothel. We did not delve into this thoroughly and did not seek collaboration. There was no brothel.'

She turned on the investigations unit. 'They were roundly disliked in the newsroom,' she said, particularly when they negotiated salaries that overtook those of many senior editorial managers. She often had to 'clean up behind them'.

Once, soon after she took office as editor, she was attacked by a ministerial spokesperson for being unethical. It turned out that the investigations unit had provided documentation to the opposition party in a parliamentary ethics inquiry into a minister that had arisen from their reporting. Or, as Oppelt put it, the unit reporters 'had unilaterally decided to support a parliamentary ethics inquiry'. The minister complained to the press ombud and the *Sunday Times* was cleared, but the incident made Oppelt 'conscious of the dangers that lurked within a unit that believed it had carte blanche'.

Her anger was aimed not just at the *Sunday Times*, but at the entire world of journalism: 'I have come to accept that the profession I once loved is no longer the same as when I entered it in 1994. These days it is about grandstanding and sucking up to bosses who will reward your sycophancy and newsroom managers who are less concerned with the texture and nuances of life, but rather the stark lines of black and white. I have no desire to re-enter a profession of which I am ashamed.'

*

Oppelt had spoken to me on the condition that I showed her what I wrote. She did not trust me, she said in an email exchange, as I had previously written 'mean, hostile, unfair and inaccurate commentary' about her. 'What assurance can you give me that you would give me a fair hearing and that what I tell you would be accurately reflected, both in context and as my words, in your book?' she asked.

I could only tell her solemnly that I wanted to get this right. As a show of goodwill, I would let her read what I wrote about her, and I would correct any factual inaccuracies she pointed out and give a serious hearing to any objections she had to my depiction of her. It is always risky to show a subject what one writes about them before publication, and it most often leads to dispute and sometimes attempts to stop publication. So I was very careful not to give her any veto over what I wrote.

I was most surprised when she read what I sent her and wrote back a polite note, in a much gentler and more self-reflective tone than a year earlier, when we had first talked. She wanted to add some thoughts, she said.

First, she wanted to pay her respects to some of her *Sunday Times* colleagues. She had previously talked about how little talent and skill she found when she arrived at the paper. 'There were certainly times that I felt the *Sunday Times* could have benefited from having more experienced journalists. But there were both journalists and managers who were excellent and brought significant skills and talent to the paper,' she wrote.

'Here I am reminded of Archie Henderson, who came out of retirement when I became editor and whose steady demeanour and experience made the world of difference. So too people like Nadine

Dreyer, Patrick Bulger, Barry Smit, Carlos Amato and many others.'

She was no longer ashamed of the profession of journalism and was wistful about not being part of it. 'Despite my own experiences, [the profession] remains a noble one. I might not be a part of it any longer, but I still read local and international newspapers and I know that without those journalists who shine a bright light on dark, dank places, our world would be so much poorer for it.'

And then she did what few of her colleagues had done: she took full, unqualified responsibility for what had happened. 'It has been years since the SARS stories were published,' she wrote, 'and I still do not know who sought to sway the *Sunday Times* with the information – whether it was merely sources within the Revenue Services or more powerful players. The buck stopped with me, however, and I know the significant and negative impact that those stories had on many people.

'I regret this and the fact that people were hurt.'

*

The role of the tobacco industry should get more attention. That this had become a gangster sector in which spying, tax evasion, smuggling and illegal surveillance were rife has been well documented by journalists and in Johann van Loggerenberg's book, *Tobacco Wars*. It seemed there were very few players in the sector – big and small, traditional grandees and newbies alike – that didn't cross the legal line in the interests of market share, or pay others to do it for them.

Most of the allegations against SARS originated from tobacco-industry agents, such as Belinda Walter and Mike Peega. That apartheid assassin Craig Williamson was among them, running one of the small new tobacco manufacturers, was an indication of an industry that attracted and was a playground for the most unscrupulous and ruthless. Williamson had set up his tobacco company after being sequestrated following a lawsuit by the Schoon family, whose activist mother Williamson had killed in the 1980s.

287

These elements found common ground with the SSA, Crime Intelligence and elements of the ANC in wanting to undermine SARS's work. In the process, they managed to capture the Illicit Tobacco Task Team – BAT sat on the task team, along with the Hawks, Crime Intelligence, the SSA and the NPA, but with SARS excluded – and cause lasting damage to the tax system and the national economy.

As early as 2014, *amaBhungane* was reporting on how the major tobacco companies, particularly BAT and Lonrho's Rollex, appeared to be able to manipulate law enforcement to their own benefit. By working closely with police and state security, BAT was reportedly able to get them to focus on their smaller rivals, and Rollex to escape when caught red-handed in illicit trade. BAT was able to push the boundaries of the law in spying on its competition. 'The evidence shows,' *amaB* wrote in the *Mail & Guardian* in March 2014, 'how vulnerable the security agencies are to manipulation by big private players with deep pockets, who do so often under the guise of "support" for official projects.' Both companies were quoted denying any wrongdoing, but did little to contradict the growing pile of evidence.

The claims that SARS was running a 'rogue unit' appear to have originated in the Illicit Tobacco Task Team and were stoked by those close to both the tobacco industry and the SSA. BAT's risk partner, FSS, employed Peega, the former SARS agent who'd been fired for poaching, and who'd peddled the 'rogue unit' narrative. BAT and TISA were said to have paid FSS R50 million to build a private intelligence network to work with the SSA and other law-enforcement bodies.

In 2016 Johann van Loggerenberg said the attacks on SARS, himself and his investigative unit 'were driven by persons associated with the tobacco industry'.

Adrian Lackay said much the same: 'There are people who have a vested interest in creating confusion among state institutions. SARS is in no doubt that they are behind these [rogue unit] allegations, as they have been in the past.'

In the same year, a whistleblower named Luis Pestana released masses of internal documents that bolstered claims of BAT dirty tricks. This included having police, metro police and SARS officials on its payroll. Pestana also implicated Williamson in cigarette smuggling. Marianne Thamm reported in the *Daily Maverick* that Pestana's evidence revealed a 'story fraught with subterfuge and deception with double and triple agents all employed and deployed to protect massive tobacco profits.'

In 2011 Van Loggerenberg's investigative unit in SARS had had roughly ninety projects on the go in its bid to close the tax gap. It was the tobacco one, Operation Honey Badger, that was to prove the nemesis for the unit, SARS and the *Sunday Times*. When the unit was shuttered in 2014, the other 89 groups of high-level tax dodgers must also have celebrated.

*

Shortly after Zuma was driven from office in 2018, President Cyril Ramaphosa appointed an expert panel to look into the SSA and its role in state capture. Its High-Level Review Panel report, released in May 2019, was unequivocal and damning in its findings: 'There has been a serious politicisation and factionalisation of the intelligence community over the past decade ... resulting in an almost complete disregard for the Constitution, policy, legislation and other prescripts, and turning our civilian intelligence community into a private resource to serve the political and personal interests of particular individuals'. The SSA had become a 'cash cow for many inside and outside the agency'.

On the SSA's activities with journalists, the report said that among the 'intelligence operations which were clearly unconstitutional and illegal ... [was] infiltrating and influencing the media in order, apparently, to counter bad publicity for the country, the then president and the SSA'.

It gave no further details, at least in the redacted public report. But this was enough to confirm that the SSA had played a significant role in gathering, developing and disseminating information that was intended to influence the media: the SSA had played the media. This was what Jacques Pauw had pointed to in his version of the 'rogue unit' story, in *City Press* back in August 2014.

It was also implicit in what Chad Thomas had described in his relationship with George Darmanovic and the role he'd played in dealing with the media, including creating and disseminating dossiers of information on targets that were identified from within the SSA.

I asked a few of the authors of the high-level SSA report – on condition of anonymity – to confirm my understanding of how the SSA had operated, and all said the following was the modus operandi. An instruction would come down from above of someone or some institution that should be targeted. SSA agents would undertake surveillance and research to find some weak point of attack; sometimes, according to a member of the office of the Inspector General of Intelligence, the SSA watchdog, they 'just made it up'. The SSA agents would put together a dossier, often a mix of real and fake information, but designed to leverage that weak point, the dirt; they would often use third parties for this, to try and secure deniability.

They would then distribute the dossier, at first to a few contacts in the media, but in later days directly to their most willing and eager publisher, the *Sunday Times*. They knew whom in the newsroom to give it to, when to give it to them for maximum impact, and how to play different media off against each other. Sometimes they organised for the information to be 'confirmed' by a 'second source'.

It was standard tradecraft, the stuff of dirty-tricks operations. In the US it's sometimes called 'opposition research', derived from when political campaigns gather and use dirt on their rivals.

I asked the member of the office of the Inspector General of Intelligence if he believed any of the journalists were actually on the SSA payroll, paid from its secret slush fund for informers, sources and agents. 'There were no records,' he said, 'so I can't put names on it. But I am confident that at least some journalists were paid. That was how they worked.'

The authors of the SSA report told me that they hadn't delved deeply enough to find individual names but that they wouldn't be surprised to hear the SSA had worked with and even paid certain journalists, as it was consistent with what they'd seen of the operation. It was a failure of the system that those who knew of illegal activities felt obliged to remain silent or speak off the record, and that an official report should point to such activities but not throw them open to public scrutiny and accountability. The SSA report opened the door into a dark room, but didn't turn on the light.

Piet Rampedi told the Press Council that among his sources were 'intelligence agents'. Johann van Loggerenberg has said that Darmanovic informed him, in phonecalls after Darmanovic left the country, that 'they were told [in SSA] to look into us [Van Loggerenberg and the HRIU] with a microscope. They were told to find whatever they could against us. He apologised to me. He admitted that he'd been on a mission to discredit me.'

Others, like Paul O'Sullivan, pointed to police Crime Intelligence under the notorious Richard Mdluli as the entity that had played the media. Certainly, Mdluli's hand was present in a great deal of surveillance, disinformation and malicious leakage. Mzilikazi Wa Afrika said they'd received the Cato Manor evidence from a senior Crime Intelligence person, and it was widely accepted that Crime Intelligence was the source of the intercepted phonecall that led to the resignation of SARS's Oupa Magashula, which opened the way for Tom Moyane's ascension.

This kind of thing was standard under the apartheid government in operations such as Stratcom and military intelligence. Both of these bodies were skilled at this type of smear work: take something true or half-true, doctor it for the effect you want, and leak it. Those who came from that regime into the new, democratic one – like Mdluli and many SSA members – would have learnt their tricks in the old regime.

When the *Sunday Times* in its retractions of these stories said they'd been played but didn't say by whom, it wasn't only because they were in a hurry to defuse a situation and didn't take the time to investigate, but because a confusing array of different institutions and individuals had been involved in the misdirection around each story. Mdluli's Crime Intelligence appears to have been crucial in the 'renditions story', and had a hand in the 'death squad' story, along with corrupt business-people. The SSA was the main driver in the SARS story, but with the assistance of Crime Intelligence and some important private-sector players, notably in the tobacco industry.

And none of this would have happened without the enabling work of accounting and legal professionals like KPMG, Judge Kroon and Advocate Sikhakhane.

CONCLUSION

'Pick up your pen ... load it with ink'

In early 2018 a documentary called *Winnie* drew a great deal of attention in the emotional period after the death of Winnie Madikizela-Mandela. Filmmaker Pascale Lamche explained away serious questions about elements of Madikizela-Mandela's conduct in the 1980s by ascribing it to the notorious propaganda arm of the security police, Stratcom. Brushing aside the evidence of Madikizela-Mandela's involvement in murder and kidnapping, Lamche focused on Stratcom's campaign against the struggle icon, implicating a number of respected resistance figures in these attacks on her.

Interviewed for the film, I spoke about the impression Madikizela-Mandela's courage, strength and charisma had made on me as a young political reporter, and how important she'd been in keeping alive the voice of the ANC inside South Africa in the most repressive years. But, I said, there was real tragedy in the damage the Security Police had done to her through detention, torture and harassment, and in her more recent conduct. We had to face up to the seriousness of what had happened in the latter period.

At *The Weekly Mail* at that time, my colleagues and I had been among the first to expose the violent conduct of Madikizela-Mandela and her 'football club', a large group of young men who accompanied her whenever she attended public functions, offering her personal protection, and serving as bodyguards and errand boys. We'd covered the story, and the angry reaction of the community in which Madikizela-Mandela lived, only because the story was too serious to ignore. She was a hero, but a damaged one.

Lamche cut out everything I said from 'But'. It didn't suit her narrative. It was a crude act of documentary dishonesty, a twisting of my words to fit a predetermined story.

At the film's launch some 18 months earlier, a young *Huffington Post* reporter had interviewed Madikizela-Mandela and she'd said she was surprised to see me in the film, because when fellow journalist Thandeka Gqubule-Mbeki and I had written about her conduct in the 1980s, we 'did the work of Stratcom'.

On Madikizela-Mandela's death, *Huffington Post* and *The Citizen* newspaper grabbed this last interview and put it on their sites without taking a close look at how untrue and defamatory it was. I complained, and they both quickly took it down and published apologies.

The EFF, eager to claim Winnie Madikizela-Mandela's memory and legacy, issued a statement saying that I, Gqubule-Mbeki and others had been named as Stratcom agents, and should come clean and repent. It was a devastating accusation, all the more outrageous because *The Weekly Mail* had exposed Stratcom's work. I had personally been a target of some of its more violent activities, such as a shooting through my front door and having had my car brakes tampered with; and Gqubule-Mbeki had been an underground ANC activist from an early age, and had been detained for it.

This deeply obnoxious and baseless suggestion of treachery was taken up on social media, and we were threatened and harassed.

So I had a taste, from this, of what it was like to have the foundation of your life blown away by wild accusations made up by an irresponsible journalist, taken up by careless editors, and spread on social media, and how difficult it was to counter such smears. I was relatively fortunate in that, when the EFF refused to retract, we were able to sue and force them to apologise and pay damages. At least I was able to set the record straight relatively quickly – within two years. I couldn't remove the stain, but I could at least counter it.

Those who were unfairly treated by the *Sunday Times* – Johan

Booysen, Johann van Loggerenberg, Ivan Pillay, Adrian Lackay, Anwa Dramat and Shadrack Sibiya – fought for many years to clear their names, and saw their professional and personal lives torn apart. They faced prosecution, had to deal with massive legal costs, and were publicly pilloried. I don't want to suggest all of these people were innocent, as that isn't a word you would associate with most of these men. But neither were they guilty of the charges the *Sunday Times* laid against them, and they didn't deserve to have their lives destroyed.

Van Loggerenberg was the most persistent. In June 2020 he documented all he had done over the years to extract apologies, rulings and retractions. This included retractions from the *Sunday Times, Carte Blanche*, Belinda Walter, the Public Protector's office, tobacco-industry companies Phoebus and Carnilinx, Judge Frank Kroon, SARS, FITA and Malcolm Rees. 'I cannot believe that anyone in their right mind cannot by now see that the entire nation was fooled, and that the entire saga was a complete and deliberate sham fed by many with overlapping nefarious motives and agendas. The evidence is overwhelming,' he said.

Was he satisfied? No. 'I will now … bring civil suits against private individuals and entities, former or current state officials, operatives and contractors, relevant state organs and any other related party.' In addition, he undertook to 'follow up on formal complaints laid at various law-enforcement agencies, oversight and professional bodies … and register further formal reports and complaints.'

*

Interviewing many *Sunday Times* people over the course of the research for this book, I was struck by how damaged all of them also were. Almost everyone I spoke to talked about the trauma of being in the newsroom at that time and how deeply it had scarred them. They spoke of it with lasting pain as an unhappy, damaging, low period of their lives. They talked of it as toxic. They, as much as their targets, had been wrecked by the experience. Good journalists like Pearlie Joubert and Songezo Zibi left the media. Some, like Malcolm Rees, were still struggling to rehabilitate themselves.

Most journalists at the centre of the scandalous reporting received settlements from Tiso Blackstar in exchange for their silence. They left or were asked to leave, but at least some of them were paid out to accept non-disclosure agreements. The company wanted to put a cap on the controversy, and were prepared to prevent them from talking about it. The effect, though, was to leave those reporters better off than the ones who'd resigned out of principle, to skew the benefits towards those who'd got it wrong and away from those who'd tried to stop them. It was the ultimate sign of how journalism values had been turned upside down in the *Sunday Times* newsroom.

*

Individuals were hurting, but the social and economic damage to the country was, of course, much greater. Key institutions such as SARS, the Hawks, the NPA and police Crime Intelligence were reduced to shadows of their former selves, deeply dysfunctional in a way that would take a generation to rebuild. The country's revenues were down, and the state's capacity to put a stop to corruption by holding culprits accountable was deeply compromised. The cost of the corruption was measured in the hundreds of billions of rands.

In a country where a strong state was needed to fight crime, deal with gross social inequality and build a new inclusive economy, the institutions of state authority had been severely weakened. The two that stood out, the only two that had some distance from the government, and which could still enforce some accountability, were the judiciary and the media. So it was particularly significant that some media had played a powerful role in countering state capture, while others enabled it.

*

The *Sunday Times* story is the most graphic illustration of how much harm the media can do. We have to remind ourselves of how much good it can do, too.

A few years ago I received an email out of the blue from someone I didn't know, Nathasha Long. Her father, this woman said, now an old man, had told her for the first time how I'd been 'part of our lives without us even knowing'. And without me ever knowing, too.

Back in the early 1980s, Hu Lau Long had called me, a young political reporter on the *Rand Daily Mail*, to tell me how he, of Chinese origin, was fighting to keep his newly built house in what had been designated a white area, and how its loss would devastate him and his family. It wasn't an unusual story at the time, when the Group Areas Act was still being ruthlessly implanted to segregate the cities. I wrote a brief account, and it – the story of just one man's pain in a sea of pain – probably only made the newspaper's pages because it was a quiet day.

I didn't follow up the story. It was one of many hundreds.

Thirty years later, Nathasha told me that after I phoned the authorities for comment and wrote up the story, the powers that be held off, and transferred the house into Hu Lau Long's name. He and the family still lived in that house.

It was a clear reminder of how doing a simple job of reporting a story can, in ways we least expect, do more good than harm.

I don't want to suggest that there was some kind of 'golden era' of South African journalism, some high point from which our news media has fallen. Our media has been shaped – or, more accurately, warped – by its 200-year history in a society of racial inequality and censorship. Broadcasting was entirely controlled by an authoritarian state determined to use it as a propaganda tool until recently, as was the Afrikaans press, which before 1990 saw itself as part and parcel of the Afrikaans nationalist project. And we inherited an English-language newspaper industry with a mixed record in dealing with apartheid: a mainstream media compromised by racial division, censorship and commercialism, but always with a few voices that stood out from this.

The mainstream English press was shaped and directed by its mining-industry owners from the beginning of the 20th century. While many of these papers opposed apartheid, they operated within the constraints of white parliamentary politics and the needs of a white advertising industry. The most outspoken of the liberal newspapers, the *Rand Daily Mail,* was closed down in 1985 when it started to push those boundaries, develop a mixed newsroom, cover more of black politics and life, and grow black readership.

There were highlights of powerful watchdog journalism in liberal newspapers like the *Rand Daily Mail,* the *Sunday Times,* the *Sunday Express,* the *Daily Dispatch* and the *Cape Times:* Allister Sparks's exposé of small-town political trials in which activists were getting massive sentences outside of the public eye; Benjamin Pogrund's exposé of prison conditions in the *Rand Daily Mail* in 1965; the Info Scandal, in which the *Sunday Express* and the *Rand Daily Mail* exposed the corruption at the heart of the apartheid government and its propaganda machinery; the *Sunday Times's* exposé in 1978 of the role the secretive Broederbond was playing in running the country; the *Rand Daily Mail's* coverage in the 1970s and 1980s of the forced removals of millions who lived outside of the designated black 'homelands'; the coverage of the Security Police killing of black-consciousness leader Steve Biko in 1977; and scrutiny of political trials over four decades, and the frequent evidence of torture and abuse that emerged from them.

There are other notable examples, all of which played a key role in exposing and challenging the apartheid government, and – most importantly – knocking down the notion that the truth was hidden from white South Africans. The one argument that can't be maintained is that people were ignorant of the horrors of apartheid, as there were always journalists and some media reporting it. Those who didn't know were those who chose to look the other way.

As the ANC itself put it, in its submission to the special media hearings at the Truth and Reconciliation Commission in September 1997:

> Individual media workers, and some media institutions, took great risks in their attempts to publish or broadcast the truth. Their untiring commitment to seeing that the truth came out played a vital role in bringing about the downfall of the apartheid system.

As important as at least some of these mainstream publications were, they also operated within a narrow political framework, where the focus was on the all-white Parliament and moderate black political figures and organisations that participated in the apartheid structures. The ANC and other more radical extra-parliamentary groups were out of bounds. The ANC was denounced by the mainstream media for its links to the Communist Party, its armed struggle and its support for sanctions and isolation – all policies that were core to the resistance but beyond the pale of white politics.

The furthest the mainstream papers could go – and it often cost them white readers and advertisers – was to support the small parliamentary opposition, notably Helen Suzman's lone voice of liberal protest and human-rights advocacy in Parliament. These newspapers were commercial enterprises that operated within the law, and therefore, albeit uncomfortably, within the strictures of censorship.

Some editors pulled at the leash, but in the end had to work within the more than 100 laws that limited what could be reported. Most editors adopted – of necessity – the pragmatic habits of living under enforced self-censorship, and the industry even signed constraining agreements with the military, police and prisons which were to be strongly criticised later for their acceptance of the rules of control of the key pillars of an increasingly repressive regime.

A low point was in 1976 when the world – and any South African with access to international media – knew the South African Defence

Force had secretly invaded Angola, but no South African media could report it. The most notable exception to the acceptance of censorship was in 1985, when Tony Heard, editor of the *Cape Times* from 1971 to 1987, calculatedly broke the law to interview ANC president Oliver Tambo. Heard was prosecuted and lost his job soon after, but he'd played a valuable role in breaking a political logjam.

*

Historically, the sectoral nature of the media in South Africa – separate newspapers for white, Indian, coloured and African audiences, with only marginal overlap – saw the parallel development of different journalism traditions: an Afrikaans tradition of subservience to political causes; an English tradition rooted in a critical watchdog journalism but constrained by its roots in commerce and trade; a black newspaper tradition focused much more on a political and communal advocacy role, but contained politically by both its owners and the state; and an alternative non-profit newspaper tradition that was more strident and outspoken, tied to periods of political turmoil.

The very first independent newspaper in the Cape Colony, the *South African Commercial Advertiser* – a paper 'chiefly for the use and accommodation of persons connected with trade and merchandise', a commercial product aimed at a commercial market – published this by an anonymous poet in 1820:

> What is it gives the price of stock,
> Of Poyais Loans, and patent locks,
> And Cape Wine at West India docks?
> The Paper.
>
> Abroad, at home, infirm or stout,
> In health, or raving with the gout,
> Who possibly can do without
> The Paper.

Compare this with black writer Tiyo Soga's take on the role of the newspaper, in the first of the missionary papers, *Indaba*, published in Lovedale in 1862:

> One advantage we shall reap with the coming of this journal is that we will be confident that the people now will get the truth about the affairs of the nation. As people who are always hungry for news often we find ourselves dupes of deceivers under the guise of relating genuine facts. We are fed with half-truths by travellers ... Today with your newspaper, you are initiating an enterprise for banning falsehood. So we are pleased and grateful.

It's clear that disinformation isn't a new problem – we have long been 'dupes of deceivers', to use Soga's elegant alliteration. He expressed a deep faith in the printed word and the journal, 'an enterprise for banning falsehood'.

In the first newspaper that had a black editor, *Isigidimi samaXhosa* in 1882, Isaac Wauchope wrote powerfully about the power of the pen in pursuit of rights and recognition, a celebration of journalism even before it was practised as a distinct craft or profession:

> Leave the breechloader alone
> And turn to the pen.
> Take paper and ink,
> For that is your shield.
> Your rights are going!
> So pick up your pen.
> Load it, load it with ink.
> Sit on a chair.
> Repair not to Hoho
> But fire with your pen.

These two traditions of journalism, the commercial and the communitarian, run in parallel through our media history, with the commercial defining the scope and limits of the mainstream media, and the alternative voices challenging those limits, particularly at times of political agitation. And it's these two traditions that we still see competing in the newsroom: journalists trying to do watchdog work in an overwhelmingly commercial atmosphere, and at a time of strong financial pressure; editors feeling political pressure to be less critical and outspoken.

The rich tradition of investigative and watchdog journalism comes from distinct elements of the country's media: overwhelmingly in the print media, rather than broadcast; largely in the English-language newspapers rather than Afrikaans (until the emergence of *Vrye Weekblad*), though some important work was hidden in the newspapers of the other indigenous languages; and most strongly in the 'alternative' press.

This isn't difficult to understand, as it's precisely because certain papers struggled financially that they chose the path of exposé and outrage. Having no money meant they had to shout louder to be heard, and therefore favoured the big exposé. And having little advertising gave them the freedom to confront difficult issues. At *The Weekly Mail*, for example, we were owner-editors with few advertisers, a precarious but ideal state that allows journalists – perhaps encourages them – to be bolder, to be more outspoken, and to take more risks.

And it is boldness and risk-taking that lead to the most interesting journalism.

*

The *Sunday Times* wasn't the worst of the media culprits in enabling state capture. That position is hotly contested between three contenders: the Gupta's own ragtag media group, New Age Media; Iqbal Survé's rogue Sekunjalo Independent group; and the national broadcaster, the SABC – all of which became open, active and committed participants in the state-capture project.

These institutions boasted of their support for those who controlled the ruling party and were turning those relationships to their own benefit. All of them asserted they were doing it in the name of 'economic transformation' and 'black empowerment'. All of them became vehicles of individual self-enrichment or aggrandisement rather than journalism.

These three were direct examples of the growing phenomenon of media capture, where the media lost their autonomy and their ability to act with a will of their own, and their primary function of informing the public became secondary to servicing vested interests. These vested interests had long played a role in influencing the media, through ownership, advertising influence or political pressure, but in the case of these three institutions, this rose to a new level of direct and complete control, where the idea of serving the public interest wasn't just compromised but entirely subjugated, and there was little pretence of media autonomy.

The Guptas' media operation started with the launch of a newspaper called *The New Age*, a name evoking the left-wing struggle newspaper of the 1940s to 1960s that had been banned by the apartheid government. While both these *New Age* titles of different eras were aligned with the ANC, the original was the voice of a movement mobilising against the government, while the more recent one was the voice of the party in power, or, more accurately, one distinct and kleptocratic faction of that party.

The Guptas' *New Age* was built on the business model set by the Afrikaans press in the apartheid era: they would give favourable coverage to their government allies, who faced a critical, sometimes hostile media, and in turn they would get government advertising, sponsorship and other forms of support. The Guptas looked to the government for lucrative contracts with state-owned enterprises, and the placement of police and tax officials who would look the other way while the three brothers accumulated untold wealth (and shared it with their allies and proxies in these positions). They promised more positive news coverage, and contrasted themselves with the existing media, which they considered insufficiently transformed to meet the needs of the democratic era – a view that found favour with a party in power that was facing strong and, it felt, hostile and unfair media scrutiny and criticism.

Both the Guptas and Survé – who copied their model when he bought Independent News and Media – called on political reporter and ANC activist Karima Brown, who promised to 'challenge the dominant neo-liberal narrative' and craft a new developmental storyline. Brown had a remarkable propensity to read the changes in ANC internal politics, and switch between different ANC factions depending on who was becoming dominant at any particular time. Since government and the parastatals were the biggest advertisers in the country, and there were severe deficiencies in media diversity, this deal appeared to have some financial promise.

A key person in developing this strategy was Essop Pahad, who had been President Thabo Mbeki's right-hand man and who, when Minister in the Presidency, had advocated for the government to consolidate its advertising budget and withhold it from media that he viewed as too critical. Pahad had studied how this had been done by the Afrikaans press under apartheid, though it had to be adapted to a more open and accountable democracy, and one in which the printing of telephone books and school textbooks wasn't as big a tender as it had once been.

When he left government in 2009, Pahad joined the Guptas' media company and set up home in the Gupta newsroom, and they gifted him with his own intellectual journal, *The Thinker*.

Along with Brown as deputy editor, *The New Age* recruited some key political journalists to head the operation, notably Vuyo Mvoko as editor-in-chief and Vukani Mde as editorial-page editor – a team that gave it weight in the ANC.

I visited *The New Age*'s offices on the eve of its first publication and spoke to both management and editorial. When they gave me entirely different accounts of their target markets – Mvoko said they were going for a popular working-class market, while one of the Guptas told me they were going for influencers and leadership – I left thinking the operation was already in trouble, under a management that had little idea about running news media. Sure enough, it blew up before they even got an edition out, with the editorial top team walking out the night before the scheduled launch, saying the paper wasn't ready to be released.

Undaunted, the Guptas recruited respected editor Ryland Fisher and experienced newspaper manager Nazeem Howa, and launched two months later. This pair had inherited a design that could only have come from those who knew little about newspapers, with at least one page a day in every edition devoted to each of the nine provinces. Intended in theory to diversify coverage, giving attention to the areas outside of the big cities in a way the existing media seldom did, what it meant in practice was filling these pages with soft, 'positive' news that was of little interest to those outside of each province. It was enormously costly, as it required reporters all over the country, and it created distribution headaches, as the company sought to get small numbers of the newspaper all around the country to the small towns and rural areas they were covering.

In fact, *The New Age*'s distribution was overwhelmingly free hand-outs through government and parastatal offices. The presidency pushed government departments to take bundles for their staff, and the papers were handed out at airports and on university campuses.

There were three big obstacles to the success of the newspaper's model. The first was that the government wanted and needed its advertising to work if its recruitment advertising was to be successful, and its messages of progress and success were to gain an audience. But *The New Age* didn't bother to join the industry's Audit Bureau of Circulations, which certified the number of copies printed, sold and given away, and which was the basis for any advertising strategy. This meant that advertisers in *The New Age* had to have blind faith, and a willingness to defy the rules of public finance, which would require advertising in the most cost-effective outlets. And the government had to make a political decision to ignore the newspapers, such as the *Sunday Times*, that were most powerful in the recruitment advertising market.

The second obstacle was that government was broadly divided at the time between Gupta-aligned and Gupta-opposed forces, and had difficulty acting in concert. So some advertising and sponsorship moved to the Gupta outlets, but others in government went their own way. James Maseko, the head of government communications, for example, was pushed aside for, among other things, declining to go along with the Gupta scheme.

And third, there was the reader and consumer on which the newspaper depended. South African audiences have long been familiar with government propaganda outlets and are used to a more critical media. The Gupta's television station, ANN7, started off so amateurishly and was so crudely propagandistic that it never gained much ground. Their newspaper treaded more carefully, and carried some voices that gave it weight and credibility, but it had the problem of being unable to tackle what was the biggest story of the time: the growing influence of the Guptas on state decisions and expenditure, and the enrichment of Zuma, his friends and family.

*

More insidious was the impact of the takeover of one of the country's biggest newspaper groups, Independent Newspapers, by a deluded narcissist named Iqbal Survé.

When, in 2013, Survé bought this company, which owned the dominant English-language dailies in each of the four biggest cities of Cape Town, Johannesburg, Pretoria and Durban, there was a sigh of relief that it was being liberated from the hands of Irish magnate Tony O'Reilly, who'd bled it dry to help deal with his financial problems back home.

When it emerged, however, that Survé had paid R2 billion with the help of a large loan and investment from the PIC, questions were asked about why anyone would pay such an inflated price in an industry that was already in sharp decline, and why the PIC would put public servants' pension monies into such a purchase. It emerged later that ANC figures had enabled the deal, in order to ensure that a major newspaper group fell into friendly and malleable hands.

I phoned Survé when he was announced as the new owner in 2013, and after a twenty-minute conversation I put down the phone and said to myself, 'This man is going to be a problem owner.' He had talked most of the time about himself, telling me, unsolicited, what a 'struggle hero' he was, and what a modest and simple life he led. He boasted about his ties with Nelson Mandela, and how his first call to Mandela had been to tell him, 'We have brought the newspapers home, Tata.'

He also said that I'd known him and his commitment to a free press during the years of struggle. I had not.

I had no idea of what a problem he would become, however. Perhaps it's best summarised in one cameo related in *Paper Tiger: Iqbal Survé and the Downfall of Independent Newspapers*, the joint memoir of two respected editors he quickly got rid of, Alide Dasnois and Chris Whitfield. When Survé first came to meet the nervous newspaper staff, they wrote, he had himself ushered in by a string quartet, hired for the occasion.

Survé moved quickly against anyone who showed any independence, chasing from the group a fine core of journalists who had anti-apartheid backgrounds and who had made the *Cape Times* an important voice in the parliamentary capital. It turned out that his purpose wasn't so much to assist the ruling party as to promote himself and his business interests. He would appear in his own newspapers multiple times a week, and the papers would viciously attack his critics and write praise poetry about his generosity and brilliance.

Perhaps the epitome of this egocentric publishing was in February 2016, on the day of the annual State of the Nation presidential address. With the country's rich and powerful gathered in Cape Town, his newspaper pushed aside the report on the speech for an announcement that Survé was launching a new socially responsible investment fund.

But Survé didn't just promote himself and drive out good journalists who wouldn't go along with this. He and the Guptas pulled out of the Newspaper Press Union (now the Newspaper Association of South Africa), the South African National Editors' Forum, the Audit Bureau of Circulations and the Press Council, systematically undermining the institutions that held together the industry and set the standards for journalism and newspapering. It was destruction in the name of reform, and it accelerated the downward trend of an industry already in trouble.

The circulation of these newspapers plummeted, along with the quality of their journalism, and it seemed that the rogues wanted to take down the industry with them.

*

The SABC, which commands by far the biggest media audience in the country with its dominance of national television and radio, produced its own sad saga of state capture. The Zuma government systematically undermined its independent board of directors until they could put their people in place, and they in turn appointed a management that was not just corrupt and compromised but incompetent.

The broadcaster's finances collapsed as quickly as its credibility, setting back by twenty years what had been a grand democratic project to transform an apartheid state institution into an independent public-service broadcaster. It was saved only by a core group of staff members, who came to be known as 'the SABC Eight', who fought back, and by the demise of the Zuma government.

Media24's sister company, MultiChoice, was itself badly tainted by state capture, and exposed by its own News24 for having entered into a secret agreement with the SABC to give them a generous pay-TV broadcasting deal – including a bonus for CEO Hlaudi Motsoeneng – in exchange for the SABC's support. In essence, MultiChoice paid the

SABC to go against government policy, public interest and their own interests. It was another indication of how deep and wide the cancer of state capture had spread, including in the media industry.

A rebuilding of the SABC is now under way, under a new board and management. The real lesson of the period, though, was that no single media institution should have such size and dominance.

*

Where the *Sunday Times* differed from New Age Media, Sekunjalo Independent group and the SABC – and where it probably had more impact – was in dressing its reporting in a cloak of neutrality and credibility. It also had much more, long-established clout. While observers and activists – and some journalists who worked in these institutions – were fighting for the SABC's independence and exposing the Gupta and Survé self-serving shenanigans, the *Sunday Times* lurked behind a shroud of journalistic respectability and independence, even while it was driving out those who dissented. It saw itself as a watchdog of those with power, using its own independence and authority for the public good – but it was a watchdog chasing its own tail.

The paper suffered from what economist Joseph Stiglitz called 'cognitive capture', the most subtle kind, the hardest to prove, the most corrosive. It's what happens when journalists come to think like those vested interests: they don't need to be bought or pressured, because they become part of the echo chamber that amplifies and gives credence to conventional wisdom.

The *Sunday Times* case demonstrates how the rot of state capture spread through not just the institutions of government, but the private sector and the media industry, even among those who were horrified by having found themselves in this role. And the *Sunday Times* case demonstrates how developments in our media world – where technological change, declining revenues and changing readership patterns were undermining the capacity to maintain journalism standards of

311

verification, fact-checking and balance – opened the way for them to be captured and played.

*

In South Africa, attempts to manipulate the news weren't new. On the contrary, the apartheid security police had honed the techniques of distortion and disinformation to a fine art. But never had one of our major newspapers been more vulnerable to it.

This doesn't exonerate the individuals at the centre of the scandal. Their sin was not so much the original errors – anyone could have made those, though perhaps it would have taken some application to do it with such regularity. Their culpability lies in their willingness to sustain those errors over months, even years, to defend the indefensible, and to insist relentlessly on not allowing competing narratives to be heard, digging themselves deeper and deeper into their hole as these counter-narratives grew louder and louder.

As I have attempted to show, this behaviour – and the arrogance that sustained it – was built into the *Sunday Times* newsroom's DNA, the journalistic culture and practice. They lived in a world where they believed they were still all-powerful, and failed to recognise when they stood alone and isolated, that the internet had empowered their critics and weakened their own authority. It was the ignominy of those so set in their ways that they can't see that the world has changed around them.

*

As I finished this book, and despaired at the state of our media and its capacity to play its rightful role in our democracy, I took a few days off to read through the entries to the 15th annual Taco Kuiper Award for Investigative Journalism. They revived my faith in my chosen profession.

There were 25 entries, from print and television, a couple in more than one medium, and even a podcast for the first time – a powerful use of new journalism tools and techniques. There was collaborative work.

There was some riveting story-telling.

As always, most were about corruption, with strong entries about not just national-government, but local-government and private-sector malfeasance. There were also stories dealing with the environment, land issues, sexual abuse, police killings and the functioning of the national lottery. The range and quality were inspiring.

What was striking was that there were only one or two entries from traditional outlets, and most of them were from relatively small internet-based operations that had been springing up on the fringe: *amaBhungane*, *Oxpeckers* (which specialises in environmental investigation), Moneyweb (a financial and business site), GroundUp (a local, bottom-up, reporting initiative) and the Organized Crime and Corruption Reporting Project (OCCRP), an Eastern-European-based anti-corruption initiative. This was where the interesting journalism was coming from, as well as the crucial investigative work. These were all non-commercial operations, dependent largely on support from philanthropic foundations or individuals.

Finding one entry that stood out from the rest as worthy of the award was going to be a tough task. And as our panel of judges chose a shortlist, it became clear that any of the top six could stand as an exemplar of powerful, innovative, courageous, ground-breaking journalism.

'There is nothing wrong with the Fourth Estate,' one of my fellow judges, a non-journalist, remarked. I might have differed with him on the overall state of our news media, but he was correct that there remained powerful pockets of accountability journalism, mainly because there were individuals or small groups who continued to do the work that shone a spotlight on those who wielded power.

*

Today, with the spread of Covid-19, and South Africa and the world's economy in serious decline, never has it seemed more important to have accurate, reliable information delivered in ways that are easy to absorb, understand and share. And never have we been so vulnerable to the spread of disinformation that can cost lives and exacerbate the impact of any cataclysmic event. It's a world in which trust and vigilance are at their most essential, and in short supply.

It's the golden age of Twitter, as people around the world, in big groups and small, share videos, memes, jokes and great stories that both bring home the weight of the crisis and lighten it. It's the time of Zoom, when we can hold meetings, reunions and discussions more efficiently than ever before. New tools promote communication and enable journalism.

But it also feels like the dark days of social media, when truths, half-truths and malicious manipulations flourish, and fact-checkers and truth-tellers run after them, trying to catch up, where noise drowns out news, and we have to struggle each day to pick the few truths from the mass of untruths that flood our spaces.

Africa Check, the continent's leading fact-checking operation, for which I currently chair the board of trustees, saw a four-fold increase in its website audience in the first two months of the coronavirus crisis. It was a clear indication of the need and hunger for accurate information, a time when the work of journalists – selecting, verifying, storifying, editing, double-checking, fighting disinformation, drawing people together around a common understanding of the problem and potential solutions – is most needed. And that applies particularly to watchdog journalism, ensuring that government and the private sector do what's required in these times, and don't abuse the opportunity of the crisis to grasp excessive power or profiteer. Many of our civil liberties have been curtailed by the emergency, and it will take a vigilant media to ensure such compromises are not extended beyond it.

The coronavirus crisis is accelerating the changes we've been watching in our media for the past decade, boosting social media, speeding the decline of slower, analogue media like traditional newspapers, proliferating both disinformation agents and fact-checkers, and with less investment in the basics of reporting and editing. The decline in advertising that will result from the economic downturn will lead to further shrinking of newsrooms and fewer resources for journalism.

In these conditions, it becomes clearer that the crisis in news media is not one the markets alone can solve. It's not merely a business-model problem, but a political and community problem, a crack in the functioning of democracy. An open democracy will not remain open for long without institutions that will fight to keep it open.

In South Africa, traditional media institutions might be vulnerable, but we keep faith in those pockets of excellence, those individuals or groups of journalists who continue to shine light into dark corners.

ABBREVIATIONS

ANC: African National Congress
BAT: British American Tobacco
CCB: Civil Cooperation Bureau
DIRCO: Department of International Relations and Cooperation
DoD: Department of Defence
EFF: Economic Freedom Fighters
FITA: Fair Trade Independent Tobacco Association
FSS: Forensic Security Services
HRIU: High-Risk Investigations Unit (SARS)
ICD: Independent Complaints Directorate
ICIJ: International Consortium of Investigative Journalists
ID: identity
IPID: Independent Police Investigative Directorate
JSE: Johannesburg Stock Exchange
MK: Umkhonto we Sizwe
MP: Member of Parliament
NPA: National Prosecuting Authority
Outa: Organisation Undoing Tax Abuse
PIC: Public Investment Corporation
SABC: South African Broadcasting Corporation
SAPS: South African Police Service
SARS: South African Revenue Service
SSA: State Security Agency
Stratcom: Strategic Communications (an apartheid Security
            Police network)
TISA: Tobacco Institute of South Africa
WMC: white monopoly capital

ACKNOWLEDGEMENTS

Many people have given generously of their time to assist me in understanding the events described in this book. I have named some of those I interviewed in the text – and a few who refused to talk to me – but I can't list all as some spoke only on background or on condition it wasn't for attribution. I greatly appreciate their candour and preparedness to give me insight.

The University of the Witwatersrand provided, as always, a stimulating working environment that enabled the work to be done, and my colleagues in the Journalism Department gave me support and encouragement.

I was fortunate to spend memorable time in a Logan Non-Fiction Writing Fellowship at the beautiful Carey Institute in Rensselaerville, New York, snowed in with inspiring company from a wonderful group of fellow writers, and pampered by generous hosts.

My colleagues in the Wits Creative Writing MA class have been kind and helpful in their critique of my work and I have enjoyed the interaction with them. In particular, I am grateful to Bronwyn Keene-Young, Gerrit Olivier, Ivan Vladislavic, Phillippa Yaa de Villiers, Terry Kurgan, Jonathan Cane and Achal Prabhala for their insight and guidance.

The commitment and care of the Jonathan Ball publishing team make them a pleasure to work with, and Jeremy Boraine's patience and firmness is – in retrospect, at least – a blessing. Editor Tracey Hawthorne knocked me and this manuscript into shape with care and dedication.

Most importantly, my wife Harriet and my children Jesse, Georgia and Jana were there with support and encouragement when I was flagging. We will remember this time in coronavirus lockdown for many things, including the whisky rationing and my complaining about the ordeal of referencing, but mostly for being together.

REFERENCES

PART 1

3   'She sent an email in September 2010 to the Sunday Times with a tip-off…':
     Stephen Hofstatter, email, 9 February 2010; Ray Hartley, interview, 27 February
     2019.

3   'Stephan Hofstatter wrote in 2015…': Stephan Hofstatter, 'Film-Maker's View'.
     www.aljazeera.com, 19 November 2015.

3   'Wa Afrika said on one occasion…': Wa Afrika quoted in Noseweek, issue 150, April
     2012.

4   'What the reporters told…': Bongani Siqoko, interview, Rosebank, Johannesburg,
     February 2019.

5   'In 2020, Hofstatter would only say…': Stephan Hofstatter, email, 8 March 2020.

5   'And Hofstatter said they spoke…': Stephan Hofstatter, email, 8 March 2020.

6   'It was more than a year later…': Ray Hartley, interview, Johannesburg, 27 Febru-
     ary 2019; Johan Booysen, interview, Midrand, 12 December 2018.

7   'Booysen told me that in the interview…': Johan Booysen, interview, Midrand,
     12 December 2018.

8   'Hofstatter denied showing Booysen…': Stephan Hofstatter, email, 8 March 2020.

15   'Hofstatter told me he'd informed police communications officials…': Stephan Hofstat-
     ter, email, 8 March 2020.

16   'When Booysen later complained…': Johan Booysen: 'Complaint against the Sunday
     Times', Press Ombudsman, November 2015.

16   'Wa Afrika wouldn't…': Mzilikazi Wa Afrika, email, 14 May 2019.

16   'Hofstatter took a different view…': Stephan Hofstatter, email, 8 March 2020.

19   'The headline would have been familiar…': Bheki Cele, 'Police must shoot to kill,
     worry later', quoted on www.iol.co.za, 31 July 2009.

19   '… who'd militarised police structures…': Mail & Guardian, 'Cele upbeat over new
     police ranks', 12 April 2010.

19   'He'd later denied this phrase …': Bheki Cele, quoted in www.timeslive.co.za,
     6 November 2019.

20   'The paper had also established a policy…': Phylicia Oppelt, interview, Johannes-
     burg, 9 February 2019.

20   'All bylined writers were given the chance …': Stephan Hofstatter, email, 8 March
     2020.

26   'The paper grew consistently…': Audit Bureau of Circulations, www.abc.org.za.

26   'Myburgh was accused…': John Matisonn, God, Spies and Lies, Quivertree, 2015.

27   'The paper for the people…': Joel Mervis, The Fourth Estate, Jonathan Ball, 1989;
     Nadine Dreyer, A Century of Sundays, Zebra, 2006.

28   'The contradictions came to a head…' David Bullard, Sunday Times, 6 April 2008.

28   'ANC leader Pallo Jordan said…': 'SA does not need Bullard', News24, 22 April
     2008.

29 'City Press *reported that the ICD ...*': Paddy Harper of *City Press*, quoted in *Noseweek*, issue 165, 1 July 2013.

30 '*Now that the dust has settled ...*': *Sunday Times*, 1 July 2012.

30 '*Police said that in searches ...*': *Noseweek*, issue 165, 1 July 2013.

31 '*It took seven years ...*': Johan Booysen, 'I feel vindicated', www.dailymaverick.co.za, 9 July 2019.

32 '*...memorably called "the first rough draft of history" ...*': The origin of this phrase tells its own story about the journalistic complications of accuracy and verification. It's widely and repeatedly attributed to Philip Graham, former *Washington Post* publisher in a 1963 speech to *Newsweek* correspondents in London, quoted in the 1997 memoire of his wife, Kate Graham, *Personal History* (Alfred A Knopf). But some internet sleuthing by media critic Jack Shafer in *Slate* (30 August 2010) found it in a 1943 *New Republic* book review by Alan Barth, and in *The Washington Post* itself in an editorial on 13 June 1948 (authored by an editorial board but published under Graham's name). A variation (without the word 'rough') appears repeatedly in *The Washington Post* in the 1940s, even before Graham became publisher. Etymologist Barry Popik (www.barrypopik.com, 3 July 2004) found another variation, with the word 'rough' but without 'first', in print in 1905 in 'The Educational Value of News' by George Helgesen Fitch (*The State*, Columbia, 5 December 1905). The *Yale Book of Quotations* quotes author Douglass Cater in 1959 writing 'The reporter [is] one who each twenty-four hours dictates a first draft of history'. Where does the credit belong? Perhaps it's best shared.

33 '*When I pointed out ...*': Johan Booysen, emails, 28 September 2018 and 16 October 2018.

34 '*Booysen gave me the first draft ...*': Most of the details on pages 39-43 come from 'Draft Affidavit for the Zondo Commission of Inquiry' by Johan Wessel Booysen, given to me in 2019.

35 '*In 2012 it emerged in newspaper reports ...*': *Sunday Tribune*, 25 March 2012; *Noseweek*, issue 149, 1 March 2012.

39 '*When the* Sunday Times *editor ...*': Bongani Siqoko, interview, Rosebank, Johannesburg 2019.

39 '*Hofstatter told me that Panday ...*': Stephen Hofstatter, email, 8 March 2020.

39 '*Journalists from other newspapers ...*': Interviews with multiple individuals. Also, *Noseweek*, issue 149, March 2012, reported, 'Panday's associates only approached the paper [*Sunday Times*] after they had failed in their attempts to "sell" the story and pictures to at least three KZN papers. All three have told *Noseweek* they rejected the story when they realised they were being recruited into a smear campaign being run by crime suspects.'

39 '*Booysen discovered that...*': Johan Booysen, interview, 2019.

39 '*These were all the dealings that Stephan Hofstatter admitted ...*': Stephan Hofstatter, email, 8 March 2020.

40 '*Booysen said to me, "If Wa Afrika denies my version ..."*': Johan Booysen, interview, Midrand, 12 December 2018.

40 '*They would've had to ignore what rival newspapers such as the* Sunday Tribune *...*': 'Booysen sticks to his guns', *Sunday Tribune*, 28 September 2014.

41 '*There was much more to this tale ...*': 'Who is Johan Booysen?' *Sunday Times*, 11 December 2011.

42   'Nose*week took on the* Sunday Times *in a series of long ...*': 'The wrong man', *Noseweek*, issue 149, March 2012; 'KZN death squad controversy', *Noseweek*, issue 150, April 2012; 'The Death Squad that wasn't', *Noseweek*, issue 165, July 2013; 'Update: Cato Manor', *Noseweek*, issue 167, September 2013; 'Booysen to sue Sunday Times for massive damages', *Noseweek*, issue 174, April 2014; 'I shall return', *Noseweek*, issue 175, May 2014.

42   *'The* Sunday Times *threesome said it was "poppycock" ...*': Rob Rose, Mzilikazi Wa Afrika and Stephan Hofstatter, 'Truth is the first casualty', *Sunday Times*, 4 March 2012.

43   *'The* Sunday Times *treated* Noseweek *...*': 'Noseweek's Cato Manor story is pure invention', *Sunday Times*, 1 July 2012. The same article appeared that day in the *Weekend Argus* and the *Sunday Tribune*.

43   *'When Martin Welz wrote a piece ...*': *Weekend Argus* and *Sunday Tribune*, 24 June 2012.

44   *'A further* Sunday Times *article in February 2015 gunned for ...*': 'A trail of bodies and ton of lies', *Sunday Times*, 1 February 2015.

46   *'Some years back, the* Sunday Times *introduced ...*': Paula Fray, Anton Harber, Franz Kruger, Dario Milo, 'Sunday Times Review Panel Report', December 2008.

46   *'Editor Phylicia Oppelt, who was ...*': Phylicia Oppelt, unpublished statement, 2019.

46   *'In 2013 the* Sunday Times *investigations unit came up with ...*': Stephan Hofstatter, Mzilikazi Wa Afrika and Rob Rose, 'Cato Cop comes clean on "hit squad"', *Sunday Times*, 24 February 2013.

47   *'The same witness featured in a documentary ...*': 'South Africa: Echoes of apartheid', https://www.aljazeera.com/programmes/africainvestigates/2015/11/south-africa-echoes-apartheid-151118121841557.html

49   *'As an example, Phylicia Oppelt ...*': interview, 2019.

49   *'Wa Afrika's 2015 memoir ...*': Mzilikazi Wa Afrika, *Nothing Left to Steal*, Penguin, 2014.

49   *'As one reviewer put it ...*': Leon de Kock, 'Fearless corruption buster', *Mail & Guardian*, 30 December 2014.

53   *'... Wa Afrika turned to his other great love ...*': See https://www.traxsource.com/label/46323/bomba-afrika and https://youtu.be/o484kiMdnrU.

54   *'... took down the Minister of Communications, Dina Pule, she brought this up*': Statement by Minister of Communications in response to *Sunday Times* smear campaign, 22 April 2013.

54   *'It emerged that Martin Welz ...*': '[Welz] told me that he had employed Mzilikazi wa Afrika after Wa Afrika had left the *Sunday Times* under a cloud in 2004. He quickly came to the conclusion however that wa Afrika's reporting was ethically suspect and terminated his association with him.' Ed Herbst, 'Top journalists duke it out in Sunday Times fake news controversy', Biznews.com, 22 October 2018.

54   *'Hartley said that when he took over in 2010 ...*': Ray Hartley, interview, Johannesburg, 27 February 2019.

55   *'And Munusamy proved them right ...*': 'Journalist Ranjeni Munusamy placed on special leave ...', News24, 18 September 2019.

55   *'Stephan Hofstatter had a stellar career ...*': Most of these details were provided by Hofstatter himself, email, 2020.

56 '*In a radio interview in 2017 ...*': 'Is journalist Stephan Hofstatter genuinely contrite about the SARS rogue unit story?', interview with Eusebius McKaiser, www.702.com.

57 '*Former* Sunday Times *subeditor Jeremy Gordin told me ...*': Jeremy Gordin, interview, Johannesburg, 2019.

57 '*On its launch ...*': 'Minister Faith Muthambi congratulates African Times ...', www.gov.za, 31 August 2016.

58 '*The phonecall came ...*': Rob Rose, interviews, 2019.

60 '*Across town, at the rival* City Press *...*': Jacques Pauw, interview, 2019.

61 '*IPID investigator Humbulani Khuba ...*': Humbulani Innocent Khuba, Warning Statement in the matter between The State and HI Khuba, 3 March 2016.

62 '*... a dubious figure caught up in ...*': Stephen Grootes, 'The rise and fall of Richard Mdluli', *Daily Maverick*, 17 January 2018.

63 '*It emerged later that Mdluli ...*': 'Mdluli's letter to Zuma shows crime intelligence "involved in party politics"', TimesLive, 20 September 2019.

63 '*The story took another turn ...*': Robert John McBride, Affidavit for Zondo Commission, 13 February 2019.

65 '*It helps to know ...*': Bryan Rostron, *Till Babylon Falls,* Coronet Books, 1991, and *Robert McBride: The Struggle Continues,* Tafelberg, 2019.

68 '*Nhleko commissioned a firm of private lawyers ...*': Sandile July, 'Report on the IPID Investigations Regarding the Illegal Renditions of Zimbabwean Nationals', Werksmans Attorneys, 24 April 2015.

69 '*The report was quickly leaked to the Sunday Times*: 'Charge McBride for Dramat Case', *Sunday Times*, 3 May 2015. The *Sunday Times* went so far as to write it as a call for prosecution of McBride, Dramat and Sibiya, and the reader had to get to the third paragraph to see that it was the report that said this, rather than the paper itself.

70 '*The charges against them were dropped*': www.timeslive.co.za, 8 October 2018.

70 '*But while he was on suspension ...*' Robert John McBride, Affidavit for Zondo Commission, 13 February 2019.

70 '*... the autobiography of journalist Mzilikazi Wa Afrika ...*': Mzilikazi Wa Afrika, *Nothing Left to Steal,* Penguin, 2014.

73 '*In the words of* Washington Post *writer ...*': David S Broder, 'Speech to the Pulitzer Prize Winners', 1979, quoted in *Behind the Front Page,* Simon and Schuster, New York, 1987, p12.

74 '*Polela wrote later ...*': 'Crime Intelligence played reporters', *Mail & Guardian*, 19 October 2018.

75 '*He swore in an affidavit in March that year ...*': Report by Colonel Kobus Demeyer Roelofse to the Anti-Corruption Task Team, 2 March 2012. Available at https://www.politicsweb.co.za/documents/a-report-on-the-mdluli-investigation--col-kobus-ro.

77 '*The spokesperson for the ...*': Johann van Loggerenberg, *Rogue,* Jonathan Ball, Cape Town, 2016, p19.

78 '*In 2005 SARS had teamed up ...*': Much of the detail in this section comes from Van Loggerenberg's two books, *Rogue* (Jonathan Ball, Cape Town, 2016) and *Tobacco Wars* (Tafelberg, Cape Town, 2019); and Ivan Pillay, 'SARS Submission to

the Sikhakhane Committee', 24 October 2014.

79   *'And as another journalist ...'*: Pearlie Joubert, interview, Cape Town, 2019.

80   *'When the* Sunday Times *approached SARS ...'*: Adrian Lackay, email to Malcolm Rees and Rob Rose at the *Sunday Times*, 8 August 2014.

81   *'Then Walter suddenly withdrew ...'*: Belinda Walter, email to Rob Rose at *Sunday Times*, 7 February 2014.

86   *'Sam Sole and Lionel Faull ...'*: 'Big tobacco in bed with SA law enforcement agencies', *Mail & Guardian*, 20 March 2014.

87   *'In July 2014 Angelique Serrao ...'*: 'SARS target of tobacco industry backlash', Independent Online, 31 July 2014.

87   *'Malcolm Rees himself wrote ...'*: 'BAT's smoke and mirrors', *Sunday Times*, 30 March 2014.

87   *'But it was Jacques Pauw's story in* City Press ...*'* Jacques Pauw, 'Sex, Sars and rogue spies', *City Press*, 10 August 2014.

88   *'As political theorist Hannah Arendt wrote*: Hannah Arendt, 'Truth and Politics', *New Yorker*, 25 February 1967.

88   *'Oppelt spoke that same Friday ...'*: Adrian Lackay, interview, Johannesburg, 25 January 2019.

88   *'Rees was later to say ...'*: Johann van Loggerenberg, Rogue, Jonathan Ball, Cape Town, 2016, p149.

90   *'The project to fix and modernise SARS...'*: Much of the detail in this section comes from Van Loggerenberg's two books, *Rogue*, Jonathan Ball, Cape Town, 2016, and *Tobacco Wars*, Tafelberg, Cape Town, 2019; Ivan Pillay, interview, 21 January 2019.

90   *'The tax net had grown ...'*: Media Statement by the Minister of Finance, Mr Pravin Gordhan, on the Preliminary Outcome of Revenue Collection, 1 April 2012.

92   *'... a dubious character called James Nkambule ...'*: 'Mbeki to be quizzed about Nkambule', Independent Online, 13 May 2001; 'Man behind hit-squad claims', *Sunday Times*, 10 October 2010.

92   *'... and there was the Browse Mole report ...'*: 'Inside the Browse Mole Report', Biznews.com, 1 May 2019; 'Special Browse Mole Report', https://mg.co.za/tag/special-browse-mole-report/.

93   *'It was a dossier that the SSA ...'*: 'Gordhan called back over "plan to meet coup plotters"', www.businesslive.co.za, 29 March 2017.

93   *'One day during this period ...'*: Pearlie Joubert, Archie Henderson, interviews, Johannesburg, 2019.

94   *'One of these was "Project Snowman" ...'*: Ivan Pillay, 'SARS Submission to the Sikhakhane Committee', 24 October 2014. Johann van Loggerenberg, *Rogue*, Jonathan Ball, Cape Town, 2016, p90.

95   *'In 2012 alone ...'*: Ivan Pillay, 'SARS Submission to the Sikhakhane Committee', 24 October 2014.

99   *'The day after the article appeared ...'*: Johann van Loggerenberg, personal correspondence.

99   *'... in a 2019 statement ...'*: Malcolm Rees, letter to Johann van Loggerenberg, 8 September 2019.

100 *'To me, though, she said, "Perhaps I did ...'*: Phylicia Oppelt, interview, Johannesburg, 9 February 2019, and unpublished statement, 2019.

100 *'...but he showed me internal reports ...'*: Johann van Loggerenberg, WhatsApp message, 4 April 2020.

100 *'Van Loggerenberg did, in fact, join the police ...'*: Johann van Loggerenberg, personal communication, 2020.

100 *'... Mastenbroek, who'd held a senior position...'*: Rudolf Mastenbroek, interview, 2020.

102 *'My first personal encounter ...'*: Johann van Loggerenberg, email, 19 April 2018.

102 *'I'd written an article for the* Daily Maverick *...'*: 'Celebrate the good while addressing the bad in journalism', *Daily Maverick*, 10 November 2017.

104 *'... a "Pretoria Mata Hari" ...'*: 'Is she SA's Mata Hari?', *City Press*, 17 August 2014.

107 *'The man at the centre ...'*: Andries Janse van Rensburg, email to Piet Rampedi, 9 October 2014.

107 *'SARS sent the* Sunday Times *...'*: Adrian Lackay, email to Piet Rampedi, 3 October 2014.

108 *'Piet Rampedi later told the Press Council ...'*: Ruling by the Press Ombudsman, Johann van Loggerenberg vs Sunday Times, 16 January 2016.

111 *'The material had been offered ...'*: Andrew Trench, interview, Johannesburg, 28 February 2019.

PART II

115 *'John (not his real name) picked up one ...'*: 'John', interview, Cape Town, 2019; and Stefaans Brümmer, interviews, Cape Town, 2017/18/19/20.

117 *'WMC was a useful phrase ...'*: AmaBhungane and Scorpio, 'How Bell Pottinger sought to package SA economic message', *Daily Maverick*, 6 June 2017.

118 *'He showed Ajay Gupta ...'*: Jonathan Shapiro, 'Willing Buyer, Willing Seller', cartoon, 27 June 2017.

121 *'"We're not political in any way," ...'*: Rebecca Davis, '#GuptaLeaks whistle-blowers speak out for the first time', *Daily Maverick*, 15 August 2018.

123 *'I need some advice ...'*: Brian Currin, interviews, 2019/20.

125 *'News24 reported that there were nine ...'*: '9 mysterious cases of intimidation ...', News24, 20 March 2017.

126 *'It included some of the country's ...'*: 'Cyberattacks on female journalists threaten everyone', *Mail & Guardian*, 6 March 2019; Ferial Haffajee, 'The Gupta Fake News Factory and Me', HuffingtonPost.com, 6 June 2017; 'Dark day for female newsmakers', The Media Online, 30 June 2017.

127 *'Should they put the raw data ...'*: ICIJ Offshore Leaks Database, www.offshoreleaks.icij.org.

127 *'The first such major data dump ...'*: 'Luxembourg Leaks: Global Companies' Secrets Exposed', https://www.icij.org/investigations/luxembourg-leaks/.

128 *'... Julian Assange's WikiLeaks ...'*: Julian Assange, *The Unauthorised Autobiography*, Canongate, London, 2011; David Leigh and Luke Harding, *WikiLeaks: Inside Julian Assange's War on Secrecy*, Guardian Books, London, 2011.

130 *'I thought I had a rocket in my head ...'*: Branko Brkic, interviews, Johannesburg, 2018/9.

132 *'Was it vodka or tequila?'*: Stefaans Brümmer, interviews, Cape Town, 2017/18/19/20.

135 *The Star newspaper and specialist publication* IT Web *...'*: 'Sahara wins substantial stake in Gauteng Online tender', *IT Web*, 8 December 2003; '1 100 Gauteng schools online by March 2004', Africa News Service, 10 December 2003.

135 *'In the event, Sahara Computers ...'*: 'Gauteng Online slammed as R3bn flop', *The Star*, 29 July 2009; 'Gauteng Online provider utterly failed', *IT Web*, 15 May 2012.

135 *'... in a story about the Guptas' attempts ...'*: 'Too slick operators', *Noseweek*, issue 105, July 2008. The article was prescient: 'Leverage is what they call it when political connections win you that government contract ...[but] their over-hasty name-dropping and careless use of company names lost them their bid ...'

136 *'Reporter Mandy Rossouw ...'*: Chris Roper, 'The day we broke Nkandla', *Mail and Guardian*, 4 December 2013.

137 '*"When the #GuptaLeaks emails were released later ..."*': Nic Dawes, 'The truth about President Zuma laid bare' in Anton Harber (ed), *Southern African Muckraking*, Jacana, 2018;

139 *'Stories did flow ...'*: www.amabhungane.org.

140 *'When Eyewitness News reporter ...'*: Barry Bateman, telephone interview, 2018.

142 '*"The brazenness of this act of entitlement ..."*': Richard Poplack, 'Hell's Wedding Bells – How the #GuptaLeaks reveal that South Africans paid for the whole damn thing', *Daily Maverick*, 30 June 2017.

142 *'The Guptas issued a statement ...'*: 'Radio 702 "misrepresented" facts over Gupta jet', The Media Online, 30 April 2013.

142 *'But the Department of International Relations ...'*: 'We didn't give Waterkloof permission ...', News24, 30 April 2013.

142 *'Then the DoD ...'*: 'SANDF unaware of Gupta's air base use', News24, 30 April 2013.

142 *'And then the ruling party ...'*: Gwede Mantashe, 'The landing at Waterkloof', 30 April 2013.

143 *'The opposition parties ...'*: 'Debate on Use of Air Force Base Waterkloof by Gupta Family', *Hansard*, 21 May 2013.

143 *'In their 2017 book ...'*: Adriaan Basson and Pieter du Toit, *Enemy of the People*, Jonathan Ball, Cape Town, 2017.

144 *'There were reports that the family ...'*: 'It'll be all white on the night: Gupta racism row over whites-only hiring policy', Biznews.com, 14 June 2017.

145 *'Unknown middle-ranking Free State politician ...'*: 'Mosebenzi Zwane sworn in as mineral resources minister', *Mail & Guardian*, 23 September 2015.

145 *'In December that year Nhlanhla Nene was suddenly axed ...'*: 'Nhlanhla Nene removed as finance minister', *Mail & Guardian*, 9 December 2015.

145 *'Under massive public pressure ...'*: 'President Zuma has fired finance minister', *Mail & Guardian*, 30 March 2017.

145 *'In March 2016 Deputy Finance Minister Mcebisi Jonas said ...'*: 'The day I turned down R600 million ...', TimesLive, 3 November 2016.

145 *'Eccentric ANC MP ...'*: 'Guptas offered me ministerial role – Vytjie Mentor', Independent Online, 17 March 2016.

146 *'Another ANC member, Themba Maseko ...'*: 'Bullying Guptas wanted diplomatic passports', TimesLive, 12 May 2013.

147 *'Scholars climbed in ...'*: Mark Swilling (convenor) et al, *Betrayal of the Promise, How South Africa is being stolen,* PARI et al, May 2017.

147 *'Church leaders followed ...'*: SACC Report to the Church Public on the Unburdening Panel, www.sacc.org.za, 18 May 2017.

147 *'The Organisation Undoing Tax Abuse ...'*: 'Organisation believes charge sheet has ...', www.thesouthafrican.com, 28 June 2017.

148 *'Brkic got a sample ...'*: Stefaans Brümmer, interviews, Cape Town, 2017/18/19/20; Branko Brkic, interviews, Johannesburg, 2018/9.

150 *'... the* Sunday Times *must have insisted ...'*: Shantini Naidoo, 'Magda Wierzycka's mission', *Sunday Times,* 21 January 2018.

151 *'... lambasting rival fund manager ...'*: 'Wierzycka raises the alarm ...', Biznews, 10 March 2017.

151 *'At the height of Zuma's presidency ...'*: Liesl Peyper, 'Wierzycka's 10-point plan to get SA back on track', Fin24, 30 October 2017.

151 *'She teamed up with ...'*: 'Helen Suzman Foundation, Magda Wierzycka team up ...', CNBCAfrica.com, 14 December 2017.

152 *'Later, she took on the Public Investment Corporation ...'*: 'Wierzycka paints a gloomy picture for PIC billions in Iqbal Survé's hands', TimesLive, 21 February 2019.

152 *'Wierzycka tried to buy back ...'*: 'Survé breaks silence on Ayo scandal by attacking Wierzycka', *Business Day,* 12 December 2018.

156 *'By contrast, amaB is fervently non-partisan ...'*: https://amabhungane.org/about-us/.

157 *'This tradition goes back to ...'*: *The South African Commercial Advertiser,* South African Library, Cape Town, 1978; Wessel de Kock, *A Manner of Speaking: The origins of the press in South Africa,* Saayman and Weber, Cape Town, 1982.

158 *'Their publications were small ...'*: Les Switzer (ed), *South Africa's Alternative Press,* Cambridge, 1997.

158 *'Key founder Pixley ka Seme ...'*: Peter Limb (ed), *The People's Paper,* Wits University Press, 2012.

158 *'... the small, struggling* Guardian/New Age ...': James Zug, *The Guardian,* Unisa, Pretoria, 2007.

163 *'Stung by losing the first round ...'*: 'Editorial: The GuptaLeaks revealed', https://amabhungane.org/stories/editorial-the-guptaleaks-revealed/, 1 June 2017.

167 *'As The Wall Street Journal put it ...'*: 'Inside the Political Scandal Rocking South Africa', *The Wall Street Journal,* 10 October 2017.

168 *'Even ANC spokesman Zizi Kodwa ...'*: 'Investigate GuptaLeaks, says Kodwa', *The Citizen,* 15 September 2017.

168 *'Groups of political thugs ...'*: 'BLF in shocking protest outside Peter Bruce's home', Independent Online, 29 June 2017.

168 *'... accused by Lord Peter Hain and Treasury ...'*: Radio 702, 23 May 2018. Peter Hain said, 'Hogan Lovells turned a blind eye to the looting for the tax agency. They took a fat fee and ignored the truth.' Ismail Momoniat said, 'The law firm issued an

incomplete, fatally flawed whitewash of a report' which helped 'state capture and corruption take root in South Africa.' http://www.702.co.za/articles/304811/hogan-lovells-fingered-role-in-state-capture-plays-the-victim-in-parliament

169 *The amaB/Daily Maverick team, for example, published a devastating series* … ': The McKinsey dossier, Parts 1-6, 14 September/3 October/9 October/12 October/23 October/25 October 2017; 'Gupta spin machine commissioned BLF's Mngxitama', 24 July 2017; 'KPMG missed more money laundering red flags', 26 November 2017.

169 *'KPMG's South African heads* …': 'Heads roll at KPMG', *Mail & Guardian*, 15 September 2017.

169 *'McKinsey suspended South African director* … ': 'Now McKinsey SA director Vikas Sagar has been suspended', BusinessLive, 9 July 2017.

169 *'SAP at first denied* …': 'SAP initiates disciplinary action ...', *IT Web*, 26 October 2017.

170 *'He called her Lady Macbeth* …': Branko Brkic (ed), *We have a Game Changer*, Daily Maverick, Johannesburg, 2019.

171 *'It took some prompting* … ': Magda Wierzycka, email, 27 April 2019.

172 *'You have shown yourself* …': Anton Harber, email, 13 May 2019.

172 *'The safety of my family* …': Magda Wierzycka, email, 14 May 2019.

172 '*… the reply – and a threat – came from* … ': Rael Gootkin, Werksmans Attorneys, email, 9 January 2020, 9.30am.

172 *'But she had second thoughts* …': Rael Gootkin, Werksmans Attorneys, email, 9 January 2020, 9.32am.

173 *'I replied* …': Anton Harber, email, 13 May 2019, 10.35am.

173 *'Nine months after* … ': Rael Gootkin, Werksmans Attorneys, email, 9 January 2020, 1.36pm.

176 '*… probably the greatest investigative* …': William Saunderson-Meyer, 'GuptaLeaks: Let's hear from the horse's mouth', Independent Online, 29 July 2017.

176 '*… wrote Adriaan Basson and Pieter du Toit* …': Adriaan Basson and Pieter du Toit, *Enemy of the People*, Jonathan Ball, Cape Town, 2017.

176 *'In March 2018, I convened* …': Remarks of the Judges, Taco Kuiper Awards 2017, 16 March 2018. https://journalism.co.za/new/wp-content/uploads/2018/03/Taco-Kuiper-Speech-2018.pdf

177 '*… sharing the 2019 Global* …': Global Investigative Journalism Network, 'Investigations from Peru, Philippines, South Africa Win Global Shining Light Award', 28 September 2019. https://gijn.org/2019/09/28/investigations-from-peru-philippines-south-africa-win-global-shining-light-award/

177 *'Small contributions from the public* …': AmaBhungane, Audited Financials for 2016/7, 2017/8, 2018/9, https://amabhungane.org/about-us/

177 *'The amaB model took off* …': MNN Centre for Investigative Reporting, Lesotho https://lescij.org/; INK Centre, Botswana https://inkjournalism.org/; Mídia Lab, Mozambique http://www.midialab.org/; CIJM, Malawi https://www.investigative-malawi.org/; CIJZ, Zimbabwe https://www.facebook.com/cijzimbabwe/.

179 'Currin, as an intermediary, had had a tough time …' Brian Currin, interviews, 2019/20.

180 *'South Africa has legislation* …': Protected Disclosures Act (no 26 of 2000).

PART III

184 *'Two key journalists … were let go'*: 'Sunday Times parts ways with Mzilikazi wa Afrika and Stephan Hofstatter', Eyewitness News, 14 October 2018.

185 *'In the SARS case …'*: Ruling by the Press Ombudsman, Johann van Loggerenberg vs Sunday Times, 16 January 2016.

185 *'Pete Richer, one of the …'*: Video: Questions over SARS rogue unit from Pete Richer, YouTube, 21 September 2018. https://youtu.be/ds788N4U5-4

185 *'One of the country's best-known …'*: Max du Preez, 'The case for *Sunday Times* journalist to come clean', News24, 16 October 2018.

186 *'Investigative journalist Jacques Pauw said …'*: Jacques Pauw, 'Come on Sunday Times, pay back the money!!!!!', Facebook, 24 January 2014; Jacques Pauw, 'Exposing the puppet master behind the Sunday Times scandal', News24, 16 October 2018.

186 *'Another commentator, Chris Vick …'*: 'Black marks on its name that a media icon has yet to properly erase', *Sunday Times*, 21 October 2018.

187 *'Mukoki's complaint to the press ombudsman …'*: Mr Alan Mukoki, former CEO of the Land Bank, against the Sunday Times, Ruling, 13 March 2008.

189 *'Two weeks later the* Sunday Times *published a front-page retraction …'*: *Sunday Times*, 7 September 2008.

189 *'I was one of four people commissioned …'*: Paula Fray, Anton Harber, Franz Kruger, Dario Milo, *Sunday Times Review Panel Report*, December 2008.

191 *'Even* The New York Times *suffered …'*: 'Repairing the Credibility Cracks', *The New York Times*, 4 May 2013.

192 *'George Darmanovic held court …'*: This section is based on extensive interviews with Chad Thomas, Johannesburg, 13 and 19 December 2018 and 7 January 2019, and others (anonymously), and draws on Jacques Pauw, *The President's Keepers*, Tafelberg, 2017.

204 *'A critical moment …'*: Rob Rose, interview, 2019.

204 *'Media24's parent company …'*: Anton Harber, *The Gorilla in the Room*, Mampoer Shorts, 2013.

207 *'In a decade,* Sunday Times *sales …'*: Audit Bureau of Circulations, www.abc.org.za.

208 *'And then the rise of the search …'*: Anton Harber, 'The big balancing act', *Financial Mail*, 16 November 2017.

209 *'Alan Rusbridger, editor of the UK's* The Guardian *…'*: Alan Rusbridger, *Breaking News: The remaking of journalism and why it matters now*, Canongate, Edinburgh, 2018.

211 *'The State of the Newsroom 2018 report …'*: Alan Finlay, *Structured Unstructured*, Wits Journalism, 2019.

219 *'Phylicia Oppelt drove into …'*: Phylicia Oppelt, interview, Johannesburg, 9 February 2019.

226 *'They'd reported that cricket hero …'*: 'Apology to Graeme Smith', TimesLive, 17 May 2015.

226 *'… they reported that a cousin of comedian Trevor Noah …'*: Trevor Noah, Twitter, 24 May 2015.

228 *'… four reports into SARS were commissioned …'*: Report of the Kanyane Panel, 2014; Investigations Report, Conduct of Mr Johann Hendrikus van Loggerenberg,

South African Revenue Service, by Adv Muzi Sikhakhane, Assisted by Advocate Nasreen Rajab-Budlender and Advocate Patrick Ramano, 5 November 2014; Report of the SARS Advisory Board, Judge Frank Kroon, 2015; Report to the SA Revenue Service on allegations of irregularities and misconduct, KPMG Services, 3 September 2015.

228 *'These reports – or versions of them ...':* 'Our stories on rogue SARS unit are backed by three probes', *Sunday Times*, 6 December 2015; 'KPMG report confirms our story', *Sunday Times*, 4 October 2015.

230 *'SARS's acting commissioner, Ivan Pillay ...':* Ivan Pillay, the Report of the Sikhakhane Panel of Investigation, undated.

231 *'In August 2019 I wrote to ...':* Anton Harber, email to Adv Muzi Sikhakhane, 20 August 2019.

231 *'His response was ...':* Adv Muzi Sikhakhane, email to Anton Harber, 20 August 2019.

232 *'... and apologised for his findings':* Judge F Kroon, apology, 19 May 2019.

234 *'It turned out to be worse ...':* Ruling by the Press Ombudsman, Johann van Loggerenberg vs Sunday Times, 16 January 2016.

236 *'Van Loggerenberg was given less than five hours ...':* Ruling by the Press Ombudsman, Johann van Loggerenberg vs Sunday Times, 16 January 2016.

237 *'Gordhan was given three hours ...':* Ruling by the Press Ombudsman, Pravin Gordhan vs Sunday Times, 15 December 2015.

237 *'The first mention of Gordhan ...':* Marianne Thamm, 'SARS Wars, season two', *Daily Maverick*, 24 January 2016.

238 *'Moyane moved swiftly ...':* Commission of Inquiry into Tax Administration and Governance by SARS, Judge R Nugent, Interim Report, 27 September 2018; Final Report, 11 December 2018.

240 *'Phylicia once asked me ...':* Pearlie Joubert, interview, Cape Town, 2018.

244 *'Oppelt launched a malicious ...':* 'Joubert is an embittered person', Eyewitness News, 17 December 2018.

245 *'A few weeks into the ...':* Songezo Zibi, Twitter, 29 September 2018. https://twitter.com/SongezoZibi/status/1045995457279913984

247 *'In fact,* Carte Blanche *had been warned ...':* Julian Rademeyer, email correspondence, 14 July 2020.

247 *'Van Loggerenberg took* Carte Blanche *...':* Van Loggerenberg, *Rogue*, Jonathan Ball, Cape Town, 2016.

248 *'Bingwa, though ...'* Radio 702. https://www.702.co.za/articles/279656/bongani-bingwa-gets-a-mention-in-the-president-s-keepers

250 *'... Johan Retief repeatedly savaged ...':* Rulings by the Press Ombudsman in the cases of Pravin Gordhan vs Sunday Times, 15 December 2015; Ivan Pillay vs Sunday Times, 16 December 2015; Johann van Loggerenberg vs Sunday Times, 16 January 2016.

252 *'"Damning findings," Marianne Thamm wrote ...'* Daily Maverick, 15 December 2015.

252 *'The paper did win one, secondary case ...':* Ruling by the Press Ombudsman, Pearlie Joubert vs Sunday Times, 27 January 2016.

257 *'In Rampedi's 2 000-word letter of resignation ...':* Piet Rampedi, 'Here is a copy of my resignation letter ...', Twitter, 17 October 2018. https://twitter.com/pietrampe-

di/status/1052570718385393665?lang=en

259   'Siqoko had a series of meetings ...': Bongani Siqoko, interview, January 2019.

263   '... but in September 2018 he held a launch of a book ...': 'Journalist's book launch hit by protests over SARS "rogue unit"', TimesLive, 20 September 2018. The fact that this was reported by Hofstatter's newsroom colleagues (who reintroduced the quotation marks around 'rogue unit') indicates the conflictual views in the organisation on his work. Video of part of this event can be found at https://youtu.be/ds788N4U5-4.

265   'The next day, radio host ...': 'Is journalist Stephan Hofstatter genuinely contrite about the SARS rogue unit story?', interview with Eusebius McKaiser, www.702.com.

267   'O'Sullivan was a formidable enemy ...': Paul O'Sullivan, interview, Johannesburg, 2019.

268   'Come on, Mr Tau ...': Paul O'Sullivan, email to Poloko Tau, 13 September 2018. The email was cc'd to Khomotso Phahlane, police spokesperson Major General Sally de Beer, and Robert McBride at IPID. Also Paul O'Sullivan email to Andrew Gill, Sunday Times, 18 September 2018.

268   'Two weeks later the Sunday Times ...': 'A transformed Sunday Times you can trust', Sunday Times, 7 October 2019.

269   'One example, from the early 1990s ...': Garson recorded this in some detail in her book, Undeniable: Memoir of a Covert War, Jacana, 2020.

272   'O'Sullivan's response?': 'That's better, Sunday Times, but you're not yet out the woods', BizNews, 15 October 2018.

273   'He told me that he'd thought of the reporters as friends ...': Johann van Loggerenberg, personal communication, 2020.

274   'Rose argued to me that he'd come in late ...': Rob Rose, interview, 2019.

275   '... his detailed response to ...': 'Former Sunday Times editor Ray Hartley's blistering response to "death squad" criticism', News24, 21 October 2018.

277   '... Rees agreed to write a letter ...': Malcolm Rees, letter to Van Loggerenberg, 8 September 2019.

278   'He later named me ...' Piet Rampedi, Twitter, 12 July 2019, https://twitter.com/pietrampedi/status/1149615535228723200.

280   Wa Afrika and Hofstatter refused ...': Erik van der Berg, 'Withdrawal of Taco Kuiper Award', letter to Harber on behalf of Wa Afrika and Hofstatter, 28 March 2019.

280   'Wa Afrika emailed ...': Mzilikazi Wa Afrika, email, 14 May 2019.

281   'Hofstatter and Wa Afrika wrote a long letter ...': To the Organisers of GIJC19, 26 September 2019.

281   '... but agreed to answer questions ...': Stephan Hofstatter, email, 8 March 2020.

282   'Some years after her fall from grace ...': Phylicia Oppelt, interview, Johannesburg, 9 February 2019, and unpublished statement, 2019.

287   'The role of the tobacco industry should get more attention': Johann van Loggerenberg, Rogue, Jonathan Ball, Cape Town, 2016, and Tobacco Wars, Tafelberg, Cape Town, 2019.

288   'As early as 2014, amaBhungane was reporting ...': Sam Sole, 'Big Tobacco in bed with SA law enforcement agencies', Mail & Guardian, 20 March 2014.

288   'In the same year, a whistleblower named Luis Pestana ...': Marianne Thamm, 'SARS

Wars: Massive data leak alleges British American Tobacco SA's role in bribery and corruption', *Daily Maverick*, 16 August 2016.

289 '*Shortly after Zuma was driven from office ...* ': The Presidency, Republic of South Africa, 'President Ramaphosa releases Review Panel Report on State Security Agency', 9 March 2019; Sarah Evans, 'Cleaning up the SSA: "The Vault is now closed"', News24, 1 December 2019.

CONCLUSION

295 '*In early 2018 a documentary called* Winnie ...': *Winnie*, written and directed by Pascale Lamche, Pumpernickel Films, 2017.

295 At The Weekly Mail *at that time ...* ': Irwin Manoim, *You have been warned ...*, Viking, Johannesburg, 1996.

296 '*The EFF, eager to claim ...* ': EFF condemns Sanef's silence on Stratcom Revelations, Statement, Economic Freedom Fighters, 12 April 2018.

296 '*... we were able to sue ...* ': Judgement in the matter between Thandeka Gzubule-Mbeki, Anton Harber and EFF, Mbuyiseni Quintin Ndlozi, Gauteng Local Division of the High Court, 24 January 2020.

297 '*I will now ... bring civil suits ...* ': Johann van Loggerenberg, Facebook, 9 June 2020.

298 '*The cost of the corruption ...* ': 'R250bn lost to state capture in the last three years, says Gordhan', *The Citizen*, 29 November 2017; 'State Capture wipes out third of SA's R4,9-trillion GDP', *Daily Maverick*, 1 March 2019.

300 '*There were highlights ...* ': Anton Harber (ed), *Southern African Muckraking*, Jacana, 2018.

300 '*... in its submission to the special media hearings ...* ': ANC Submission on Media to the Truth and Reconciliation Commission, 30 September 1997.

302 '*... published this by an anonymous poet*': *The South African Commercial Advertiser*, South African Library, Cape Town, 1978.

303 '*... Tiyo Soga's take on the role of the newspaper ...* ': *Indaba*, vol 1, no 1, August 1862, Lovedale.

303 '*... Isaac Wauchope wrote ...* ': Isaac Williams Wauchope, 'Fight with the Pen', *Isigidimi samaXhosa*, 1882. Hoho was Chief Sandile's mountain refuge.

308 '*More insidious ...* ': This episode is best documented in Alide Dasnois and Chris Whitfield, *Paper Tiger: Iqbal Survé and the downfall of Independent Newspapers*, NB Publishers, 2019.

310 '*It was saved only by ...* ': Foeta Krige, *The SABC 8*, Penguin, 2019.

310 '*Media24's sister company ...* ': 'MultiChoice and SABC in cahoots over control mechanism ...', *Mail & Guardian*, 8 October 2019.

311 '*... what economist Joseph Stiglitz called ...* ': Joseph E Stiglitz, 'Toward a taxonomy of media capture', in Anya Schiffrin (ed), *In the Service of Power: Media capture and the threat to democracy*, CIMA, Columbia University, 2017.

312 '*... the entries to the 15th annual Taco Kuiper Award ...* ': https://journalism.co.za/tacokuiper/.

314 '*Africa Check, the continent's leading ...* ': www.AfricaCheck.org.

INDEX

www.ingramcontent.com/pod-product-compliance
Lightning Source LLC
Chambersburg PA
CBHW052120270326
41930CB00012B/2697